Dietrich Fischer
Wilhelm Nolte
Jan Øberg

WINNING PEACE

Strategies and Ethics for a Nuclear-Free World

Published in cooperation with the
Transnational Foundation for Peace and Future Research

CRANE RUSSAK
A Member of the Taylor & Francis Group
New York · Philadelphia · Washington, DC · London

USA	Publishing Office:	Crane, Russak & Company 79 Madison Ave., New York, NY 10016
	Sales Office:	Taylor & Francis · Philadelphia 242 Cherry St., Philadelphia, PA 19106-1906
UK		Taylor & Francis Ltd. 4 John St., London WC1N 2ET

Winning Peace: Strategies and Ethics for a Nuclear-free World

First published 1989
Printed in the United States of America

Library of Congress Cataloging in Publication Data

Fischer, Dietrich, 1941–
  Winning peace.

  Includes index.
  1. Peace.   2. Nuclear disarmament.   3. Security,
International.   I. Oberg, Jan, 1951–   .   II. Nolte,
Wilhelm.   III. Title.
JX1952.F594 1989 327.1'72   88-25731
ISBN 0-8448-1574-8
ISBN 0-8448-1575-6 (pbk.)

Contents

PART I: AN ACTIVE PEACE POLICY

PART II: PREVENTING WAR—PROTECTING PEOPLE

PART III: CHANGING OUR WAYS OF THINKING

List of Figures and Tables

Figures

Tables

Preface

To "win" has many meanings. In plays and games it is mostly fun; in conflicts and war it may imply mass killing of fellow citizens.

Peace should not be won through a war. What we all have to do is to explore, invent, discuss, re-search, and imagine ways and means to help further change toward a peace culture. The moment we think we have arrived at a peaceful situation or think we know for sure what peace *is*—it is not peace. We could never be too curious and persistent in going through our ideas and proposals and revising them in the light of experience from dialogues and social change.

Preventing war and other types of violence is important, of course. But so is it important to abolish war as a social institution altogether. And so is it important to develop security and secure development toward a pluralistic peace culture encompassing the whole human community. That is, recognizing that peace is not just the absence of something, but the active presence of us all being—acting and creating a better future.

We don't postulate, of course, that we know the world would be peaceful if leaders, countries, bureaucracies, and public opinion change policies according to the thoughts and ideas presented in this book. But we have written it because we think that our ideas could be a modest contribution on the way to a more humane and peaceful world. We hope that the book may serve as one of the millions of water drops scooping out the hardest of stones.

Thus we don't claim to know how to win peace. We claim a right to contribute and to do so "against the prevailing winds," which push us toward catastrophe. We believe ourselves to be critically aware of something being very, very wrong in our policies and deeper ways of thinking—but we would not have met and written the book had we not had hopes, had we not had faith in the emotional and intellectual powers of fellow citizens and humanity to change the course.

The problems are of our own collective making—although some are more responsible for having created the mess than others. It will also be of our own to invent a more secure and morally acceptable future for all.

We wrote the book in a new environment. We met periodically at the Transnational Foundation for Peace and Future Research (TFF) in Lund, Sweden, which is a private, nonprofit, and very small foundation, set up to further the type of constructive thinking about world affairs that is not typical at our respective universities and academies. We worked together there and wrote and revised manuscripts in our spare time, summer vacations, and such in Princeton, Hamburg, and Lund.

Each of us has written extensively on the basic issues before—Dietrich Fischer mainly in his "Preventing War in the Nuclear Age" (1984), Wilhelm Nolte together with his brother Hans-Heinrich Nolte in "Civilian Resistance and Autonomous Protection" (1984, in German) and Jan Øberg in his "Developing Security and Securing Development: An essay about Militarism and Peace" (1983, in Danish/Swedish). Having met a couple of times, having studied the thought and writings of each other carefully, we decided to make a common effort and locate it with the TFF and its research program.

We come from different backgrounds—Switzerland and the United States, West Germany (Wilhelm Nolte was born in what is now East Germany), and Denmark/Sweden, trained in computer science and economics, military science and practice, and in sociology and peace research, respectively.

We saw a challenge in combining our competence and trying a cooperative effort in spite of differences in language, style of writing, perspectives, and many other variables. We did it, first of all, because we knew each other well as human beings, not only as professionals. We shared a basic concern about world developments, an awareness of the need for alternative thinking cutting across established standards and the limitations of our daily professions. And we found it humanly very rewarding to dig into the problems together in mutual respect and without an urge to "streamline" and water down our individual arguments in the final version.

You may find that "Winning Peace" can be read in a cyclical movement. You will find it rewarding to start from the first page and go on—but you will also find that your perspectives on the issues have changed after reading the third part on ways of thinking so that rereading the first two parts offers a new experience. We see the parts and their chapters as building blocks— but we would never maintain that the exposition as such is free of contradictions. Each of us took primary responsibility for a portion of the book (Fischer Part I, Nolte Part II, and Øberg Parts III–V), which we thoroughly discussed with each other. Yet we deliberately did not want to leave out aspects or values that could enrich an open mind just because it turned out that one of us placed the emphasis somewhere else.

You may find that we have drawn on a broad variety of perspectives and ideas and borrowed freely from contributions within several sciences. We simply don't believe that one school of thought will do if we take our existential situation serious. It is explained throughout why we deal with the matters in the way we do, and we deem this "eclectic" attitude important for the creative process, almost like the archeologist who, while digging, carefully collects everything that looks important for further analysis. We tend to think that there is much too much emphasis on limitation, specialization, and narrowing of perspectives in conventional science. We also believe that the eclectic attitude serves well our attempt to think in "both/and" terms where so many other expositions in security and peace research build implicitly on "either-or."

"Winning Peace" is just a steppingstone in a process, integrated in our lives. We have not attempted to make it a "testament"; rather we see it as a challenge and invitation to you to reflect and enter a dialogue—with us as well as others.

The three of us have given lectures and public speeches to very different audiences in Central Europe, Scandinavia, Spain, and Yugoslavia, in the United States, Canada, and elsewhere during the last five to ten years. They have always stimulated criticism, counterproposals, and—to a certain degree—a combination of sympathy and skepticism. This is as it should be; we believe in the constructive dialogue, intellectually challenging debates, and broad decision making about what to do.

"Winning Peace" is not meant as a blueprint for peace. It does not say "just do as we say, then . . ." We have not hesitated to take up big issues—sometimes more because we find them essential rather than because we believe that we command them as experts. But we have hesitated to offer clear-cut solutions. What we do *must* be part and parcel of the democratic, participative process—based on information and challenging analyses. If our book in some ways can help you find out what to do and why, we are satisfied—as experts in some sense of the word we are, however, *not* out to convince you that our thinking is the only good one. We try, instead, to be humble when facing all the authors and writers who are "deep" experts in fields we just touch—and to be humble as citizens in influencing you.

Believing that peace is a process that involves anyone who wants to take part, *we* should not monopolize the field just because we are academically trained. Rather, we should take part in the global, transnational dialogue on a par with anyone else concerned and listen to his or her views. This is why we invite you, toward the end, to respond to our opening statement "Winning Peace."

We would like to thank those thousands of people, including students and colleagues, who over the years have commented on our thoughts in speech and writing. The meeting of human beings is still *the* single most rewarding activity on earth—much more so than reading books. But one need not exclude the other, of course.

We also thank our publishers who have encouraged us to take a keen interest in the creation process. We are grateful to Vicki Golich who carefully read the entire manuscript and made many helpful suggestions. Dietrich Fischer wishes to acknowledge a Social Science Research Council/ MacArthur Foundation Fellowship in International Peace and Security Studies. Last but most important, of course, our heartfelt thanks to our wives and children who not only allowed us to have such great fun in working together and spending our evenings, weekends, and vacations on the writing, but also encouraged us in so many and important ways.

Yugoslav political writer and former vice president Milovan Djilas is believed to have said about the partisan resistance against the Germans of World War II—in which he played a major role: "Had we known that what we did was impossible, we would never have succeeded."

As long as humanity, each single one of us, does not know that the struggle for peace is an impossible one, we may still succeed. In winning peace.

Dietrich Fischer	Wilhelm Nolte	Jan Øberg
Princeton,	Hamburg,	Lund,
United States	Federal Republic of Germany	Sweden

Overview

1. First we erect ten barriers against war for our world full of conflicts and describe an

   ACTIVE PEACE POLICY.

2. Next we present a concrete proposal for a strategy that frees us from the responsibility for nuclear weapons and includes nonviolent resistance:

   PREVENTING WAR—PROTECTING PEOPLE

3. Next we seek to address a challenge by Albert Einstein; we develop a cosmology of new thinking and plead for an expansion and strengthening of ethical norms:

   CHANGING OUR WAYS OF THINKING

4. With this background we seek to give security a new meaning; we show conditions for a policy that aims at nothing less than a future:

   SECURITY AND SOCIETY

5. Finally, we deliberate how these insights can be put into daily practice; we conclude that we need your, the reader's help:

   SI VIS PACEM, PARA PACEM

In the Appendix we

Name the authors and their works to which we refer.
Present ourselves.
Say something about the editor of this book, the TFF.

Part I

An Active Peace Policy

1

Taking the Adversary's Security into Account

Security Through Redundancy

Driving along the highways of Switzerland, one can observe rows of covered holes in the pavement every few kilometers, where the road is cut between steep cliffs. In case of an invasion of the country, steel rods would be inserted in those holes to block advancing tank columns. There is not just one such barrier but a whole series, at least four or five from the border inward, in every direction. If the first barrier is broken, there is another. If that one breaks down, there is a third, and so on. The Swiss do not want to take any chances. They seek security through redundancy.

These rods of steel are physical barriers against a potential invasion. In addition, Switzerland has taken a whole series of economic, political, and diplomatic measures to avoid war.

The next three chapters outline ten barriers against war. The last barrier, protective defense, is a physical barrier against attack. All the others are institutional and social barriers. The purpose of such a comprehensive approach is to achieve greater security through redundancy. As long as at least one of these ten barriers withstands the pressure to which it may be exposed, war can be prevented. For war to erupt, all ten of them, one by one, must collapse. If efforts are made to strengthen all ten of these components, this should provide effective protection against the eruption of war.

Similar to the rods of steel to block tanks, the barriers against war outlined here do not threaten the security of anyone else. On the contrary, by reducing the probability of war, they help improve everyone's security.

The ten barriers can be grouped into three types of approaches: (1) cooperation, (2) conflict resolution, and (3) defense. If the two parties agree,

3

they can find numerous ways to cooperate for their mutual benefit. If they have a conflict, they may still agree to seek a peaceful solution. Only if the other side refuses to negotiate or accept legal procedures is defense a last resort to prevent or resist aggression. But even then, as we shall see, non-military methods can play as important a role as military defense.

The ten barriers against war considered here are shown schematically in Figure 1. They form a sort of multiple fence, insuring that we cannot fall into the abyss of nuclear extinction.

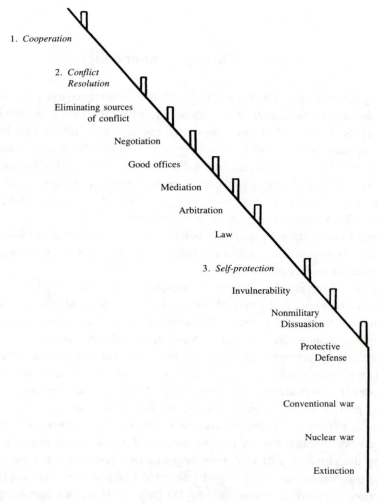

1. *Cooperation*

2. *Conflict Resolution*

Eliminating sources of conflict

Negotiation

Good offices

Mediation

Arbitration

Law

3. *Self-protection*

Invulnerability

Nonmilitary Dissuasion

Protective Defense

Conventional war

Nuclear war

Extinction

Figure 1.   Ten barriers against war.

The peace strategies outlined in the following pages rest on four premises:

1. Unilateral security at the expense of the security of other nations has become impossible in the nuclear age, at least in the longer run. Only *common security* can protect us. If we are perceived to represent a threat to the security of others, to such an extent that they wish we would disappear from the face of the earth and if they have the means to make us disappear, we cannot be very secure. To be truly secure we should see to it, on the contrary, that we are so useful, preferably even indispensable to other countries, that they would be disappointed if we did indeed disappear.

2. We can no longer afford to wait until another world war breaks out, and then seek to minimize our losses. That would be too late. It could mean the extinction of humanity. We must actively take measures to *prevent* a nuclear holocaust before it occurs. Since a nuclear war could result from the escalation of a conventional war, it has become more urgent than ever to prevent any form of war. There will always remain conflicts of interest. It would be an illusion to hope for a world of complete harmony and agreement. But we must learn to deal with conflicts by other means than war. The more successive barriers between conflict and war that we erect, the safer we are. In the following pages, an entire sequence of such barriers is considered.

3. We must seek *cooperation* with other nations to establish a new, improved world order. Negotiations with that purpose should be pursued relentlessly. But negotiations should never be used as an excuse for not taking steps toward peace and greater common security that we can undertake on our own, *autonomously*. If we wait for others to make the first move, we may wait until it is too late. Somebody must seize the initiative to break the deadlock. There exists a whole range of measures that can be taken by one country after another, independently, without risk to its security. As the economist and peace researcher Kenneth Boulding once said, agreement is a scarce resource, and if we can do something for peace without depending on agreement, we should not hesitate.

4. There is no single solution to all conflicts, in the same way that there is no single cure to every disease. As the Norwegian sociologist and peace researcher Johan Galtung pointed out, if we want to stay healthy, it is not enough to rely only on surgery, or only on inoculations, or only healthy food, or only exercise. We may need a little of each. Similarly, a whole range of efforts, all working in parallel, are needed to avoid war. *Redundancy* provides greater security.

It is difficult to arrange all the methods that can help prevent war in any simple, logical sequence. In some way, they are all interrelated. The way we deal with this problem here is to begin with a brief overview and return to the various proposals, filling in detail gradually. The same method is normally used to paint a picture. We do not start at the top left corner of the canvass and fill in every detail until we arrive at the bottom right. We begin with a rough sketch of the entire picture, and then fill in details gradually. However, the authors do not pretend to fill in every detail. The strategies described here will remain sketches. We invite you, the readers, to help us fill in the missing details. In fact, this painting will have to be redone and refined by every succeeding generation. It will never be complete.

What is conflict?

A conflict is the pursuit of incompatible goals. It may involve several parties and several conflict issues.

One of the simplest types of conflict is one that involves only a single person who tries to pursue two goals that are in some contradiction with each other. This is usually called a dilemma. For example, a student may be equally interested in two different subjects but can enroll in only one program. She or he must somehow make a choice. A country may wish to increase its investment in development projects, and also increase its population's current consumption, but resource constraints may not allow it to do both to a full extent. It must find some balance between these two goals.

Another basic type of conflict involves two parties and a single issue. One spouse may want to write a book, and the other spouse may want her to help in the garden instead. Two drivers may want to pass the same intersection at the same time. If both go ahead with their plans, they end up in a collision. Someone has to yield. (We use the analogy of conflict in traffic repeatedly in this book, because we can relate to it from our personal experiences. Few of us are in a position regularly to make decisions affecting the fate of a nation. But most of us have to confront competing road users daily. Certain systems and mechanisms have been developed to deal with such conflicts, and although these methods do not work perfectly, we can learn from them and apply some of them to international conflicts.)

What are some typical issues involved in international conflicts? Two countries may want to exert sovereignty over the same piece of territory, or exploit the same natural resources. One country may want to impose its own political or economic system, or its religion or ideology on another country, against its will. (For simplicity, in the following pages we often refer to a "country" pursuing a goal, when, in fact, it is only that country's current leadership, which may or may not act in accordance with the wishes of the majority of its population. But to carry that distinction throughout the book would make many sentences too complicated.)

What is the East–West conflict about? "Issue number one is this superpower urge to have societies around the world that are essentially copies of themselves; a reproduction by cloning" (Galtung 1984, 42). This urge is deeply rooted in the missionary drive that is part of occidental religions. People who believe they have discovered the truth are convinced that they not only have a right but a duty, even a burdensome, holy duty, to bring that truth to others, by force if necessary. This is one of the primary sources of conflict in the world today. The thirty-year war between Catholics and Protestants in Europe was ended in 1648 with acceptance of the principle "*cuius regio, eius religio*"—letting the ruler of each region choose its own religion, without any further attempts to impose religious beliefs from outside. Today, most countries allow their citizens to choose their own faith. Concerning political beliefs, we should now at least take the first step and allow each country to choose its own political and social system, without outside intervention.

There also exist more complex conflicts involving several issues and several parties. The Law of the Sea negotiations, an international assembly that first met in Geneva in 1958 and drafted an accord concerning control of the high seas in 1980, involved about 150 parties and roughly the same number of issues. In some sense such conflicts are harder to solve, because agreement among many parties is required. But in another sense the solution may be easier, because many more possibilities for trade-offs among different issues open up. A party that yields on one issue can expect to be compensated by getting its way on another issue. A brief classification of solutions to conflicts is given in the next section.

Not all conflicts are open, or manifest. Two parties may have opposing interests, but one or both of them may not be aware of it. For example, the interests of the inhabitants of the former colonies had from the beginning been in contradiction with the interests of their colonial masters, who wished to exploit the colonies. But for a long time the people in the colonies were not fully aware of being exploited. They had to realize what was going on, to raise their consciousness, before they began to understand the source of their misery. Only then did this latent conflict become articulated. Movements emerged that demanded, and finally won, independence from colonialism. In some cases (particularly in India, led by Mohandas K. Gandhi) the struggle for independence was nonviolent. In other cases (for example, in Algeria) a war of liberation was fought. When the colonial powers began to realize that they would have to fight against one war of liberation after another in a futile attempt to maintain colonialism, they began to grant independence to their former colonies. Most former colonies were lucky in the sense that they did not have to repeat the same kind of sacrificial struggle for independence that other colonies had fought before them.

One latent conflict, which has not yet become fully manifest, is the conflict of interests between the national security elites in some countries and the people of the world. Some of these elites have a new kind of spirit of martyrdom. In the pursuit of their political or ideological goals, they are willing to make enormous sacrifices, not so much of their own lives (hoping in vain to survive in deep bunkers), but of their entire nations, as well as other nations. The people of the world may not agree to be sacrificed, but they have not been asked. Often, they are not even aware of it. Worse, they don't want to hear it if they are told, because the thought is too painful. The seventeenth-century French philosopher Blaise Pascal observed aptly that "it is easier to die without thinking about it than to endure the thought of death without dying" (quoted in Schell 1982, 148).

The massacres carried out by tyrants of the past pale before the absolute power exercised by these "security" managers. Not even Nero, Attila the Hun, or Genghis Khan could have wiped out entire nations at the push of a button.

Albert Einstein was once asked, "With what weapons will World War III be fought?" He replied, "That I don't know. But World War IV will be fought with sticks and stones." Today we know that he was optimistic. There may be nobody left to fight a fourth world war.

It has been said that a nuclear war will not happen, because nobody wants it. But as long as we rely on the threat of nuclear war for political purposes, walking along the brink of extinction, a catastrophe is bound to occur sooner or later. It does not necessarily take a deliberate decision to get us there. Disasters, big or small, can also occur due to a technical malfunction or human negligence. Nobody wanted the space shuttle *Challenger* to explode, but it did. Nobody wanted the nuclear power plant at Chernobyl to explode, but it did. To avoid human extinction, the *possibility* of nuclear war must be eliminated.

One of these days, the people of the world may finally wake up to realize how their future is being gambled with, and put an end to this nuclear insanity, before it is too late.

What is a solution to a conflict?

Let us concentrate on one of the simplest types of conflict, involving only two parties and a single issue. As mentioned, there is some obstacle that prevents both parties from getting all they want. Take as an example the conflict between Japan and the Soviet Union over the Kurile Islands, a chain of four islands north of Japan, stretching to the southern tip of Kamchatka. These islands used to be Japanese but came under Soviet control at the end of World War II. Japan wants them back. The Soviet Union is reluctant to return them, fearing that they might be converted into U.S. military bases, and that yielding in this case could open the floodgate for a whole series of territorial claims by other neighbors.

A number of possible solutions to this conflict are immediately apparent. One is to leave things as they are, with the Soviet Union keeping full control. Another solution is that they be handed over to Japan. A third solution is a *compromise*, giving two of the four major islands to Japan, and leaving two with the Soviet Union. It would also be possible for the Soviet Union to keep three of the islands and return one to Japan, or vice versa.

All of these solutions have the property that they are "efficient" or "pareto-optimal." A solution is called efficient in this context if everything available is divided up in some way, that is, it is impossible to give more to one side without taking away something from the other. In the possible solutions mentioned, neither side could gain more of the islands without the other side giving up some of them.

More precisely, an efficient solution is reached when it is no longer possible to make one side better off without making the other side worse off. An inefficient solution would clearly result if Japan and the Soviet Union fought a war over control of the islands and in its course made them uninhabitable. *Both* could be better off if they divided them equally (except if denying them to the other side is more important for the conflicting parties than possessing them).

War is *always* an inefficient solution to a conflict. To prove this, it is sufficient to show that for *every* possible war there exists *some* outcome that would leave *both* sides better off than if they fought a war: in principle, they could simply sign the peace treaty that finally emerges, without fighting. This would spare losses and suffering to both sides in every case.

Besides efficiency, another property of solutions to a conflict is *fairness*. A solution is fair if neither side envies the other. If there is agreement that the contested objects should be divided equally, a simple method is having one party divide them in half, and let the other choose. If the one that is left with the remainder is unhappy, it did not divide the objects fairly and has only itself to blame.

Of course, the two sides may not agree that both should be entitled to the same share. Each side may want the whole thing. In that case, a quarrel may persist.

A related concept of fairness has been proposed by John Rawls (1971): Those who are least well off should be made as well off as possible. This may or may not imply equal sharing. It may require to give more resources to those who can use them most efficiently, if that helps make everybody a little better off.

A solution can be fair and yet inefficient. If two parties fight over a Chinese vase, they may break it and divide the shards equally, but both would clearly be better off if they sold it intact and shared the proceeds.

If the two parties have different preferences and value judgments, it is possible to invent *superfair* solutions, which give each side more than half of the total, in their own view (Baumol 1986). Each side may prefer what it gets and would not want to exchange with the other side. A simple example was given by Fisher and Ury (1981). Two sisters fight over an orange. Finally they agree to split it in half. One eats half the orange and throws the peel away. The other uses half the peel to bake a cake and throws the fruit away. If they had only communicated better, both could have gotten all they wanted. This illustrates how important it is to talk with one another and to state one's preferences clearly and openly, while being flexible and imaginative in seeking solutions that satisfy both sides at the same time.

One could also imagine more creative solutions to the conflict between the Soviet Union and Japan over the Kurile Islands. They could agree to administer them together, demilitarize them, and jointly explore mineral reserves on the islands and offshore, sharing any resulting benefits equally. Such a solution would save the Soviet Union the cost of maintaining military installations on the islands. It would save Japan the cost of military installations on Hokkaido facing those islands. And it might give some economic benefits to both sides.

What are some of the procedures for arriving at a solution to a conflict? A solution may be reached through voluntary agreement, through legal procedures, or through a power struggle. Before going into greater detail regarding the various methods of dealing with conflict, let us take a quick overview. It is instructive to compare the methods that have gradually evolved to resolve conflicts in traffic with the very different, quite primitive approaches that are still used to deal with international conflicts.

The worst approach to deal with conflict is through quarrel, which can turn out deadly if it is unrestrained. Conflicts over the right of way on a road were occasionally settled in this way in ancient times. According to Greek mythology, Oedipus got into an argument over whose horse carriage arrived first at an intersection, drew his sword in anger, and killed the other traveler. As he learned later, the traveler had been his father, whom he had not known. (His parents had sent him abroad as an infant to prevent fulfillment of the prophesy that he would kill his father and marry his mother.)

That approach is, of course, exceptional. One side or the other usually gives in, sooner or later. Until the late nineteenth century, essentially no traffic rules existed, and vehicles somehow negotiated their way past each other, moving either to the left or to the right, as pedestrians on a sidewalk still do today. But with the advent of motorized vehicles, collisions became more frequent and more deadly, and a better solution had to be found.

One could imagine some system of central planning and control. Anyone who wanted to use a congested stretch of road would have to go to a central office in town that keeps a large road map, indicate what roads he wanted to use at what times, and give a sufficient reason for doing so. If there was still space available, the applicant would be issued a permit indicating the times and places where he is permitted to travel. Such a solution would be unsatisfactory, for several reasons: First, it would be time-consuming, both for the public, the bureaucracy required to issue the permits, and the large police force that would have to check these permits periodically. Second, it would invite corruption. The official issuing the permits could say, "Actually that road is already very busy, but for you I can perhaps make an exception," indirectly soliciting a bribe.

This approach is used in a number of countries (and even in the Pentagon) to issue permits to do certain types of business, with predictable results.

A much simpler and better solution has been discovered to solve traffic problems. All vehicles are required to drive on the right-hand side (or the left in a few countries) to avoid collisions. This rule is *self-enforcing* once adopted. Anyone who violates it and drives on the wrong side of a two-way street takes a grave risk and will probably soon end up in an accident. Furthermore, no time can be saved by driving on the wrong side. Little police supervision is needed to enforce that rule, and there is little temptation to cheat, much less to pay a bribe to get permission to cheat.

Additional rules involve stopping at red lights, speed limits, the prohibition of drunk driving, and so on. Such rules do need to be enforced by police, because some people are tempted to violate them to save time, even though they endanger themselves in addition to other road users. Insufficient enforcement of such existing rules is responsible for most traffic accidents.

Even though traffic still takes a heavy human toll, the situation would be much more chaotic and dangerous in the absence of any rules.

All of these rules are designed to *prevent* accidents, not merely to react to crises. We do not passively wait for accidents to occur and then rely only on safety belts or ambulances, although we need those, too. We have also taken many steps to actively prevent accidents in the first place.

This contrasts sharply with most countries' current national security policies, which are essentially reactive. Enormous sums are spent for military arsenals to deter aggression or defend a country in case a crisis should erupt into war. Comparatively little effort is devoted to actively building peace for the long term. Too little efforts are devoted, figuratively speaking, to preventing accidents by building safer cars, safer roads, and observing traffic rules, and almost all the energy is absorbed with attending to the numerous accidents resulting from such a short-sighted policy.

Some clue of what an active peace policy might look like can be gained from a comparison with measures to improve traffic safety:

1. We observe certain traffic rules.
2. We drive carefully and skillfully, beyond the minimum required by law.
3. We learn to drive and must pass a test before obtaining a license.
4. We build safe roads, wide enough for two cars to pass, with fences along cliffs, and so on.

What should we do if we were to follow a security policy based on analogous principles?

First, we would adhere consistently to *international law*, in our own long-term interest, and work with other nations to expand law into areas that are now left to a power struggle. The U. S. mining of Nicaragua's harbors in 1984 backfired. It may have inspired Libya to mine the Red Sea shortly afterward. Some governments argue that they cannot respect international law because other governments don't either. But even if others cross red lights, it does not help us to imitate their folly. Some fear international law would restrict their freedom and sovereignty. But only by adhering to certain mutually beneficial norms can we gain better control over our destiny. Clearly, traffic laws restrict our freedom to drive on the left side of a road, or drive in zig-zag, if we feel like doing so. But only by observing such rules can we gain the more important freedom to go where we want quickly and safely.

Without such rules, we would suffer from hopeless traffic jams and frequent collisions.

Second, we would deliberately *avoid provocative behavior*, beyond the minimum required by international treaties. The best way to avoid wars of liberation from colonialism was to grant independence to the former colonies. We should search for potential causes of war and eliminate them, not only out of altruism, but also out of self-interest. By driving with caution we do not only improve the safety of others, but primarily our own. A policy of brinkmanship, seeking to push adversaries right up to the edge of war, does not help us. Similarly, if we see a heavy truck approaching an intersection without stopping, it does not help us to insist on our right of way. A memorable tombstone inscription says: "May he rest in peace. He had the right of way."

Third, we would require national leaders to obtain training and pass a test in conflict resolution before taking control over the awesome military machinery of a modern state. A pledge to defend the constitution is not sufficient. We would never allow someone to drive a car based on a mere "pledge" to drive skillfully. Of course, we would not want to choose our leaders only on the basis of their performance on a test. We want to choose someone who instills confidence in us. But we should do so only among qualified and trained candidates. We do that when we choose a surgeon, or even a lawyer or plumber. We want to choose someone we trust, but only among those who have learned their profession. Good intentions alone are not sufficient. We would not let an untrained person do open heart surgery on us, not even our own mother, even though we have no doubt that she wishes us well. Acquired skills to manage and defuse tense and dangerous situations are as important for leadership as popularity and charisma alone. Imagine a group of air travelers choosing one among them saying, "He's the nicest guy; let him be our pilot." That could be a prescription for disaster.

Finally, we would cooperate with other nations to improve the security and living conditions of everyone. By better managing the earth's resources, avoiding ecological catastrophes, combating hunger and disease, ending the arms race, we can make everyone better off. Similarly, building safer roads improves everyone's common security, not just our security at the expense of others.

Let us now do the reverse and see what would happen if the principles guiding today's national security policies were applied to road traffic.

First, extended *nuclear deterrence*, the current U.S. and NATO strategy, threatens the first use of nuclear weapons in case Western Europe should be attacked with conventional weapons (Fischer 1986). This may well contribute to deterring a deliberate attack by a coolly calculating, rational opponent. But it would not deter an opponent who thought that this threat was merely a bluff. Moreover, it is not always obvious exactly who started a war. For example, Israel believes that Egypt started the 1967 Mideast war when it blocked the passage to Israeli vessels at the Bay of Aqaba. Egypt believes that Israel started the war when it subsequently bombed Egyptian airfields. The United States held North Vietnam responsible for the Vietnam War, whereas North Vietnam blamed it on U.S. intervention. Either side can always find *something* that the other side did first. Two antagonists may slide into war unintentionally, if they are not careful.

Even at the interpersonal level, conflicts are not always started intentionally. Hardly anyone gets up in the morning and decides, "Today I want to start a big quarrel with my spouse." Yet misunderstandings or little accidents tend to occur from time to time, and if we don't watch out, they can escalate into a big argument. Similarly, not every war begins with intentional aggression by one side. Many wars have started out of a misunderstanding or an accident. World War I was precipitated by the act of an individual assassin when Austrian Archduke Ferdinand and his wife were assassinated on June 28, 1914, at Sarajevo.

If a war begins, for whatever reason, escalation to the first use of nuclear weapons could bring total destruction to both sides. It is doubtful whether a nuclear war, once started, could be halted after the exchange of a few nuclear weapons. It has taken the superpowers more than forty years of negotiations before reaching the first modest agreement to eliminate some nuclear arms. How could we be certain that they would be able to negotiate an end to a nuclear exchange within minutes, given that rational thinking tends to be one of the first casualties of war? (Beyond War 1985, 2)

Adopting a strategy of first use of nuclear weapons to seek to deter war is as if we loaded our car with dynamite, wired to explode on impact, to kill the driver of any car that might hit us. This should certainly deter anyone from hitting us intentionally. But we might also collide accidentally. Moreover, it would kill us, too.

The proponents of a second doctrine, "*nuclear war fighting*," hold deterrence as unreliable, because an adversary might fail to be deterred by the threat of retaliation. They advocate seeking "victory" by destroying the nuclear forces of an opponent before he or she can use them, if war appears imminent. That would be like mounting a machine gun or laser weapon on our car, threatening to kill the driver of any car that veered dangerously close to ours. That would, of course, invite others to do the same, and in a critical situation they might panic and kill us before we could kill them. If those were the methods used to avoid collisions, it would be advisable to stay off the road.

President Reagan and Soviet leader Gorbachev publicly agreed in Geneva in November 1985 that nuclear war cannot be won and must never be fought. Gorbachev proposed a plan to rid the world of all nuclear weapons by the year 2000. Reagan has also rightly criticized deterrence as immoral. In his so-called Star Wars speech of March 23, 1983, he said: "I have become more and more deeply convinced that the human spirit must be capable of rising above dealing with other nations and human beings by threatening their existence." We fully agree. But this does not mean that the answer is *Star Wars*. Relying on defense against nuclear weapons is totally inadequate. It would be like driving over the edge of an abyss wearing a safety belt. Even worse, maintaining a nuclear arsenal while building a defense against retaliation (even if that defense should turn out illusory) must appear to an adversary like a system designed for a first strike. It would put pressure on the other side to seek a way to penetrate the system, escalating the arms race. It would also entrust the fate of the earth into an extremely complex technical system, which could go wrong catastrophically. The tragedies of Bhopal, the Challenger, and Chernobyl warned us.

There are better alternatives than Star Wars! Many questions remain, but a research program on new approaches to conflict resolution, foreign policy, and defense could be generously funded with a small fraction of what is currently spent each year for research on new weapons systems. Such a research program could add far more to each nation's own security, and to global security, than research into ever more sophisticated methods of fighting wars.

Nuclear war would lead to mutual destruction and is not a realistic option for solving conflicts. Since any war could escalate into a nuclear holocaust, war itself has become too risky an approach to conflict. Conflicts will always emerge anew. It would be illusory to expect a future world in which there are no disagreements or conflicts of interest. But nations can and must develop nonviolent methods to deal with conflicts instead of war.

In the world of business, nonviolent methods to compete and to decide the outcome of conflicts have long taken hold. For example, the International Business Machine Corporation (IBM) and the American Telephone and Telegraph Corporation (AT&T) are locked into a gigantic struggle for the conquest of the U.S. computerized telecommunications market. But they would never dream of bombing each other's headquarters, or initiating organized massacres among each other's employees. They compete through price wars, advertisements, better services, strategic purchases of subsidiaries, and, as a last resort, battles in court.

Business competition has not always been peaceful, however. In the early hectic search for oil, some companies had the oil wells of rivals bombed out. But businesspeople soon learned that such methods are more costly and inefficient than nonviolent competition. It is also noteworthy that when Japan tried before and during World War II to build a "co-prosperity sphere" using military means, it failed miserably. Since then, it has essentially succeeded with the same goal, through mutually beneficial trade and investment, rather than through the use of force.

The more barriers we erect between conflict and war, the safer we are. The following sections list some such barriers, but there are many more. The reader is invited to help in the search for additional barriers of this kind.

Those who advocate the abolition of war are often scornfully decried as utopians and illusionaries by those who call themselves realists. But as international lawyer Richard Falk has pointed out, those who falsely believe that we can survive the nuclear age by pursuing politics as usual are actually clinging to an illusion. Those who recognize that nuclear weapons force us to find new ways are the true realists.

2

Promoting International Cooperation

One of the most effective ways to avoid war is not to focus on conflict itself, but to take the initiative in developing mutually beneficial cooperation in areas of common interest. A goal that is in the joint interests of two parties, but cannot be reached by either side alone, is called a *superordinate goal*. The pursuit of such goals has been observed to be one of the most effective means of overcoming mutual hostility.

One of the observations that led to this discovery was a famous experiment in social psychology, the so-called Robbers' Cave experiment (Sherif et al. 1961; Sherif & Sherif 1969). Muzafer Sherif, who was born and raised in Turkey, had a horrible experience in World War I. At age fifteen, he was among a group of civilians who were shot by enemy soldiers. Half buried under a pile of bodies, he lay motionless. Because the soldiers thought he was dead, they left him. After that experience, Sherif decided to do everything he could to understand better how conflicts emerge and how they can be overcome.

In the early 1950s, in some boys' summer camps in the U.S. Midwest, Sherif and his American wife experimented repeatedly with different groups of boys, of course, without their knowing it. Over and over they observed the same results. A group of newly arrived boys from the same town, who had no grudges against each other, would be subdivided randomly into two smaller groups of about a dozen boys each. The members of each group lived in their own separate cabin, chose a name of their own, and worked and played by themselves. Then the two groups were led to play competitive games with each other, such as football, tug-of-war, competing in building a bridge across a stream as fast as possible, and so on. The boys began to develop a very strong identification with their own group and hostile feelings toward the other group. It was "us" versus "them." They began to call each other bad names. Some broke into each other's cabins and ransacked them.

Some even fought mock battles, using apples as projectiles. The atmosphere became very tense. Then the researchers tried a number of ways to improve relations between the two groups. They had adults lecture to the boys about the advantages of mutual cooperation, but with no visible effect. However, they found an approach that worked. They put the boys, again without telling them, into a situation where they had no choice but to cooperate if they wanted to achieve a certain desirable goal. After a long hike, when the boys returned to camp hungry and tired, the experimenters secretly arranged for the food delivery truck to get stuck in a puddle of mud. Neither of the two groups alone was strong enough to get the truck out of the puddle. If they wanted to eat, which they wanted very badly, they had to cooperate. So, after some futile separate attempts and lengthy discussions, they reluctantly began to help each other, pushing and pulling together, and got the truck moving again. That experience changed the whole atmosphere in the camp. From that day on, the boys began to talk with each other, concluded friendships, and considered themselves as one larger group solving common problems.

The same mechanism has also worked to fuse individual farmers or small village communities into some of the first high civilizations, thousands of years ago. Farmers in the Nile and Euphrates valleys were plagued by periodic floods and droughts. To control these forces of nature, it was necessary to dam up the rivers and release irrigation water in a controlled way. Such a task was clearly far beyond the capacity of any single farmer. Thousands of people had to cooperate to complete such huge projects. This necessity for organization and planning led to the emergence of the first advanced civilizations in Sumer and Egypt, about six thousand years ago.

Today the world community faces a host of problems that affect all of us but that cannot be solved by any of today's sovereign nation-states alone. They require global cooperation for their solutions. Maybe these problems confronting humanity will guide us to the establishment of some form of global civilization, just in time to avoid extinguishing each other.

Modern technology has made some degree of global organization inevitable, and also feasible. It is noteworthy that when the United States was founded two centuries ago, it took a minimum of ten days to carry any message from New York to Washington by horseback riders. On July 4, 1776, King George of England wrote in his diary: "Nothing of importance happened today." Three months later he learned via a sailboat that on that day the American colonies had declared themselves independent. Today we can reach almost any point on earth within seconds via telephone, and within hours by plane. The global exchange of information, the transportation of goods, and exchange of people throughout the world today is at a much more intense level than it was within today's nation-states when they were founded. The seams of national boundaries are ready to burst.

Many problems can no longer be handled by individual nation states. They require global cooperation. A typical example is the greenhouse effect. Burning coal and oil releases carbon dioxide into the atmosphere, which forms a layer that traps the heat from the sun inside, like the glass roof of a greenhouse. This effect is warming the earth's atmosphere, and during the next century, scientists fear it will expand deserts, disrupt agriculture, and cause other profound changes on our planet. It can melt the polar ice caps, leading to the flooding of huge land masses close to sea level, including some of the world's major coastal cities. Obviously, it is in everyone's interest to prevent that catastrophe. But no country, not even the superpowers, can do so alone. As long as one single major industrial country continues to burn excessive amounts of fossil fuel, the whole world will suffer. This is a typical superordinate goal whose solution requires global cooperation.

A similar problem is involved in saving the ozone layer from depletion through a number of industrial gases. The ozone layer protects us from ultraviolet radiation, which can cause skin cancer and kill single-cell organisms that are at the basis of our food chain. As long as a single country continues to release significant amounts of those gases, all will be affected. Similarly, no country alone can prevent pollution of the oceans or the extinction of certain rare species. As long as one nation continues to wantonly catch and destroy endangered species, they may become extinct for everyone.

There are also problems that could spell immediate disaster. The United States and the Soviet Union may differ on many nuclear weapons issues, but they both agree that they don't want nuclear weapons to spread to additional countries, and particularly not to terrorist groups. For this reason, they jointly signed the 1968 nonproliferation treaty. But that treaty could be significantly strengthened. As long as a single nation possessing nuclear technology makes plutonium or enriched uranium—the raw material for bombs—accessible to a terrorist group, or to an unstable government, the whole world is threatened. To keep tighter control over these materials, worldwide, is in the global interest, but can only be achieved through global cooperation.

There are a number of other problems for whose solution global cooperation is not indispensable, but still helpful. For example, the United States and the Soviet Union can each explore outer space independently, but they could achieve more and avoid duplication if they cooperated more closely

(Deudney 1985). On the other hand, if they seek to counter each other's efforts by expanding the arms race into space, they will spend enormous amounts, with zero (or perhaps negative) net effect. What we should do is to create a global space agency in which all countries enjoy the benefits and contribute according to their means. Research results, once they are discovered, can be shared without limit, at practically no additional costs. Such an entity could undertake large and fascinating projects. It could set up an astronomical observatory on the moon, where the entire electromagnetic spectrum can be observed clearly, without being blocked or distorted by the earth's atmosphere. It could construct permanent space stations with materials mined on a small asteroid, from where it can be transported without having to overcome the earth's strong gravity field. In May 1988 Mikhail Gorbachev invited the United States to join the Soviet Union on a mission to explore Mars. Seeing television pictures of joint new discoveries in our living rooms could help us see all of humanity as one large group solving common problems.

There is already some limited cooperation in space exploration. For example, after the United States cancelled plans to send a space probe to meet Halley's comet in 1986 for budgetary reasons, the Soviet Union agreed to carry some experiments of American scientists on one of its two Vega spacecraft sent to meet the comet. In 1975, a U.S. Apollo and a Soviet Soyuz space station linked up in outer space, with astronauts and cosmonauts shaking hands. Scientific observations from space probes are shared worldwide. Scientists generally do not seem themselves working against each other; they welcome cooperation in order to find solutions to common problems. Such cooperation could be vastly expanded.

Another successful precedent for global scientific cooperation is the International Geophysical Year of 1957. Scientists from the United States and the Soviet Union and many other countries cooperated to do research on the earth's climate and explored Antarctica together. With the development of computers, communications and space technology that has taken place over the last three decades, such an understanding could be repeated today on a much more thorough and comprehensive basis. By means of observation satellites, an inventory of the earth's planet and animal life could be undertaken, to estimate available renewable resources and avoid their over-exploitation. New mineral deposits could be systematically explored. The mechanisms determining long-term weather changes could be studied, so as to avoid climatic catastrophes and irreversible damange to our environment.

East and West, North and South could also cooperate, in their mutual interest, to do research on renewable and safer sources of energy, including solar, wind, and wave energy, as well as energy-saving transportation and production technologies and better insulation of homes. The cost of developing such technology is the same regardless of whether it is used by a single country, or by 150 countries around the world.

There could be a joint global effort to fight cancer, not only by working on cures for existing cases, but also by systematically investigating its causes for more effective prevention. The World Health Organization (WHO) had an impressive success in eradicating smallpox at a cost of $80 million worldwide, half the cost of a single MX missile. Malaria and other diseases could also be eradicated if we were to devote the necessary resources to such efforts.

Cooperation does not always have to begin with the most difficult and controversial issues, such as arms control. It may be much easier to reach some initial agreement in areas that are noncontroversial, where there is a very obvious joint interest, even if they may be less significant in themselves. But a series of easy agreements may pave the way for tackling more difficult issues later, after a more favorable climate for successful negotiations has been created. For example, the improvement of relations between the United States and China did not begin with an arms control treaty, or an agreement on the future of Taiwan. If agreement on those issues had been made a precondition for closer relations, the mutual suspicion and nearly total isolation of two decades ago might still persist. Instead, the first contact was made by a Ping-Pong team. Some scientific exchanges followed. One of the next steps was President Nixon's lifting of the total ban on the import of Chinese-made gifts and souvenirs by American tourists returning from abroad. This measure hardly affected the trade balance between the two countries, but it was a symbolic gesture that paved the way for more significant agreements. Today about 27,000 Chinese students are in the United States, and about a quarter-million Americans visit China each year. China is interested in buying U.S. technology, and American consumers benefit from low-priced Chinese imports. Such mutually beneficial relations and close people-to-people contacts have removed much of the fear and the danger of war.

Some claim that the key factor that brought the United States and China closer together was their common fear of the Soviet Union. They argue that the perception of a common enemy is a precondition of cooperation. But it is not necessary that such a common threat be a personalized enemy. What unified the Sumerians was not the fear of a foreign invader, but the danger of recurrent floods. Besides, there are numerous instances where people are brought together by a common interest, not just by a common fear or a common enemy.

Hostility is not a constant that must be increased in one direction if it is to be decreased in another. It can be decreased in all directions simultaneously. And it certainly could also be increased in all directions.

An improvement in U.S.–Soviet relations does not mean that there must be a corresponding deterioration of U.S.–Chinese relations. There is no need to play a "Soviet card" against China, nor are better U.S.–Chinese relations necessarily a ploy to play the "China card" against the Soviet Union. Fear on the part of some U.S. officials that an improvement in Chinese–Soviet relations must hurt U.S. interests are totally unfounded. On the contrary, if there is less danger of a war in Asia, this is in everyone's interest, including the United States.

U.S.–Soviet relations could benefit greatly from expanded trade between the two. Nonagricultural U.S.–Soviet trade is only at the level of about half a billion dollars per year, less than U.S. trade with Trinidad and Tobago! Some Americans claim that whereas the Soviet Union would be interested in buying certain high-technology products from the United States, there is little that the Soviet Union has to offer in return. The United States does not need Soviet coal or oil, and its natural gas is too far away. Soviet consumer products do not meet American tastes. On the other hand, the United States has long complained about its huge trade deficit with Japan, close to 70 billion in 1987, and has begun to take drastic measures to seek to curtail that deficit. Japan, lacking domestic natural resources, could make good use of imports from the Soviet Union, particularly coal, oil, and a variety of minerals from nearby Siberia. If Japan were to increase its imports from the Soviet Union, and the Soviet Union would use a trade surplus with Japan to purchase goods from the United States, then trade could balance in a triangular relationship, to the advantage of everyone. An obstacle to such a solution is currently the Japanese–Soviet dispute over the Kurile Islands. But maybe progress in one area could facilitate progress in another. The process resembles untying a knot, where one must loosen each string little by little, in turn.

Of course, not everybody would like to see an improvement in East–West relations. For arms producers, a sudden thaw in U.S.–Soviet relations could be their worst nightmare.

We need not rely only on governments to take the initiative in improving international relations. Individuals can make personal contacts across borders and help build bridges between countries whose governments consider each other as enemies. Many communities have established special relations with twin communities in other countries, some between the United States and the Soviet Union or China, some between industrialized and Third World countries. It is also significant that the largest group of foreign volunteers helping Nicaragua in its development projects comes from the United States. There are more Americans working in Nicaragua than Russians and Cubans combined.

An example of a private initiative to help create U.S.–Soviet cooperation by pursuing a superordinate goal is a project on the joint development of high school curricula in computer-based education in mathematics and science. The project has been conceived and funded partially by the Carnegie Corporation of New York, a private foundation, in cooperation with the Soviet Academy of Sciences. Approval from the U.S. State Department and the National Science Foundation was sought and received beforehand, so that the project would not run into obstacles later. The basis for mutually beneficial cooperation is that Soviet schools have been successful in introducing concepts of higher mathematics and physics to students at an earlier age than in the United States. The United States is ahead in introducing computers and programming at the high school level. By cooperating, both sides can gain from each other.

Individual citizens and private organizations are hardly in a position to affect the military arsenals directly. They can seek to put public pressure on governments to disarm, but by themselves they cannot even dismantle a single missile. However, they *can* make a difference in establishing person-to-person contacts, and in this way alter mutual perceptions and break down stereotyped enemy images and prejudices.

Before even resorting to methods of conflict resolution or defense, the first step should be to seize the initiative in developing better relations. We should not only react to fires and fight them after they erupt (although we need to do that, too). We must also actively build fireproof structures, to prevent fires in the first place. Governments today are so overwhelmed by reacting to day-to-day emergencies that they often do not take the time to give sufficient attention to the longer term challenge of helping build a peaceful world. Therefore they are overwhelmed by the endless crises caused by the lack of a deliberate, active peace policy.

At the Geneva summit in November 1985, President Reagan said to General Secretary Gorbachev that if the earth were attacked by aliens from outer space, the United States and the Soviet Union would surely become allies to fight this common enemy. But we don't need to wait for an enemy from outer space. There are plenty of common enemies right here on earth: hunger, disease, poverty, ignorance, and many more. Our greatest common enemy is the threat of nuclear extinction. Let us jointly fight against that threat without delay, and win.

3

Conflict Resolution

Eliminating sources of conflict

Despite the best efforts at fostering mutual interests and cooperation, conflicts will undoubtedly emerge from time to time. The next barrier against war is to seek to eliminate the sources of conflict. To win peace, we must systematically "search and destroy" the causes of conflict.

If we want peace, it is in our own interest to seek to understand what may appear as intolerable injustice or provocation to others, and may lead them to seek change by force. For example, as mentioned, the best way to avoid wars of liberation from colonialism was for the colonial powers to grant independence to the colonies. The best method to avoid peasant uprisings is to institute just land reform, giving land to the tiller. The best way for the Soviet Union to avoid the guerilla war in Afghanistan is to end its unconditional support for an unpopular regime, as it has begun to do. The best way for the United States to help avoid Communist guerilla wars in the Third World would be to stop supporting right-wing dictatorships. Maybe the withdrawal of support for Marcos in the Philippines and Duvalier in Haiti is a sign that the United States is slowly beginning to learn that lesson. But if it continues to support the Chilean Junta and the South African regime, it should not be surprised if in the future those countries will see the emergence of governments that are suspicious of the United States and seek allies elsewhere.

The fact that the Sandinista government in Nicaragua has sought role models not in U.S. capitalism, but in Cuba and the Soviet Union, is a direct result of repeated military intervention in Nicaragua by the United States. For decades, it supported the corrupt dictatorship of the Somoza dynasty. The Reagan administration has created an army of "contras," whose avowed goal is to overthrow the popularly elected government of Nicaragua. The contras,

who include many of Anastasio Somoza's former national guardsmen, have
been trained, financed, and armed by the United States. Even one of their
instruction manuals (the infamous "murder manual") was supplied by the
CIA. Such measures only confirm the Nicaraguan's view of the United States
as an imperialist bully. It will take much goodwill and patience to help overcome the bitter feelings created by this policy, and heal old wounds.

The U.S. role in the plot to overthrow the government of Mossadegh in
Iran in 1953 after it nationalized the oil industry, bringing the shah back to
power, was considered a great success for U.S. interests at the time. But it
led to growing resentment among the Iranian people. Iranian students complained during the 1960s and 1970s that most positions of responsibility in
their own country were held by foreigners and blocked to them. The shah
invited large numbers of foreign advisers and technicians to help modernize
Iran. At some point, over 100,000 foreigners, mostly Americans, were busy
converting Iran into a Western industrialized nation in the image of the United
States. Some Americans find it hard to understand why the Iranians are not
grateful to them for that help. But let us try to imagine a reverse situation.
Suppose the Ayatollah Khomeini had used secret agents to overthrow the
U.S. government and installed a monarchy, or a fundamentalist ruler sym-
pathetic to the Iranian revolution. He had then sent 100,000 mullahs to teach
the Americans how best to convert their country into an Islamic Republic
in the image of today's Iran. The American people probably would not be
too enthusiastic either about receiving such "help." It is true that Khomeini's
fundamentalist regime has brought great suffering to Iran. But it is important
to understand how U.S. behavior in Iran made Khomeini popular, to avoid
similar mistakes in the future.

When the Mexican government of Cardenas nationalized the oil industry
in 1938, President Roosevelt had the good sense not to overthrow the Mexican government. Otherwise the United States might face strongly anti-
American sentiments in Mexico today, and might have experienced a "Mexican hostage crisis" long ago.

There is a Chinese saying: "If a spear is sticking in someone's body, it
is not sufficient to break off only the visible part that is sticking out. It is
necessary to pull out the spear's tip from the body—or else a festering wound
will persist." Similarly, it is not enough to deal only with the visible symptoms of a conflict. One must find the root cause, and remove it.

The same principle also applies to a successful strategy against terrorism.
A two-pronged attack is needed: (1) apply the full force of the law to ap-
prehend and punish terrorists, and (2) eliminate the sources of grievance that
breed popular support for terrorist causes.

Both aspects are essential. It is important not to reward and further en-

courage terrorist acts by paying ransom or by giving them excessive attention in the news media. Every step possible should be taken to foil terrorist
attacks, without endangering those who are innocent. For example, the hi-
jackings of passenger planes of Israel's airline El Al declined significantly
after it included armed guards on every flight. But such measures alone are
not enough. They only deal with the superficial symptoms of terrorism, not
its underlying causes. Terrorism will simply emerge in other forms, for example, attacks at airports, on ships, in dance halls, and other places. Seeking
to control terrorism by dealing only with its symptoms would be like "trying
to control steam escaping from a cauldron with a lid, while allowing the fire
to blaze underneath it unabated," to paraphrase Gene Sharp (1973, 10).

To prevent terrorism effectively, one must also make an effort to explore
and remove the sources of grievance and frustration that lead people to threaten
others' lives and risk their own. Otherwise, success in the fight against terrorism will be only temporary. Such a policy does not imply sympathy for
terrorists. But burying one's head in the sand and pretending terrorism has
no cause is a short-sighted, ineffective policy that hurts one's own interests.

The British government has long tried to control terrorism in strife-torn
Northern Ireland with military force, but so far without success. The source
of the problem appears to be that Catholics feel dominated by the Protestant
majority in Northern Ireland and would prefer to become part of Catholic
Ireland rather than Great Britain. The Protestants of Northern Ireland fear
their fate as a minority within Ireland. A very similar conflict emerged in
Switzerland in the 1950s and 1960s when a Catholic, French-speaking minority in the Jura region of the Canton Bern felt constantly overruled in
parliament by the Protestant, German-speaking majority. Some extremists
in the Jura wanted to secede from Switzerland and join France. Others called
for the formation of their own canton within Switzerland. Feelings grew
tense, and some sporadic acts of political violence began to emerge. There
were cases of arson against some farm houses, although no people died.
However, there is little doubt that if the problem had been left unsolved,
this conflict could gradually have developed into a civil warlike situation as
in Northern Ireland. After prolonged discussions, the Bernese government
finally agreed to hold a referendum in the contested region. About half of
the districts voted in favor of forming a new canton and were allowed to do
so in 1978. The other districts had majorities in favor of staying with the
canton of Bern, and stayed. Since then, the violence has disappeared. It
may be worthwhile to try that solution, local self-determination, in similar
conflicts elsewhere. Political unity can only last if it is voluntary and perceived as beneficial by the people involved. Otherwise it breaks down.

Decisions are best made at the lowest level that involves all people affected by the outcome of the decision. If decisions are made by authorities who are far removed, and the outcome is bad, people will have understandable grievances against those authorities. If they make a decision on their own, even if they make an occasional mistake, they have nobody but themselves to blame. Thus granting local autonomy in local matters is a method to eliminate a possible source of conflicts.

It is worth noting that the Bernese government did not give in to the extremist demands of those who wanted secession from Switzerland, who did not enjoy majority support. Instead, it permitted a reasonable solution, local autonomy for those who preferred it. In this way it isolated the more extreme elements from popular support.

It is often said that the grievances leading to terrorism cannot be removed, because terrorist groups make unacceptable demands. Some Israelis argue that it would be useless to set up a Palestinian homeland on the West Bank of Jordan, because Palestinian terrorists demand far more, the elimination of Israel. But meeting legitimate aspirations of the majority of the Palestinian people would isolate the extremists who want to destroy Israel. Seeking to defend an unjust, indefensible policy is self-defeating in the longer run. By seeking voluntarily to remove sources of justified grievances, one is in a much stronger position to defend what is essential. Moshe Dayan was right in criticizing the Israeli policy of replacing popularly elected Palestinian mayors with Israeli officers. He predicted that this would undercut support for Israel among residents of the West Bank.

The current South African government makes the same mistake. It argues that it cannot share political power with the black majority, because the blacks want total control of the government. There may be some blacks who make that demand. But white rule in a country with a black majority is a totally unjust and indefensible position, which cannot last. By adopting a more reasonable position of proportional representation in the government now, the whites of South Africa might still be able to stave off a civil war, with far greater losses for everyone involved.

President Reagan's approach to terrorism was to deal exclusively with the symptoms. He accused Colonel Qaddafi of Libya of financing and training Palestinian terrorists. Yet the Reagan Administration has financed and trained contras who entered Nicaragua and killed civilians, in much the same way as he accused Libya of doing, only on a far larger scale, with thousands of Nicaraguans killed over the last eight years. After an American soldier and a Turkish woman in Berlin were killed by a terrorist bomb, Reagan ordered an airstrike against Tripoli and Benghazi in Libya, killing scores of civilians, including Colonel Qaddafi's infant daughter. No evidence of Libyan responsibility was made public, and none was found later. Let us compare this with Holland's reaction when one of its citizens was killed in New Zealand in a similar terrorist attack. French secret service agents, using forged Swiss passports, entered New Zealand and planted a bomb on the Greenpeace flagship *Rainbow Warrior*. When the bomb exploded at night, it killed a sleeping Dutch photographer on board. The Greenpeace leadership happened to be at a meeting on shore, otherwise they could all have been killed, too. The two agents were apprehended and admitted in court that they had acted on orders from the French defense ministry. The Dutch government did what is normal in such cases, let the New Zealand police and courts handle the matter. Imagine if the Dutch government, in alleged "self-defense under Article 51 of the United Nations Charter," had bombed Paris and Marseilles and killed President Mitterrand's daugher. Or if the Sandinista government were to bomb New York and Washington and kill Reagan's baby daughter (if he had one). The United States would probably go to war. Why should Reagan expect the Libyan and Nicaraguan people to be more forgiving?

It is much easier to avoid a war at an early stage, before emotions and hostile fervor have been stirred up by demagogues. The longer one waits, the more difficult it becomes. Another example of this is the policy of the victors of World War I. At the 1919 peace talks at Versailles, French Prime Minister Clémenceau insisted that Germany be declared the sole country guilty for the war and pay huge reparations to France over the next fifty years. Lord Keynes, a member of the British delegation to Versailles, warned that the imposition of such heavy payments would paralyze the German economy and lead to social unrest and future troubles. When his advice was ignored, he resigned in protest. As it turned out, he was right. Dissatisfaction with the Versailles Treaty and economic depression made it easy for Hitler to campaign on a promise to abrogate the treaty and revive the German economy. It might still have been possible to stop Hitler when his troops marched into the Rhineland in 1936, before the rearmament of Germany had reached its peak. It finally cost fifty million lives to defeat Hitler in World War II. If we have a World War III, there may be no survivors.

Keynes's advice was heeded belatedly after World War II, when the United States provided reconstruction aid to its former enemies, as well as its allies (except for the Soviet Union) in the form of the Marshall Plan. If the United States had insisted on large reparations from Germany and Japan, it might have revived old enmities, instead of turning its former enemies into allies. If it had included the devastated Soviet Union among the recipients of assistance under the Marshall Plan, it might have avoided the dangerous period of the cold war with the Soviet Union.

It is much easier to *prevent* an avalanche by planting some trees on a slippery slope to stop the snow from starting to slide. Once an avalanche is set in motion, it takes a much greater effort to stop it. It may be impossible before it has run its course.

How to Negotiate Successfully

If we cannot remove the source of a conflict by ourselves, the next step to take in order to resolve it is to talk to the party with whom we have a disagreement and see whether we can arrive at a mutually satisfactory solution.

There appears to be a dilemma in facing a negotiating partner: should we be tough and unyielding and risk a breakdown of negotiations? Or should we rather give in to try to reach agreement and risk sacrificing our interests, or even encourage escalating demands from the other side?

Both of these approaches are frought with danger. As we mentioned earlier, Prime Minister Clémenceau of France took a tough stand at the 1919 peace negotiations in Versailles. He was able to force Germany to sign the accord, since it was in a weak position, right after having lost the war. But the agreement did not last, since it did not satisfy Germany's interests. German resentment of the huge reparations payments imposed on it in the Versailles Treaty may have been one of the factors that led to the emergence of Hitler and to World War II.

But giving in to unreasonable demands can be just as dangerous. Chamberlain thought he had learned the lesson of Versailles when he gave in to Hitler's demands to annex part of Czechoslovakia in the Munich agreement of 1938. However, failure to stand up to Hitler in time encouraged him to seek the conquest of Europe. Is there a way out of this dilemma?

The two approaches discussed above are not the only alternatives. It is not necessary that we yield in order to satisfy the other side's interests, or that we ignore the interests of the other side in order to defend our own. To achieve an agreement that can last, we must seek to satisfy *both* side's legitimate interests simultaneously. (This point is discussed extensively in Fisher and Ury 1981.) It may take greater ingenuity, but by exploring the interests of the other side, it is often possible to discover solutions that can last.

Consider the following example. Every twenty years (last in 1980), a worldwide radio conference is held to allocate frequencies on the radio spectrum to different countries. The needs of developing countries have grown steadily. A potential clash could have arisen with the developed countries, which traditionally dominated the spectrum of radio frequencies. But an ingenious compromise was found. Some of the developed countries gave up frequencies at the lower end of the spectrum that had been assigned to them earlier in return for broader bands at the very high end of the spectrum. These high frequencies are more difficult and expensive to use and therefore not of much value to developing countries, but they satisfy the needs of industrially advanced countries. Through this approach, a new global agreement could be reached, and chaos on the radio spectrum, which would have hurt everyone, could be avoided.

Many believe that trying to understand the interests of the other party in a conflict is being soft and yielding. But if we want to protect our own interests, we must come up with a proposal that also has something attractive for the other side. How could we expect the other side to sign a totally one-sided agreement? Even if we can force the other side to yield temporarily, it may seek to overturn an agreement it considers unfair at the first opportunity. It is in our own interest to find solutions that are also acceptable to the other side. Otherwise we will fail to reach a lasting agreement, and will hurt our own interests.

One obstacle that hampers successful negotiations is the widespread false belief that anything that helps them, harms us, and anything that harms them, helps us. Morton Deutsch (1983, 28) wrote about possibilities for U.S.–Soviet cooperation: "Clearly, it helps them if their control over nuclear missiles is such as to prevent accidental firings. But does this harm us? Clearly, it helps them if their children have available the Sabin polio vaccine. But does this harm us?"

Lasting agreements are built on mutual self-interest, not on blind trust. When disarmament negotiations resumed in Geneva in 1985, an American businessman was asked, "Can you trust the Russians? If you sign an agreement with them, do they live up to it?" He laughed and said, "We don't trust their goodwill. When we write a contract, we make sure that if they break it, they hurt their own interests, not only ours. We trust their self-interest." This is no different from business deals made within the United States, or any other country. No company would say to another, "Come over and help yourself. Take as much as you like."

One basic principle of negotiating is that one may submit any proposal, even an outrageous one that is very unlikely to be accepted by the other side. But if the other side unexpectedly accepts it, one cannot backtrack and add new conditions. That would destroy one's credibility.

In terms of arms control negotiations, the Reagan Administration has not always lived up to that principle. It refused to negotiate a nuclear test ban treaty, saying that without on-site inspection such a treaty could not be adequately verified. When Soviet General Secretary Gorbachev offered on-site inspections in December 1985 and extended a unilateral Soviet test moratorium, the Reagan Administration shifted its stand and said that it needed to continue testing to develop new nuclear weapons and was not interested in a mutual test ban.

When Ronald Reagan proposed the zero-zero option for theater nuclear weapons in Europe, demanding the dismantling of all Soviet SS-4, SS-5, and SS-20 missiles west of the Ural in return for a cancellation of U.S. plans to deploy 576 cruise and Pershing II missiles in Western Europe, many people expected that this was not a negotiable proposal. One could not trade missiles on paper against missiles already built and deployed. The Soviet Union under Yuri Andropov was willing to reduce some of its medium-range missiles, but insisted on retaining a number equal to the French and British missiles. The Reagan Administration took the position that it could not negotiate on behalf of Britain and France. It would match only U.S. against Soviet medium-range missiles. If the Soviet Union wanted to deal with Britain and France, it would have to talk to their governments directly, not to Washington. On January 15, 1986, General Secretary Gorbachev outlined a proposal for complete nuclear disarmament by the year 2000, and as a first phase essentially accepted the zero-zero option, dropping Soviet insistence to match British and French missiles, asking only that their numbers should not be increased and that U.S. nuclear missiles should not be transferred to other governments. But the Reagan Administration, not satisfied, came back with additional demands. It declared that it was now negotiating also on behalf of the Japanese and Chinese governments, and wanted the Soviet Union to reduce its SS-20s in Siberia. This led the former U.S. chief negotiator of the SALT II treaty, Paul Warnke, to quip, "They won't take yes for an answer."

In December 1987 an agreement on the elimination of U.S. and Soviet medium-range nuclear missiles from Europe was signed in Washington, after West Germany agreed to dismantle 72 Pershing I missiles with American nuclear warheads. The Soviet Union will eliminate about four times as many nuclear weapons as the United States under this agreement. The Reagan Administration credits the treaty to its unyielding stance, which, it claims, forced the Soviet Union back to the negotiating table. But the agreement may be more the result of the change in leadership in the Soviet Union. It is hard to imagine that if the Soviet government had called the United States an evil empire and President Reagan a liar and cheat, Reagan would have concluded that they are serious and that therefore he better sign an agreement with them. But it is quite plausible that if there had been a fundamental change in leadership in the United States, a new government might have tried to break through the prolonged deadlock and achieve a first agreement by making some significant concessions. It appears that this is what happened in the Soviet Union. It is now in the U.S. interest to pursue this new opportunity for reaching mutually beneficial agreements by being forthcoming and imaginative. If Gorbachev should have nothing to show for his efforts to achieve mutual disarmament, it would make it more difficult for him to succeed with his reform proposals. That would neither be in the U.S. nor the Soviet interest.

If we want to reach agreements that are in our interest, we must also offer something that meets the interests of the other side. If we blindly pursue only our own interests, without trying to see the situation from the point of view of the other side, we often end up hurting each other, even unintentionally.

A good illustration of such a situation is the so-called dollar auction, which has been analyzed extensively by game theorists. It works as follows. A dollar bill is sold to the highest bidder, but all those who make a bid must pay the amount they offered, regardless of whether they win the dollar or not. Let us take a case with only two bidders. They may start with very low bids, but are likely to compete with each other, perhaps until one bids 49 cents and the other 50 cents. If the lower bidder goes on to 51 cents, they collectively pay more than one dollar. But buying a dollar for 51 cents is still a bargain. They may hesitate again when one bids 99 cents and the other one dollar. Does it make any sense to pay $1.01 to buy one dollar? Not normally, but in this situation the choice is between losing 99 cents for nothing, or paying $1.01 for a dollar and losing only one cent. The choice seems clear. But it does not stop there. Suppose one side has bid $4.99 and the other side $5. The choice is now between losing $4.99, or paying $5.01 for a dollar and losing only $4.01, and so on. Sooner or later, one of the two realizes his or her folly in continuing this mutually destructive process and stops, but often not before both have bid several dollars. Demonstrating this auction in a classroom or to a group of friends can be a profitable undertaking and teaches them a long-lasting lesson, which they hopefully need not learn twice.

If the two sides had cooperated, instead of blindly competing against each other, they could have agreed to have one of them bid two cents and the other nothing, and to divide the gain of 98 cents equally among each other.

This simple game illustrates real world processes that are far more serious but follow the same destructive logic. During the Vietnam war, the argument was often heard in the United States: "If we withdraw from Vietnam now, all the American soldiers who lost their lives in Vietnam so far have died in vain. We cannot allow that to happen. We must fight on until we win." In the end the United States did finally extricate itself from Vietnam, but only after many more Vietnamese and Americans had died. If they had negotiated earlier, both sides could have reduced their losses considerably.

Good Offices

If the other side refuses to meet with us face-to-face, it is often possible to communicate via a third party that enjoys the confidence of the other side. The third party may be approached by either side or both of the two sides, or may take the initiative to volunteer its services as a go-between.

Two sides that have been fighting a war with each other often have developed so much animosity against each other that they find it hard to sit down face-to-face and negotiate. If there is a person or party that is trusted by both sides, it may help them communicate indirectly. For example, after fifteen years of civil war in the Sudan, during which the black, mostly Christian or Animist population in the south sought autonomy from the Arabic Moslem majority in the north, both sides began to realize that neither side could achieve its maximum objectives by force, and they began to get tired of continuing the war endlessly. The two sides sent delegations to different hotels in London, but could not agree on a place to meet. Bona Malwal, a southerner, who was the former editor of a Sudanese newsmagazine and was studying in New York at the time, had been able to maintain good relations with people on both sides of the conflict. He was invited to London and shuttled between the two hotels, carrying messages back and forth. After about ten days, the two sides were able to agree to meet later in Addis Ababa for talks on a cease-fire, which were successful. In 1973 these talks led to an agreement for internal autonomy for the southern area with one regional government for the three Southern provinces. This agreement ended the first civil war.

Unfortunately, former Sudanese President Nimeiry abrogated the agreement in the early 1980s, disbanding the southern regional government and imposing harsh Islamic law, *Shariah* (including cutting off the hands of petty thieves) on the whole country. Predictably, this led to a resumption of the civil war in the south. In 1985 Nimeiry was overthrown in a military coup while he was on his way returning from Washington, where he had just been promised new aid from the Reagan Administration. But the civil war that he had helped rekindle is still continuing. In addition to the victims of the armed struggle, many refugees who are cut off from outside supplies are threatened with starvation.

It takes great effort and skill to make peace, but it is unfortunately often too easy to fan the flames of war.

During times when tensions are less acute, a third party may be able to take the initiative to host direct talks between two antagonists. For example, in 1975 the government of Finland invited all European governments and those of the United States and Canada to a conference on security and co-operation in Europe. The conference ended with the signing of the Helsinki accords, in which East and West agreed on principles of human rights, and with agreement to hold a series of follow-up meetings dealing with confidence and security building measures, family reunion, and other issues. In this way, Finland played an instrumental role in helping bring about a peace treaty in Europe, thirty years after the end of World War II.

Mediation

If the two conflicting parties are unable to come up with a mutually acceptable solution on their own, a third party may take a more active role than simply carrying messages back and forth between the two, or hosting a meeting. It may take the initiative in submitting solution proposals of its own. Which elements of such proposals are to be included in an agreement can still be left to the final decision of the two antagonists.

This role is called mediation. To be successful, it is important to be creative in devising solutions that hold something attractive for both sides. It may often be possible to construct ingenious compromises that give each side what is most important to it. Through such imaginative solutions, it is often possible to break an apparent deadlock. Fisher and Ury (1981) give an example from daily life. Two peole in a library are arguing. One wants the window open, the other wants the window closed. The librarian, disturbed by the noise, enters and asks one of them why he wants it closed. "Because I cannot stand the draft," he replies. She asks the other why he wants it open. "Because I need fresh air," he says. So the librarian opens a window in the next room, which provides fresh air, without causing draft.

Fisher and Ury also gave a striking example dealing with an international conflict. During the peace negotiations between President Sadat of Egypt and Prime Minister Begin of Israel at Camp David, hosted by U.S. President Carter, an impasse appeared. Egypt wanted every inch of the Sinai returned. Israel was willing to give up most of it, but not all. Neither side was willing to yield, and the negotiations were in danger of breaking down in failure. But with skillful advice on mediation tactics, looking for underlying needs rather than stated positions, President Carter was able to break the deadlock. It turned out that Egypt's main concern was its sovereignty. It did not want to accept another humiliation by ceding territory after centuries of being dominated by foreign powers. Israel's main concern was its security. It did not want Egyptian tanks on its borders. A compromise could be developed, which gave each side what it was most concerned about. The Sinai was officially returned to Egypt, with the Egyptian flag flying over the entire territory. But a demilitarized zone along the Israeli border, patrolled by an international peace-keeping force, satisfied Israel's concern for its security.

A mediator is not always welcome, and it takes a great deal of insight into the psychology and frame of mind of the two opposing parties. For example, Roger Fisher recounted that in 1980, then Secretary General of the United Nations Kurt Waldheim flew to Teheran to try to help end the war between Iran and Iraq. On his arrival at the airport he made a statement, broadcast over the radio, that he had come here "to mediate a compromise." Within minutes, a crowd gathered and stones were thrown at his limousine on the way from the airport downtown. He found it difficult to understand why he was met with so much hostility. Someone then explained to him that in Persian the word "mediate" had the connotation of meddling into somebody else's affairs that are none of our business. The word "compromise" had the connotation of giving up sacred principles, as in the phrase, "a virgin has compromised her virtue." Language can sometimes be a real obstacle to understanding.

An admirable effort in mediation has been played by President Arias of Costa Rica, whose peace proposal for Central America led to the signing of an agreement at Esquipulas, Guatemala, on August 7, 1987. On March 23, 1988, the government of Nicaragua and the contras signed a cease-fire agreement at Sapóa, Nicaragua. President Arias was awarded the 1987 Nobel Peace Prize for his efforts.

Another effort worth mentioning is the Five Continent Initiative, formed by President Raúl Alfonsín of Argentina, Prime Minister Andreas Papandreou of Greece, Prime Minister Rajiv Gandhi of India, President Miguel de la Madrid of Mexico, Prime Minister Ingvar Carlsson of Sweden, succeeding the late Olof Palme, and Former President Julius Nyerere of Tanzania. They have appealed to President Reagan and General Secretary Gorbachev, urging them to halt the nuclear arms race and to heed their responsibility for the survival of humanity. Their appeal reads in part: "We have faith in the capacity of human beings to rise above the current divisions and to create a world free from the shadow of nuclear war. The power and ingenuity of the human race must be used, not to perfect weapons of annihilation, but to harness the resources of the earth so that all people may enjoy a life of security and dignity." They have also called on all people around the world to defend their right to live. "For centuries, men and women have fought for their rights and freedoms. We now face the greatest struggle of all—for the right to live, for ourselves and for future generations" (The Beyond War Award 1985).

During past centuries, small independent countries have been able to maintain their security by taking a neutral position, keeping out of conflicts between other countries, and by defending their own borders sufficiently, if necessary. Today this is no longer enough. Even nonbelligerent countries, who are not the target of aggression and not participants in a war, would suffer enormous losses in case of a nuclear war, and would face possible extinction in the "nuclear winter" that could follow. Therefore, it has become essential for the people of every country to play an active role in preventing war and building peace, if they want to survive.

Arbitration

If two conflicting parties are unable to agree to a mutually acceptable solution, even with mediation by a third party, they may submit the dispute to arbitration. They will have to agree on the selection of an arbitrator who enjoys both side's confidence for being fair.

France and New Zealand recently submitted their dispute over France's bombing and sinking of the Greenpeace ship *Rainbow Warrior* in Auckland harbor, New Zealand, to arbitration by U.N. Secretary General Perez de Cuellar. France was requested to apologize to the government of New Zealand and pay compensation, and New Zealand was to release the two captured French agents who carried out the bombing into French custody in a military garrison on a small South Sea island. Both sides expressed satisfaction with the verdict.

The United States and Canada had a long dispute over fishing rights in the George's bank off Newfoundland. They finally agreed to submit it to arbitration by the World Court in the Hague, and both announced in advance that they would abide by the decision, whatever it might be. But in an unnecessary slap in the face of Second and Third World countries, the Reagan Administration insisted that out of fifteen judges, only the five from Western industrialized nations could rule in the case. The court divided the bank according to long-standing principles of international law, along a line of equal distance from the two countries' shores, and ended the dispute.

It is often easier to accept the arbitration of a neutral third party than to yield to demands made by an opponent. That might represent a loss of face.

An arbitrator need not possess power to enforce his or her decision, if both sides realize that they are better off by accepting a third party's decision than by engaging in a mutually destructive conflict. This point has been stressed by Howard Kurtz, who has long been promoting the idea of an international observation satellite to provide all nations with information about possible surprise attacks. He gave the analogy that an air traffic controller does not have any physical power to keep one plane from landing until another one has cleared the landing strip. But if two passenger planes approach an airport at the same time, even if they are from two countries that may be at war, both pilots will follow the instructions of the air traffic controller. No pilot in his right mind would signal to the other over the radio, "Watch out, my plane is bigger, I am going to land first." They know that this could mean mutual suicide.

When will the leaders of both superpowers begin to realize that they are better off by submitting disputes to a fair, neutral arbitrating commission than to pursue a collision course, which would destroy not only them, but also their helpless passengers, us?

Strengthening International Law

If two conflicting parties cannot agree to a mutually acceptable arbitrator, one of the two may take a grievance to the International Court of Justice in the Hague, Netherlands. Legal proceedings are more formal than arbitration. The court decides what evidence is admissible, and both sides can have their lawyers cross-examine each other. A strengthening of international law is long overdue.

Grenville Clarke, who wrote *World Peace Through World Law* with Louis B. Sohn, told that around the beginning of the century he rode on horseback into a town in the "Wild West" of the United States. He observed that everyone was carrying two loaded guns in his belt. A year later when he returned to the same town, he noticed that the guns had disappeared. He asked what had happened. "Shortly after you left," he was told, "there was a series of fatal shootings. A judge passed through our town and offered to come by once a week to sit to court and settle our grievances, if we agreed to appoint a sherif and give up our guns. We thought, why not try, and it has worked out well. We now feel safer than in the old times when we used to take justice into our own hands."

That elementary, sensible step still remains to be taken at the international level by the nations of the world. We live in a largely anarchic world. Some limited body of international law exists, but it is often ignored. Some national governments have a tendency to invoke international law if it serves their interest and to disregard it if they believe this to be to their short-term advantage. But if law is observed only selectively, it breaks down.

The U.S. decision not to recognize the jurisdiction of the World Court in Nicaragua's complaint against the CIA's mining of Nicaraguan harbors and supply of arms to the contras has damaged its future ability to refer disputes with other countries to settlement by the World Court.

One of the principal shortcomings of the World Court is that it has nothing corresponding to the police within states to enforce the law. To be more effective, it would have to be complemented by an international peace-keeping force that can implement the court's decisions, if necessary. It currently depends on the accused and plaintiff countries' voluntary acceptance of its decisions. This is totally inadequate. Benjamin Ferencz (1988, 82) has asked the rhetorical question, "Would you feel safe if a murderer in your town could only be tried by a court if the alleged killer agrees to it?"

Sometimes, it is in each country's interest to abide by a decision, even if it cannot be enforced, as the decision of an air traffic controller mentioned in the previous section. Until better mechanisms for the enforcement of international law can be developed, it may be best to concentrate on the strengthening of law that is self-enforcing, because it is in the obvious interest of each side.

One example of a court that functions even without a police force is the International Bank of Settlements in Basel, Switzerland. If two countries have a dispute over international loans and debt repayments, they usually refer the case to the Bank of Settlements. Even though its decisions cannot be enforced through any physical power, the contestants generally accept the decisions, because they know that ignoring them would hurt their own interests. Debtor nations would find it difficult to obtain new loans and creditor nations would jeopardize the ultimate repayment of their outstanding loans. Monetary incentives take the role of physical punishment in this case. That method of sanctions may have many other potential applications, which are probably far from exhausted.

Some visible incentive to adhere to legal decisions must be present. If such incentives do not exist automatically, some policing power is required to enforce the laws. Otherwise, laws are ineffective. Even worse, they may be counterproductive. Those who voluntarily adhere to a law may get penalized, whereas those who disregard it may gain an advantage.

For this reason, it is very important, for example, that a code of conduct for transnational corporations, regulating environmental protection, health and safety standards, and other business practices be *legally binding*, not simply a voluntary guideline. Otherwise those companies that adhere to it incur higher costs, and those that ignore it would gain a competitive advantage. That could lead to a rapid breakdown of any such code.

To be effective in the long run, law must enjoy the consent of the governed. Arbitrary and unjust decrees will ultimately be overturned by the people. For example, the arbitrary imposition of a tea tax by King George of England on the American colonies sparked a rebellion that marked the beginning of the U.S. struggle for independence. People must realize that even though they may occasionally lose a legal case, overall they are still better off than in the absence of law. That is different from voluntary compliance.

To illustrate the difference, consider the following example given by William Baumol (1952). Suppose car owners can buy a $200 device to eliminate pollution from their exhaust. If the decision to install the device is voluntary, very few people would decide to buy it, because they would spend $200 but still suffer from the exhaust of other cars. But if people are given the choice, "Are you in favor of a *law* requiring an antipollution device on every car?", they may well say yes, without contradicting themselves. Now the choice is different. They know that if they pay their $200, everyone else will be required to do the same, and they can really enjoy clean air. For this reason, it is important for people to have mechanisms through which they can make *collective decisions*, in their common interest, as Anatol Rapoport (1960) and Mancur Olson (1965) have also pointed out. Such collective decisions, codified in law, are very different from decrees that are arbitrarily imposed by a paternalistic government.

Each decision is best made at the lowest level that includes all those who are affected by the decision. Decisions about buying an antipollution device for a car should not be made at the individual level, since other people besides the car owner are affected by the car exhaust. National legislation may be required to arrive at the optimal decision. For such problems as acid rain, which pollutes across borders, international agreements must be reached (Tinbergen and Fischer 1987).

Laws should not be made at a higher level than necessary either. For example, the choice of language of instruction is probably best taken within each language group within a country. The people may still choose to learn one national language, because this gives them greater economic mobility. But if the central government *legally imposes* the use of another language on a minority group, this may create conflict. The Iranian government's imposition of Persian as language of instruction in the Arabic-speaking province of Khusistan in 1980 led to angry demonstrations and bloody clashes with the police. Iraq took this as an opportune moment to attack Iran.

To establish just laws at each level, it helps if the people governed by these laws have a voice in creating them. There are representative legislatures at provincial and national levels in many countries, but nothing comparable yet at the global level. Most democracies have a system with two legislative chambers, a lower house of parliament elected in proportion to population, and an upper house elected with the same number of representatives from each political unit. For example, in the United States there is one representative for about every half-million people, and two senators from every state of the union. At the global level, there is the United Nations General Assembly, with one vote for every country. There is an urgent need to create a popularly elected "lower house" also at the global level. Proposals have been made for a *People's Assembly*, which would have one elected representative for perhaps every ten million people. Such a body could propose legislation at the global level.

Many U.N. resolutions have been ignored by the most powerful countries, because they refuse to accept a majority decision reached by a voting system in which Luxemburg or Burundi have the same vote as the United States or the Soviet Union, and 81 states, which form a majority, pay together less than one percent of the U.N. budget. To overcome that problem, Richard Hudson from the New York Center for War/Peace Studies has made a proposal for reform of the U.N. voting system. He calls it the "binding triad." If a decision is adopted by at least two-thirds of all U.N. members, by a group of members who contribute at least two-thirds of the regular U.N. budget, and by a group of members with at least two-thirds of the world's population (of those present and voting only), it would be binding. By checking past votes in the General Assembly, he found that most resolutions that enjoyed such diverse and overwhelming support were in fact implemented. The major advantage of this proposal is that it would abolish the veto in the U.N. Security Council, which has paralyzed the world body.

If international law contradicts state law, international law takes precedence. This was clearly laid down in the Nuremberg Principles after World War II. Benjamin Ferencz, the chief U.S. prosecutor at the Nuremberg trials, played an instrumental role in helping establish these principles. They hold that individuals cannot justify crimes against humanity by saying that they

simply followed the laws of their country. Richard Falk, an international
lawyer at Princeton University, has used these principles to defend the right
of citizens to protest unjust actions by their own governments. For example,
in 1984 he was called to the defense of twenty-three citizens in Burlington,
Vermont, who were accused of illegal trespassing for having occupied a
congressman's office, trying to convince him to hold public hearings about
the U.S. policy toward Nicaragua. Falk told the jury: "Someone who breaks
through a window and enters someone else's house without permission commits a punishable offense. But someone who sees a house on fire, hears a
baby cry inside, breaks through the window and saves the baby's life is not
punished. The principle to save lives is above the principle to respect property. These people did not trespass for personal gain. They protested their
government's violation of international law, and wanted to save lives in
Nicaragua." The jury freed all twenty-three.

Is there any hope that the nations of the earth, who cling so insistently to
their sovereign rights and selfish national interests, will ever learn to cooperate and establish an effective system of international law? Cooperation
can emerge even among selfish entities if it is to their mutual advantage.
Robert Axelrod (1984) has pointed out that there exist certain forms of cooperation even among bacteria. They certainly don't have any altruistic motives. The reason is very simple. Among the millions and millions of strands
of bacteria that emerged during evolution, those who destroyed each other
died out. Those who happened to cooperate and protected each other mul-
tiplied and took over. If there were millions and millions of civilizations in
the universe, those who cooperated would survive and thrive, whereas those
who fought each other would die out. Of which type is the human civilization? It is up to us to choose. We have no indication that there are other
forms of life in the universe. Even if there are, we may never be able to
communicate with them, because it would take four million years to send
and receive a message at the speed of light even to the nearest neighbor
galaxy.

Many people, pointing to the fact that international law is currently being
trampled on by so many governments, consider the establishment of effective world law as utopian. They argue that it is a waste of time to seek to
strengthen international law and global institutions, that we should first de-
vote our efforts to more feasible short-term goals, such as the election of
less belligerent governments. Others argue that it makes little difference
whoever is in power at the national level as long as the international system
is not transformed. We should not divert our attention from the essential
long-term goal, the establishment of a new global order.

Who is right? Both and neither. *Many* efforts are required to build a world of peace. Some are short term, with small but quick results, others are long term, which may not be completed in our lifetime, but have a potentially very large impact. We all should pursue those approaches that we consider most important, and where we think we can have the greatest effect. But we should not stop others from doing what they consider most useful, and try to convince them that only our approach is worthwhile. By doing so, people would cancel each other's efforts. It would be as if two passersby would argue whether the victim of a traffic accident needs an ambulance or major surgery while the patient is slowly bleeding to death (Schell 1984). Obviously, the victim needs both, an ambulance to get to major surgery. In the same way, both short- and long-term efforts are required to guarantee human survival.

4

Self-protection

If we are unable to reach a peaceful settlement through negotiation, mediation, or legal means and face aggression by an opponent, we must find ways to protect ourselves unilaterally. Self-protection includes: (1) *invulnerability*, making oneself less vulnerable against military, economic, and psychological pressure, (2) *dissuasion*, persuading potential aggressors, without evoking fear, that peaceful cooperation is more attractive *for them* than waging war, and (3) *protective defense*, resisting aggression, without carrying out counterattacks against the homeland of the opponent. Let us briefly discuss these three methods.

Invulnerability

The notion of "strength" has two meanings: It is used in the sense of invulnerability, the fact that others cannot hurt us even if they try. It is also used in the sense of being a threat to others by possessing the power to hurt them (Fischer 1984, 29ff.). What we need to avoid war is strength in the sense of not being hurt, but not strength in the sense of being able to hurt others—*invulnerability without threat*. For if others feel threatened by us, they will naturally seek to eliminate that threat, and this reduces our own security.

Invulnerability can protect us from physical force, as well as from economic and psychological pressures.

Bomb shelters can protect us from harm to some extent without doing any harm to the one who drops the bombs. Hand-dug underground tunnels were essentially the only defense the Vietnamese had against U.S. carpet bombing by B-52s. These tunnels did not kill any Americans, but they saved many Vietnamese lives.

Similarly, the steel rods intended to block tanks advancing along a high-way in Switzerland help prevent aggression, but by themselves do no harm to anyone.

Dispersal of population and industries can also make them less vulnerable to bomb attacks. For example, the fact that the Ho-Chi-Minh-Trail used for the transport of supplies by the National Liberation Front of Vietnam consisted of a widespread network made it impossible for the United States to cut off the flow of supplies, despite heavy bombing. If one branch was interrupted, there were dozens of alternative paths to go around it. Blocking all of them at once would have been as difficult as killing a swarm of mosquitoes at one blow.

It may appear that an antimissile shield such as President Reagan's star wars proposal is a measure that protects the United States without threatening the Soviet Union. *By itself* it might do that, if it works. But together with a nuclear arsenal, it becomes a highly threatening system. A shield alone does not threaten, but a soldier equipped with sword and shield may be more dangerous than one who has only a sword. (We discuss that problem in Chapter 5.)

A country can protect itself against economic pressures and extortion by making itself economically more self-reliant. It can use domestic resources and its own labor for the production of essential goods, or at least be prepared to do so in an emergency. It can maintain reserves of strategic raw materials, develop alternative sources of supply, explore the potential use of substitutes, and have stand-by rationing plans to limit the use of scarce resources to vital uses if necessary.

President Nixon sold the United States government's stockpile of strategic metals and minerals into private hands, arguing that private enterprise would best be able to estimate what amount of reserves it was most economical to maintain. But if the welfare of an entire nation is dependent on such reserves, we cannot assume that private enterprises will take into account the importance of these reserves for the rest of the nation. One could equally well propose to let private enterprise take care of a nation's defense. Kenneth Boulding once made a simple disarmament proposal: All people should be free to contribute individually to national defense as much as they wish.

How much should a nation spend to prepare itself for a possible interruption of imports? It is clear that domestic production may be more expensive than imports. It is therefore sensible to make use of foreign trade during peace time. But in case of a cutoff of imports, it is still cheaper to depend on domestic products than to go to war.

Switzerland depends for nearly 50 percent of its food on imports, but has a stand-by plan for food self-sufficiency in an emergency and had to make use of that plan during parts of World War II. The plan calls for a restricted diet, with much less meat, and a fivefold increase in the consumption of potatoes. It is not necessary to make expensive preparations to continue the same living standard even during a total cutoff from outside. But it is wise to be prepared to survive, even if more simply.

The United States could save some of its Alaskan oil for an emergency, rather than relying on plans to use military force in an effort to maintain access to Persian Gulf oil. The threat to use "any force necessary" (presumably including nuclear weapons) to guarantee access to that oil, which was made by President Carter and reaffirmed by President Reagan, could draw the United States into a nuclear war to save its driving habits. As Richard Barnet (1981, 77) put it, "that would, of course, vaporize the oil along with the civilization that depended on it."

How can a nation protect itself against the subtle threat of psychological and ideological infiltration? The best way is to build social justice at home, so that people have a stake in preserving the system they have and are immune against hostile propaganda. A country that is internally divided between rich and poor, or along ethnic, linguistic, religious, or ideological lines, or all of the above, is highly susceptible to subversion. It is also vulnerable to foreign intervention. A foreign power may not even need to take the initiative to intervene militarily; it will probably be invited to do so by a dissatisfied group inside the country.

Nonmilitary Dissuasion

In addition to making itself less vulnerable to hostile pressure of all sorts, a country can also persuade potential aggressors that keeping peace is better for them than going to war. To *dissuade* opponents from war, one can make war less attractive for them, and peace more attractive. To make war less attractive, one can increase opponents' losses in case they begin a war, and reduce their expected gains. Similarly, to make peace more attractive, one can increase mutual benefits from peace, and voluntarily reduce losses opponents may believe to suffer in peace time.

This yields four possible approaches to dissuading aggression (Galtung 1967, 1984; Fischer 1984). Of these four, military defense focuses on only one, inflicting heavier losses on opponents in case they attack. The other three approaches are generally neglected by comparison. Yet they are just as important. In fact, inflicting greater losses on an aggressor is the least promising of the four approaches in the longer run. It creates mutual fear and can generate an escalating arms race. But if another country seeks greater security by making peace more attractive for us, we are not worried. On the contrary, we welcome such a move. If there is a mutual escalation of efforts to make peace more attractive, both sides can only benefit. And we don't have to wait for others to make the first move. We can initiate the process, autonomously, in our own interest.

It has been said that decisions about war and peace are not taken on the basis of simple economic cost/benefit analyses. Such aspects as national pride, prestige, ideological, and religious aims are equally if not more important than financial gains or losses, or even losses of life in the eyes of decision makers. This is certainly true. But it does not mean that therefore dissuasion is ineffective. It simply means that gains and losses have to be understood much more broadly than in simple accounting terms. If we want to dissuage aggression, we must seek to understand what is important for an opponent, in his or her own perception, and this may be quite different from what we might value most ourselves.

Let us consider some examples for each of the four approaches. Inflicting losses on opponents as they attack is usually considered a purely military task. But even here there exist many nonmilitary approaches. They include economic sanctions. They can also include such intangibles as inflicting loss of prestige, loss of political support, and so on. For example, when Somoza's troops killed a U.S. journalist in cold blood during the civil war in 1979, this was widely shown on U.S. television, and the public outrage forced the Carter Administration to end its supply of arms to the Somoza regime. When Nicaragua filed a complaint against the United States in the World Court and won the case in 1986, the United States ignored the verdict. But it did inflict a certain loss of prestige on the United States around the world. And it may well have been a factor in encouraging Nicaragua's neighbors to refuse permission to the United States to train contras on their territory.

For the second approach, reducing the gains an aggressor may hope to win from attacking us, we may seek to deny his or her objectives. Sweden threatened to blow up the hydroelectric dams supplying power to its iron ore and coal mines in case of a German invasion. Switzerland threatened to blow up its Alpine railway tunnels. These tactics contributed to dissuading an attack by Hitler Germany. Switzerland built factories deliberately in such a way that the removal of a few hard-to-replace key components would paralyze them. In this way they could not have been used by an occupation force. Preparations were made to destroy stockpiles of goods if otherwise they would fall into enemy hands. Bridges and railway tracks were mined to be destroyed in front of advancing enemy troops, if necessary. Such self-sabotage, which does not kill, is different from guerilla attacks on occupation forces, which could be used as justification for retaliation against the civilian population.

One important strategy for denying to an aggressor the objectives he or she might hope to achieve is *civilian-based defense*, about which Gene Sharp (1973, 1980, 1986), Theodor Ebert (1981), and others have written extensively. All rulers, including military occupation forces, depend on some degree of voluntary acceptance of their authority by their subjects in order to control them. If people refuse to follow orders, nobody can govern. It may be difficult to refuse orders openly if this risks death. But it is not necessary to show open defiance. People can do exactly what they are forced to do, but no more. This would require an enemy soldier to stand next to every worker all the time, which is not an efficient way of running a country.

People generally tend to be much too intimidated by authoritarian personalities. We should learn to defy their orders if they are unjust. We should treat them as if their voices were tape-recorded messages that deserve no particular respect. A two-year-old boy once called his friend on the telephone. Instead of his friend's familiar voice, a taped message from an answering machine was played back, which did not respond to the little boy's friendly greetings. The boy was terrified, trembling, with tears flowing from his eyes. When the parents explained to him that it was only a taped message, not a real person speaking, he calmed down. Authoritarian personalities ought to be treated as if they were mere robots with a built-in tape recorder, who deserve no special respect.

A deeply inspiring demonstration of the power of nonviolent resistance was given in 1986 by Filipino nuns, who kneeled praying in front of advancing tanks sent by Ferdinand Marcos to crush a military unit that had split from his ranks. The tank driver's conscience did not allow them to roll over innocent nuns, and they refused their orders and pulled back. If instead they had encountered armed resistance, they might well have crushed it without scruples.

The third tactic of dissuasion is to reduce any losses a potential opponent may suffer during peace time. We should not seek to make the present situation difficult, or even unbearable for an opponent, because that would reduce his or her incentive to keep that sort of peace if not reverse it. A defense guidance plan signed by former U.S. Defense Secretary Caspar Weinberger recommended that the United States should "fight an economic and technical war against the Soviet Union, as a peace-time complement to military strategy" (*The New York Times*, May 30, 1982). This does not make that sort of "peace" more attractive for the Soviet Union, on the contrary. In this way, such a belligerent strategy does not improve but reduces U.S. security.

If we want to maintain peace, we should voluntarily avoid to squeeze others economically, threaten them, or humiliate them, as long as they keep peace. If others have made a mistake, we should allow them a face-saving way out, and not interpret offers to correct their mistake as signs of weakness. Otherwise, they will be reluctant to correct their mistakes.

The fourth method of dissuasion is for a country to make itself useful, preferably even indispensable for others as long as they leave it in peace. One can offer assistance in case of natural disasters, work through the International Red Cross, cooperate in science and technology, engage in mutually beneficial trade, and so on. One can serve as an international banking center. Most people do not want to wipe out their bank account.

For example, China has long laid claim to Hong Kong, which was seized from China by Great Britain in the nineteenth century. Hong Kong is in a militarily untenable situation. It would be sufficient for China to turn off Hong Kong's water supply to force it to surrender within a few days. But by playing a useful role for China, serving as a foreign trade center through which China earns a substantial portion of its foreign exchange, Hong Kong has seen to it that it is not in China's interest to destroy it. Even though the British lease on Hong Kong will expire in 1997 and sovereignty over Hong Kong will return to China, the Chinese government has gone out of its way to seek to assure Hong Kong's business community that it does not intend to change Hong Kong's political and economic system.

Similarly, one of the central components of Switzerland's security policy, which has helped it avoid war for nearly five hundred years, is to play a useful role for its neighbors as long as it is left in peace, by hosting international organizations, serving as a banking and conference center, and so on.

This principle does not represent any new insight. It has been known for centuries. The story of Sheherazade, dating from the cruel times of the eighth century in Baghdad, is an excellent illustration: A prince was deceived by his wife and had her executed. In rage, he vowed never to marry again, but he spent each night with a new woman and had her executed the next morning, so that he could never be deceived again. One of his victims was Sheherazade. Was there any way she could save herself from the murderous prince? Maybe she could smuggle a dagger with her and kill him. But there was no chance. His heavily armed bodyguards would have easily overwhelmed and killed her. As the fatal night approached, she thought of a far more effective stategy, based not on violent force in which the prince had an advantage over her, but based on wisdom and slyness, in which she was far superior. She told him a fascinating story, which he enjoyed. Since the night was not yet over, she began another story, but left it unfinished at the most suspenseful moment when the morning arrived. The prince was torn. If he stuck to his vow, he would never find out how the story ended. Reluctantly, he postponed her execution by one day but was determined to have her executed the following day. The next night she completed the story, and began another one. The prince postponed her execution for another day, to hear the end, and so on. Altogether Sheherazade told the prince one thousand and one stories, always beginning them during one night and ending them the following night. During those one thousand and one nights, she gave birth to three sons. Gradually, she won the prince's heart and he gave up the thought of executing her and took her as his wife.

This story from a dark past sounds inconceivable and shocking today. But it does provide a striking illustration of the powerful idea that by making ourselves useful we may be able to achieve far greater security than through violent force.

Protective Military Defense

If everything else has failed, if an opponent is unwilling to cooperate with us and refuses to settle conflicts through peaceful means, if we are vulnerable to attack and unable to dissuade an opponent from aggression through nonmilitary methods, the very last resort to take is military defense. But it is essential that military preparations are purely *defensive*, not of an offensive nature; otherwise they do not protect us against war.

To stop aggression, it is important to give a potential opponent a dual message: (1) if he attacks, he will suffer, but (2) as long as he does not attack, he has absolutely nothing to fear and nothing to lose. The first of these two approaches is generally accepted and widely practiced. The second is often forgotten, but is equally if not more important. If an opponent believes he takes risks by not attacking us, he has every incentive to attack us.

Measures intended for self-protection are called *purely defensive* if they increase our own security without reducing the security of others. They are called *purely offensive* if they reduce the security of others without adding to our own security. Intermediate measures add somewhat to our security, and reduce the security of others, to varying degrees. There is a whole spectrum of measures ranging from purely offensive to purely defensive. There even exist measures that do not only add to our security without reducing that of others, but increase the security of *both sides* simultaneously. They can be called *superdefensive*. On the other hand, there exist *superoffensive* measures that reduce the security of both sides (Fischer 1984, 47ff).

Whether a country's military posture is primarily offensive or defensive depends, of course, on the whole combination of military forces, not on any single weapons system. Nevertheless, one can distinguish between weapons that are primarily useful for offensive purposes and others that *by themselves* can serve only for defense.

What are some examples? Tanks, bombers, and landing boats are primarily offensive. They can be used to attack another country and invade it. Antitank and antiaircraft weapons and shore batteries in fixed positions can be used to stop an invasion, but cannot be used to carry out an invasion. They are defensive. Stationing a U.N. peacekeeping force along a contested border protects *both sides* from harm. This is a superdefensive measure. Weapons systems that are highly threatening yet vulnerable tend to invite an attack rather than deterring one. They reduce the security of both sides and are therefore superoffensive.

The following illustration is a typical example of a superoffensive weapons system. In the 1960s, President Nasser believed that if Egypt only had a strong air force that could match the Israeli air force, it would be militarily stronger and therefore more secure. He spent vast sums, inviting scores of foreign engineers and technicians, to build an Egyptian air force. The end result was that both Israel and Egypt possessed vulnerable bomber fleets on open desert air fields, each side knowing that if it struck first in case of a war, it could destroy the other side's air force on the ground, before its planes could take off. If it hesitated, it would risk losing its air force. This was a highly unstable situation. When the situation grew tense in 1967 and war appeared imminent, Israel did not want to take a chance to wait and see whether the Egyptian air force might attack soon. It felt compelled to destroy most of the Egyptian air force in a predawn surprise attack. In this way, Egypt's bombers did not improve its own security, but reduced the security of both sides.

If both sides had possessed stronger defensive forces, like antiaircraft weapons, neither side might have wished to initiate fighting and lose its planes. Yet the surprising fact is that reciprocity is not needed in this case. *One side alone* can prevent war by shifting from an offensive to a defensive posture. Even if only one of the two sides had possessed a sufficiently strong defense and had deliberately avoided the acquisition of provocative offensive arms, it could have prevented an attack from the other side without posing any threat to it.

Sweden and Switzerland, the only two countries in continental Europe that were able to keep out of World War II, understood that principle. They deliberately avoided acquiring any long-range bombers that could have struck Berlin. They calculated that even if they did not threaten to use those weapons, merely having them stand around on the ground might invite a German air strike to destroy them "to be on the safe side." Instead, they concentrated on antiaircraft weapons and short-range interceptors to defend their airspace (Roberts 1976, 98).

Some European countries were invaded by Hitler Germany although they were neutral and did not possess offensive arms, e.g. Belgium. But they did not maintain a strong defense either. The most effective way to stay out of war is to be strong in terms of defensive capacity, without being perceived as an offensive threat. The best way to persuade an opponent that we have no offensive intentions is not to build offensive capabilities in the first place. We should design our defenses in such a way that we are *structurally incapable of attack*. What we cannot do, we certainly will not do.

A shift from offensive to defensive capabilities is different from disarmament. Disarmament must be mutual if it is to reduce the risk of war. Unilateral disarmament, beyond a certain point, could increase the risk of war by offering a weak and tempting target. But a shift from an offensive to a nonthreatening defensive military posture can be undertaken *autonomously* by any country, in its own interest, without having to wait for others to take the first step. If Sweden and Switzerland had waited for Hitler Germany to shift to a purely defensive military posture first, they would have waited in vain, to their own disadvantage.

A defense of the type advocated here has been called "nonthreatening," "nonprovocative," or "nonoffensive." We prefer to describe it by what it *is*, rather than by what it *is not*. We therefore call it *protective defense*. The purpose of true defense is to protect life and property, not to destroy it.

Johan Galtung (1984) has offered the following characterization of defensive versus offensive arms: Defensive are those types of arms that we would use against an invader, on our own territory, whereas offensive arms are those designed to be used outside of our territory. Anything that has a long range, or large-scale destructiveness is offensive. Defensive arms are either in fixed positions or mobile only over a short range, and are of limited destructiveness.

Typical defensive arms in that sense are land mines in fixed positions.

They cannot be moved into someone else's territory, and they do not cause large-scale indiscriminate destruction, but only blow up tanks if they attempt to cross the mines. Precision-guided munitions, which enable an infantry soldier to destroy a tank with a single shot, give a cost-advantage to the defense. Another defensive system would be underground pipes along a line close to the border, which would be filled with an explosive liquid and blown up if there was a threat of invasion. The resulting trench would be an obstacle for advancing tanks. They would either be stopped or at least slowed down and could be repelled with antitank weapons. A nondestructive defensive shield against tanks can also take the form of a dense forest, for example, along the East-West border in the North German plains. This would prevent tanks from advancing in either direction and would be a clear signal of purely defensive intentions.

A method to have a large defensive force ready in case of an emergency, at relatively moderate costs, is the institition of a *militia army* of militarily trained citizens who keep their personal weapons at home or in a nearby deposit. During peace time, its members pursue their normal professions and do not represent a burden on the country's economy. But if the country is threatened with an invasion, a large defense force can be mobilized rapidly.

If a country forms a military alliance with other countries, who would come to its assistance if it should be attacked, this can help it keep out of war, provided the other members of the alliance are equally careful in avoiding war. But if even a single member of such an alliance pursues an aggressive, provocative foreign policy and intervenes militarily in trouble spots around the world, this can draw all other alliance members into war against their will. Pursuing a policy of nonalignment may be safer in that case.

Of course, a nonaligned country could not defeat a militarily superior opponent by itself. But that is not required for security. Our military forces need not be stronger than those of a potential aggressor in order to avoid being attacked. What is required is only to make it clear that the expected costs of attacking our country would far outweigh any expected benefits. If the gains are small, then even a relatively small defense force is sufficient to prove that. Therefore, the smaller a country is, the smaller is the military force required to keep it out of war.

NATO and the Warsaw Pact both state explicitly that they are purely defensive military alliances. Both stress that they would never initiate war and would respond only if they were attacked first. On the other hand, if they were attacked, both have plans to pursue counteroffensives. The Soviet Union has large numbers of tanks that could be used in an attempted advance into

Western Europe. Given that the Soviet Union has been invaded from the West by Napoleon and three times in this century, it has made preparations to insure that if there was another war, it would not be fought on its own territory again. In the West, such preparations cause concern. No one wants to rely on what potential opponents promise they would or would not do. Everyone tends to base defense preparations on what an opponent *could* do. Therefore, NATO plans for the worst, assuming a Soviet "blitzkrieg"-type push into Western Europe, as long as the Soviet Union maintains military forces that could potentially be used in such an attack.

The West must assume that Warsaw Pact planners do the same, planning for the worst possible case, regardless of NATO assurances of purely defensive aims. The recent debate within NATO about the AirLand Battle concept, which calls for deep strikes into Eastern Europe to destroy command posts, supply lines, and follow-on-forces in case of an attack on Western Europe, is causing concern in the East. How could the members of the Warsaw Treaty be sure that NATO would never attack them if it builds forces that could serve offensive purposes?

The principal danger of building offensive forces and pursuing an offensive strategy, even if only in retaliation against an attack, is that it could lead to the rapid escalation of a small incident. It is not always obvious who started a war. One little step may lead to the next. One can always find *something* the other side did first. Consider the following hypothetical scenario, occurring during a tense political confrontation: Suppose a U.S. helicopter accidentally strays into East Germany in dense fog and is shot down. The crew survives and is seized by Soviet troops. The United States demands their immediate release. The Soviet Union announces it will put them on trial for espionage. NATO sends a commando force to free the crew, but it is met by superior Warsaw Pact forces. NATO sends a tank column to relieve the rescue team. Soviet forces repel the tank column and push the fighting across the border into West Germany. Both sides bring in rapid reinforcements in a mutual attempt to push the fighting onto the other side of the border. World War III may have begun.

If NATO were to pursue a defensive strategy only, this would prevent escalation. NATO would make every effort to stop Warsaw Pact advances into Western Europe, but would deliberately avoid entering Eastern Europe. This would put maximum pressure on the other side to end the fighting as soon as possible. If it continued fighting, it would continue to suffer losses. But it could be assured that as soon as it stopped fighting, its losses would end. On the other hand, if NATO pursues a strategy calling for counteroffensives, then the Warsaw Pact is under pressure to keep up the fighting, if it should ever start for any reason. Otherwise it would allow NATO to seize the initiative.

A second drawback of an offensive strategy and force structure is that it may invite a pre-emptive attack: An opponent may seek to destroy our forces before we can use them if he is afraid that we might attack him. The above discussion of the outbreak of the 1967 Mideast war illustrates this.

A third drawback of building offensive forces is that they contribute to an arms race (Fischer 1984b). Consider a competitive arms buildup between two countries, A and B. If A builds offensive arms, their main effect is to reduce the security of country B. B will want to build more arms to restore its security. This threatens A, which will build more arms, and so on in an escalating spiral. Acquiring offensive arms is like taking drugs: it produces a short-term euphoria of military superiority, but is followed by a miserable feeling of insecurity when the other side catches up. Countries pursuing an offensive arms race are victims of the "fallacy of the last move." They believe erroneously that if they can only gain military superiority, their problems will be solved once and for all. They fail to anticipate that the other side will respond with a countermove.

If a country builds purely defensive arms, this does not threaten an opponent and does not cause a spiraling arms race. With a shift from offensive to genuinely defensive arms, it is possible to end the arms race, even without any mutual agreement between the two sides.

A defensive military strategy is also the only morally acceptable one, in the sense that it can be elevated to a general principle recommended for everyone. If each country would defend itself only against aggression *inside its own borders* and never attack any other country, there would be no more war. (This theme is discussed in Part III.)

5

Nuclear Deterrence, Warfighting, Star Wars: Part of the Problem, Not the Solution

Deterrence

There is no known effective defense against nuclear weapons. For this reason Robert Oppenheimer, father of the atomic bomb, considered it to be an "inherently aggressive weapon" and he predicted that it would be used in a series of "lightning-swift aggressive wars" in which a country would be attacked with atomic bombs, without any way to stop the bombs from falling. But Bernard Brodie (1946) argued that even though a country could not physically intercept the bombs, it could threaten to do the same in retaliation, and the fear of retaliation would paralyze the finger on the nuclear trigger. This idea has since become known as deterrence theory and has formed the basis of nuclear strategy for many years.

Some people have argued that nuclear weapons have helped preserve peace since 1945. This is contrary to facts. According to Small and Singer (1982), each one of the five nuclear powers has been involved in a whole series of wars since 1945 (two for the Soviet Union, three for the United Kingdom, and five each for China, France, and the United States). On the other hand, the six neutral countries of Europe, which have no nuclear weapons and are not even under anybody else's "nuclear umbrella," have not been involved in a single war during the same period. This does not prove that the nuclear powers have been at war *because* they possess nuclear weapons. But certainly there are other factors that are more important in helping keep a country out of war, for example, a noninterventionary foreign policy.

Have nuclear weapons at least prevented another world war? The fact that nuclear weapons have not been used in war since Hiroshima and Nagasaki does not prove that they will never be used again. That conclusion has been compared to the remark of someone who jumped from a 100-story building. On the sixtieth floor, someone looked out the window and asked, "How is it going?" to which he replied, "Fine, so far!"

The threat of nuclear retaliation against a nuclear attack will deter a rational, coolly calculating opponent from launching an attack. But not all wars (in fact, the minority) start with a coolly calculated, rational decision. More often, wars start by miscalculation, accident, involuntary escalation of a smaller crisis, and hot passion. Against these dangers, deterrence offers little protection.

There are also some prominent, perfectly reasonable-looking people who cheerfully proclaim, "There are values more precious than avoiding nuclear war," and consider themselves to be rational.

As long as nuclear war remains *possible*, even if it is unlikely, it will ultimately happen with certainty if we only wait long enough. According to Murphy's law, anything that *can* go wrong, *will*. George Wald, the Nobel Prize-winning biologist, once asked a professor of government at Harvard how likely a nuclear war was. "Not very likely," he replied, "I would say about two or three percent per year." This may seem low. But assuming a two percent per year probability, a calculation shows that the probability of a nuclear war over the next 50 years would be 64 percent, over 100 years 87 percent, over 200 years 98 percent, over 500 years 99.99 percent, and over 1,000 years a virtual certainty. It is similar as if we were to throw a pair of dice each year. If a double six appears, it means nuclear war. We may be lucky for a long time. But we know that if we continue to play this game forever, sooner or later we will definitely throw a double six.

Of course, nobody knows exactly how likely a nuclear war is. But the point is that no matter how low the probability, as long as there is a finite possibility, it is bound to happen ultimately, if we only wait long enough. We must eliminate the possibility altogether. We cannot continue to rely on nuclear deterrence forever. As long as we have these weapons in our midst, they will go off sooner or later, whether by accident or madness.

Even more dangerous than basic deterrence against a nuclear attack is the current NATO doctrine of so-called extended deterrence, which threatens the first use of nuclear weapons against a conventional attack. If it fails to deter the attack, NATO faces a terrible dilemma: should it surrender, or initiate the use of nuclear weapons? There is no guarantee that the use of nuclear weapons, once started, could be halted through negotiations before the total destruction of both sides involved, and the rest of the world.

Nuclear weapons do not always deter an opponent, who may doubt that they would be used. The more enormous a threat, the less credible it is, because it would be suicidal. When the United States possessed a monopoly on nuclear weapons in 1948, this did not deter Stalin from ordering the blockade of Berlin. Great Britain's nuclear submarines did not deter the Argentine military junta from attempting to seize the Falkland Islands/Malvinas in 1982. Nobody even threatened the use of nuclear weapons in these cases, but if it had been threatened, the warning might well have been ignored. Stalin asserted that nuclear weapons were for people with weak nerves.

Thomas J. Watson Jr. (1986), former chairman of IBM and former U.S. ambassador to the Soviet Union, has offered a scenario of how extended deterrence might lead to nuclear war: "Imagine a situation in East Germany where the Communist government is trying to reform the system, as in Czechoslovakia in 1968. The Soviets try to stop it, but the East German leader falls back into West Germany with some of his forces. There he is granted sanctuary and by radio urges his countrymen to resist the Soviets. The Soviets, fearing that their empire will crumble, take the risk and enter West Germany to put an end to the danger. Fighting ensues, and NATO is pushed back. Our current policy under those conditions is to initiate the use of tactical nuclear weapons on the battlefield if our troops are being overwhelmed. That would lead, according to Soviet doctrine, to all-out nuclear war. . . . There is no guarantee that anyone involved . . . would have the fortitude to take the first step back to sanity. Each side may wait for the other to blink, and suddenly it will be too late."

Playing with threats of total destruction may invite self-destruction. Even the strongest, most "credible" threat may fail to work as intended.

Again, old folks' wisdom is a guide. Johann Wolfgang von Goethe described in one of his poems how a fearsome-looking robber baron entered a medieval town, went straight to the barber shop, pulled out his knife, and stuck it into the table. Then he pulled out a bundle of gold and casually threw it onto the table. He said to the barber: "If you shave me without cutting me, you shall have my gold and be a rich man for the rest of your life. But if you cut me even one little bit, I will kill you." The barber trembled and did not dare to try. His assistant did not dare either. But the little apprentice boy said confidently, "I will try." He sharpened the blade very carefully and shaved the robber clean without the slightest cut. The robber was impressed and handed his gold to the apprentice. As he left, he turned around and asked, "Weren't you a little afraid?" "No," replied the apprentice, "I figured that if I cut your cheek by mistake, I simply would quickly cut your throat as well." Now the robber began to tremble.

Nuclear Warfighting

The adherents of the school of "nuclear war fighting" argue that an opponent could not always be trusted to be deterred from using nuclear weapons through the threat of retaliation. Therefore, they say it was necessary in case of war to physically *prevent* the opponent from using nuclear weapons, by destroying them before they could be used. They aim at "winning" a nuclear war by disarming the opponent.

The problem with this strategy is that it does not deter nuclear war, but invites it. It makes nuclear war even more likely than relying on nuclear deterrence. If we threaten to destroy an opponent's weapons before he can use them, he has every incentive to do the same to us.

Nuclear weapons required to implement a warfighting strategy are so-called counterforce weapons, aimed at an opponent's nuclear forces. They differ from "countervalue" weapons, which are designed to deter an attack through the threat of retaliation against values, such as centers of heavy industry. Counterforce weapons must be highly accurate, fast (to surprise the opponent), and be equipped with many nuclear warheads to detroy all of an opponent's nuclear weapons. They need not be able to survive a nuclear attack, because they would be used first. Typical nuclear weapons of this type are land-based missiles with several nuclear warheads per missile, so-called MIRVs (multiple independently targetable re-entry vehicles), like the U.S. MX-missile or the Soviet SS-18. Such weapons are designed as antisilo weapons. This implies that they are first-strike weapons. As Robert Johansen (1982, 54) pointed out, "No one wants to destroy a silo after the missile it houses has left, so the weapon makes most sense for use in a surprise nuclear attack."

Building such weapons gives an opponent the reverse signal from that intended. Instead of giving the message "Don't attack us, or else you face the threat of retaliation," the other side is implicitly told: "If you don't destroy those weapons, you face a constant threat. But if you destroy them, which is easy to do, you eliminate the threat." It is not wise to give such signals, especially not to someone one does not trust too well.

Many people intuitively believe that a balance of forces is a precondition for security and that if the other side has first-strike weapons, we have no choice but to build them, too. But it can easily be shown that this is not true. A balance of forces is neither necessary nor sufficient for security. In the absence of first-strike weapons, both sides can be relatively secure, even with an imbalance of forces. But in the presence of first-strike weapons, both sides can be extremely insecure, even if there is a perfect balance of military forces.

Because this point is so important, and so little understood, it is demonstrated here. To show that balance and security are two entirely different things, it is sufficient to give an example of a force configuration that is imbalanced but leaves both sides relatively secure, and another configuration that is balanced but leaves both sides highly insecure.

Suppose two adversaries have as their only weapons nuclear-tipped, land-based missiles in silos. Assume the accuracy and explosive power of the weapons is such that on average it takes five nuclear weapons to destroy a missile in its silo. If each missile has only a single warhead, neither side can disarm the other in a surprise attack, even with a substantial imbalance of forces.

Consider, for example, a situation in which country A has 1,000 missiles with one warhead each, and country B has 3,000 such missiles. Country A could destroy at most $1,000/5 = 200$ out of the 3,000 missiles of its adversary and could not possibly disarm the enemy in a surprise attack. But even country B, which has a 3:1 military superiority, could destroy only $3,000/5 = 600$ of its adversary's 1,000 missiles; 400 would be left for possible retaliation. In this situation, both sides are deterred from attacking the other side, despite a large imbalance of forces.

Of course, this does not preclude the use of nuclear weapons due to a mechanical or human error, but at least there is no incentive for a rationally calculating decision maker to strike first.

We can now see that, on the other hand, even with a perfect balance of forces, there may be an incentive to strike first during a crisis if both sides possess first-strike weapons. Suppose each side has 100 missiles with 10 warheads each, for a total of 1,000 warheads each. Each side could wipe out all of the 100 missiles of the opponent using only 500 warheads on 50 missiles. Whoever strikes first during a grave crisis, when war may appear imminent, can totally disarm the opponent. Whoever hesitates risks being disarmed in a surprise attack. That would be an extremely unstable situation, dangerous for both sides, even though both have exactly the same weapons with the same capabilities.

If both sides would agree to a mutual step of *qualitative disarmament*, exchanging their MIRVs for 1,000 single-warhead missiles each, neither side could disarm the other, and both would be safer. But interestingly enough, it is not necessary to reach agreement in this case. One side alone can break out of this dangerous situation and restore stability, even without cooperation from the other side. If country A were to exchange its 100 MIRVs for 300 missiles with a single warhead, it now has a survivable force. Country B could destroy at most 200 of country A's 300 missiles. At the same time, country A no longer poses a counterforce threat to country B. With its 300 warheads, it could destroy at most 60 of the 100 MIRVs of its adversary. Neither side would have to fear a disarming first strike. Often it is possible to take unilateral measures that improve the security of *both sides*.

Even if an opponent makes nuclear war more likely by building first-strike weapons, it does not help us at all to imitate the mistake and make nuclear war still more likely.

In a 1979 speech to NATO foreign ministers, Henry Kissinger said, "I believe that it is either necessary that the Soviets be deprived of their counterforce capability in strategic forces or that a U.S. counterforce capability in strategic forces be rapidly built" (1982, 123). To deprive the Soviet Union of its counterforce capability (if indeed it has one, which so far is highly implausible) can reduce the danger of nuclear war. But for the United States to build a matching counterforce capability makes the situation only worse. Not only would the Soviet Union then have the potential to destroy U.S. nuclear weapons, it would also be under great pressure to do so during a grave international crisis, out of fear that otherwise the United States would do it first. Kissinger's argument in favor of balance is as if two parties were sitting at different ends of the same lifeboat and someone would say, "Those vicious people on the other side have drilled a hole in the boat. Now we have no choice but to repair that hole or rapidly drill one of our own, to restore the balance."

Star Wars

President Reagan has rightly denounced nuclear deterrence and the warfighting doctrine as immoral. As an alternative, he has proposed the Strategic Defense Initiative (SDI, widely known as star wars). He promised to make nuclear weapons "impotent and obsolete" through an impenetrable shield over the United States, formed by ground- and space-based laser beams and guided missiles that would intercept incoming nuclear warheads. "Wouldn't it be better to save lives than to avenge them?" he proclaimed.

The idea of shifting from deterrence by threatening retaliation to a defensive strategy sounds indeed attractive. Although most independent scientists not on the payroll of the U.S. government or of defense contractors doubt whether any such scheme could be implemented in the foreseeable future, this alone is no reason not to try. But there are some serious problems with this proposal, so that far from reducing the danger of nuclear war, it would rather increase it. Let us consider some of these problems.

By itself a defense against nuclear weapons would not threaten anyone. But the United States has no plans to give up its nuclear weapons entirely. *Combined* with a defense against retaliation, these weapons would become far more threatening than they are now. As long as a nuclear power is vulnerable to retaliation, no sane leader would ever want to initiate the use of nuclear weapons, knowing that this would be suicide. But if a country can protect itself against retaliation (or even if its leaders falsely believe they could protect themselves), its leadership might consider the use of nuclear weapons to serve "national interests," or at least the threat to use them for coercive blackmail.

Former U.S. Defense Secretary Caspar Weinberger wrote: ". . . a Soviet breakthrough in advanced defense technology . . . would . . . put us as great risk" (International Herald Tribune July 11, 1985, 4). In the same article he also wrote, "Such systems would save lives, not threaten them. The plan involves a visionary, moral quest." If it is a moral quest to save lives, how could it put the United States at risk if the Soviet Union developed such a system? The truth is that the United States would be terribly afraid if the Soviet Union could attack it, but the United States could not retaliate. The Pentagon is already secretly developing missiles that can take zig-zag courses to evade destruction by any future Soviet laser beam weapons (New York Times February 11, 1985). When the Soviet Union improved its air defense system, the United States did not scrap its nuclear bombers as "impotent and obsolete." On the contrary, it developed two new types of bombers, the B-1 and the Stealth with radar-evading technology, and built thousands of air-launched cruise missiles to penetrate any Soviet defense. The U.S. reaction to a Soviet antimissile defense would most likely be to build more and "better" nuclear weapons to penetrate any defense in order to maintain its capacity to retaliate against a nuclear attack. The United States must expect that the Soviet reaction to star wars, if it was deployed, would be no different. Proceeding with star wars would lead to a vast new round in the arms race, extending it from earth into space.

Even supporters of SDI concede that a 100-percent leak-proof shield that would be able to protect cities is currently out of reach. A 90-percent protection against 10,000 warheads would allow 1,000 to slip by, which would still totally destroy a country. A peace organization in Washington is selling "SDI-umbrellas" on the steps of the Capitol. They have 10-percent holes. In a heavy rain, they are, of course, totally useless.

Henry Kissinger said on a televised interview that the critics of SDI contradicted each other. On one hand they said it would never work. On the other hand they said it was very dangerous and had to be stopped. Both obviously could not be true, Kissinger remarked. But unfortunately, both *can* be true at the same time. It is not necessary that the system actually work for it to be a threat. Even if a decision maker only falsely believes the system would work, this would lead him or her to take dangerous steps. Imagine, for example, that a future Soviet leader were to announce, "Our scientists have now developed a new weapons system with which we can survive and win a nuclear war." We could all be certain that this was impossible, that it violated physical principles, and that he was wrong. But that would be of little comfort. As long as *he* seemed to believe it, we would have ample reason to be concerned.

It is very unlikely that a reliable defense against nuclear weapons could be developed. Even if ballistic missiles that pass through outer space could be intercepted with 100-percent effectiveness, such systems could not stop cruise missiles, pilotless airplanes flying at low altitudes to evade detection. And since no country can totally prevent the smuggling of drugs, how could anyone reliably prevent nuclear weapons from being smuggled in a car trunk or sailboat?

Deployment of star wars would also increase the danger of accidental nuclear war. Decisions would have to be made in such a short time that they would have to be turned over to an automated system without human intervention. From January 1979 to June 1980, the NORAD computerized warning system generated 3,804 alarms of a possible Soviet nuclear attack on the United States (*The New York Times*, October 29, 1980). All of these alarms were, of course, found to be false on human inspection. After that the Pentagon stopped publishing those statistics, so as not to frighten the public. To turn over the decision to start combat to such a fallible system would be folly.

Another danger of accidental war, besides a false warning, is the vulnerability of space weapons to accidental collisions, which might be misinterpreted as deliberate attacks. Gorbachev (1985, 434, 439) has speculated that a separated fragment of a test missile might collide with a space weapons subsystem. "All computers would be switched on, while politicians would not be able to do anything sensible . . . Decisions, irreversible in their consequences, would be taken by computers, without participation of human mind and political will . . . Such a development could result in a universal catastrophe—even if the initial impulse were an error, miscalculation or technical malfunction of sophisticated computer systems."

A false interpretation of signals under time pressure can lead to an attack by mistake. A tragic recent example is the shooting down of Iran Air's Flight 655 on July 3, 1988 over the Straight of Hormuz by the crew of the U.S. cruiser Vincennes. The Vincennes had a highly sophisticated, automated radar system that was not supposed to confuse a passenger airliner with a military aircraft. This turned out to be an empty promise, like the "unsinkable" Titanic or "safe" nuclear power before Three Mile Island and Chernobyl. Will we blindly accept similar assurances about star wars? If we turn over the decision to start war to a hair-trigger system like star wars, we could all share the fate of the passengers of Flight 655.

The computer programs necessary to control such a system have been estimated to require about a hundred million lines of computer code, written by hundreds or thousands of individual programmers (Waldrop 1986). It is preposterous to believe that such a code could be free of errors, especially since the system could never be tested under real conditions.

A study of the Cuban missile crisis by James Blight and others of Harvard's Avoiding Nuclear War Project concluded that one of the main reasons why we have not had a nuclear war up to now is the decision makers' fear of its consequences. For example, they quoted Robert McNamara as saying that as he left a meeting at the White House during the Cuban missile crisis, he observed a beautiful sunset over Washington and suddenly began to wonder whether this might be the last sunset he would ever see. He also was concerned about the fate of his children. But a computer has no such fears. It could not care less whether it will ever observe another sunset, and it has no children. It could initiate the destruction of life on earth without the slightest hesitation or remorse.

We are progressing into ever more dangerous territory. The strategy of deterrence is often called "Mutual Assured Destruction," abbreviated as MAD. The Warfighting doctrine has been described as "Nuclear Utilization and Target Selection" (NUTS). Daniel Deudney (1984) has coined an appropriate acronym for star wars: "Destruction-Entrusted Automatic Devices" (DEAD).

Other reasons have been offered in favor of progressing with star wars. Some have praised the anticipated spinoffs of new technologies that are expected ultimately to find their way also into civilian applications, including transportation, communication, and medicine (Browne 1986). But these goals could be achieved far more efficiently if they were pursued directly instead of being accidental byproducts of military research. The argument that military research benefits medicine is about as convincing as saying that washing a car helps the growth of vegetables because some of the waste water dribbles into the vegetable garden. Why not pour all of the fresh water directly onto the vegetables?

Another argument offered in favor of star wars is that it would force the Soviet Union into a costly arms race that would bankrupt the Soviet economy. The United States could thus defeat the Soviet Union without firing a single shot. But it might bankrupt the U.S. economy as well. In the meantime, it would, of course, be a feast for defense contractors.

A serious danger to U.S. security is its federal budget deficit. It has been running annual deficits in the order of $200 billion. President Reagan, who campaigned on criticizing Carter's much smaller deficits, has accumulated far more government debts than all the previous U.S. presidents from George Washington to Jimmy Carter combined. So far, this deficit has not produced much visible damage to the economy. But if private lenders should begin to lose their confidence in the government's willingness or ability to repay its loans, there could be a sudden mad rush on the treasury, resulting in economic chaos and possibly street violence. Nobody would want to be last and be left without cash. Milton Eisenhower, the president's brother, once warned that deficits were like sleeping pills. One could take one or two, perhaps even four, without much harm. But if one swallowed twenty, one could be sure to be dead. If we don't know exactly where the limit is, it is better not to try it out.

Security cannot be achieved through any technological fix. It is a political problem.

During the great debate in the United States in 1969 whether or not to build an antiballistic missile (ABM) system, a propaganda film in favor made the point that even though it was not yet technologically feasible to build a "dense" ABM system against Soviet missiles, this was not so important. The Soviet leadership was relatively reasonable and reliable. The great danger were the Chinese; they were so fanatic and unpredictable. All that was really needed was a "thin" ABM system to keep out Chinese nuclear missiles. Today the United States is not afraid of a Chinese nuclear attack, but not because of any "thin" ABM system. It is because the United States and China have developed better relations.

Security stems primarily from a skillful policy that seeks common ground with other nations, rather than from reliance on military means. If the United States had put military pressure on China, for example, by sending troops and bombers into China during the Cultural Revolution to support a more "moderate" faction, and instead had sent Ping-Pong teams and symphony orchestras into Vietnam, its relations with those two countries would probably be just the reverse of what they are today: quite friendly relations with Vietnam, and rather tense relations with China.

6

People Do Have Power

Some people say that since nuclear deterrence is immoral, we need star wars. Others say star wars is too dangerous; therefore we must continue to rely on deterrence. Both are wrong. Star wars and deterrence are not the only two alternatives. There is a whole range of instruments at our disposal with which we can build a more secure world.

Figure 2 gives an overview of the methods briefly discussed here. Much more could be said and *has* been said about each one of them.

The first thing to try is to develop international cooperation and build global institutions based on common interest. If conflicts emerge, we can first seek to remove the sources of the conflict. If we fail, we can negotiate. If we are unable to reach agreement, we can involve a third party with better access to our adversaries. They can simply facilitate communication, or mediate by making their own suggestions, or arbitrate by deciding on a fair solution. If the other side refuses to accept the arbitrator's verdict, we can seek recourse through legal means. Only if all of these methods have failed and we face aggression, need we resort to defense. Defense can consist of nonmilitary means, making ourselves less vulnerable against hostile activities, and persuading any opponents that peaceful cooperation is in *their* better interest than going to war. If nonmilitary methods fail, the last resort is military defense. But such defense must protect ourselves from harm, without posing a threat to other countries. If we are perceived as a threat to others, we invite our own destruction.

Part II of this book, which outlines the concept of *Autonomous Protection,* describes a concrete proposal for combining some elements of the last three measures in this collection of successive barriers against war: reduced nonmilitary dissuasion, vulnerability, and protective military defense.

This book is not addressed to those who plan wars of aggression; any admonitions to the contrary would probably fall on deaf ears. It is addressed

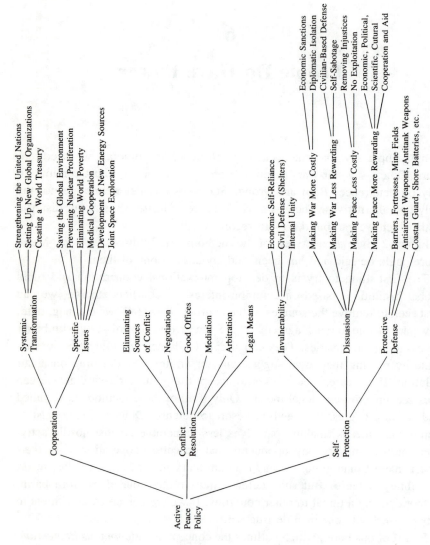

Figure 2. Components of an active peace policy: An overview.

to the potential victims of war, to empower them to prevent war more effectively. The potential victims, who don't want war, may feel they are not responsible for war. But they are certianly more motivated to prevent war than those who are prepared to go to war to further their own ambitions.

It is important for people to realize that something *can* be done to prevent war. If we *believe* that we cannot prevent it, then we will fail. "Learned helplessness" can be paralyzing, as the following finding illustrates: In an experiment, dogs were put into a cage with a metal floor and an exit to an adjacent cage. They were administered electric shocks through the floor. The dogs winced, searched around, and then escaped into the other, safe cage. Then another group of dogs were put into a cage without exit, where they were administered electric shocks. They winced, searched around, but when they found no way to escape, they helplessly lay on the floor, quietly wimpering. When these same dogs were later put into a cage with an exit and administered electric shocks, they did not search for an escape, but simply lay on the floor, in resignation. They had been trained to feel helpless. But the most interesting lesson is that dogs that had initially learned to look for an exit continued to do so, even if they were temporarily put in a cage without escape. When they later were in a cage with an exit, they found it.

Similar behavior has been observed among human beings (Worchel & Cooper 1983). If we have tried to change our conditions and failed, we may give up hope and become fatalistic. But if we have once experienced that we *can* make a difference, then we tend to continue to strive for improvements, even in the face of adversity. People also can do something that dogs cannot: *we can learn from others*. For this reason, we want to mention here three examples of individual citizens' initiatives that have shown far-reaching consequences.

A few years ago a small group of women in Ronneby, Sweden, decided that they wanted to do something for peace. They noticed that most governments profess to be in favor of disarmament but claim they cannot disarm because they feel threatened by other countries. This gave them the idea of asking governments questions of the form, "Are you willing to take steps to insure that the development, possession, storage, and employment of mass-destruction weapons including nuclear weapons, which threaten to destroy the very conditions of life on this earth, are forbidden in your country—if all other members of the United Nations undertake to do the same?" Other questions dealt with nonintervention, the prohibition of arms exports, the use of the earth's resources for the fundamental necessities of life, and the peaceful resolution of conflicts. If all governments agreed conditionally, they could then go back to them and say, "All other governments also agree under the condition that everyone else participate, so why don't you all do it at the same time?" They formed an organization called The Great Peace Journey, and in May 1985, with a grant from the Swedish government, they took this list of five questions to the governments of all small and medium-size countries in Europe. Twenty-five governments received delegations, only three declined; fifteen governments gave positive answers to all five questions, and several more to some questions. In 1986 the organization took this list of questions to most of the remaining governments of the world, including the two superpowers, with the cooperation of women's organizations around the world. The great majority of governments gave positive answers to all five questions. Even though the volunteers' ultimate goal is not yet fulfilled, they received a great deal of publicity on television, radio, and in print in many countries, and have raised the consciousness of many people.

In 1980 Michael Randle, who teaches peace studies at Bradford University in England, formed a small discussion group of about a dozen members to explore an alternative British defense policy, which would not rely on nuclear weapons. They published a report called "Defence Without the Bomb" (Alternative Defence Commission 1983), which was widely discussed. The Labour party essentially adopted their ideas in its platform. If the party wins some future elections, this proposal could become British defense policy. It is impressive to observe the far-reaching consequences that an individual's courageous initiative can have. Of course, this could not have been achieved without public concern and support. There is widespread antinuclear sentiment in Great Britain. It takes fertile soil for a seed to grow into a majestic tree. If a seed is planted into the desert, nothing can grow. But even with the most fertile soil and the most favorable climate, unless someone plants a seed, nothing will grow either. For change to occur, the conditions must be ripe, and someone must seize the initiative to make use of the right conditions.

Randall Kehler, who later became the national coordinator of the U.S. Nuclear Weapons Freeze Campaign, went to jail in 1969 for refusing military service in Vietnam. Before going to jail, he went around the country speaking out against the war at public meetings in churches, at universities, and other places. He had no idea whether this would make any difference; he did it out of his conscience. Daniel Ellsberg later said that hearing Kehler speak was what finally moved him to decide to publish the Pentagon Papers, after he had gradually become increasingly disillusioned with the war. He felt that Kehler was very sincere. Ellsberg was a Pentagon analyst with access to secret documents. When he passed these documents to several major newspapers, which published them, the American people began to realize that they had been deceived by all the government's pronouncements about the "light at the end of the tunnel." No end to the war was in sight, and the United States was not winning. When people saw this, growing numbers began to turn against the war, and this forced the U.S. government to withdraw its troops. Of course, the struggle of the Vietnamese, who made enormous sacrifices, was also crucial. But without domestic public opposition, the U.S. government could have resorted to nuclear weapons, as it did against Japan in 1945, when it had public support for its demand of unconditional surrender. At the right moment, together with help from many others, an individual's action can make a decisive difference. Speaking out in public may indirectly help end a war, or avoid a war.

There is a saying that at the right moment, a single snowflake can break the branch of a tree. Since we never know whether our action represents that critical snowflake, we should always try. And even if our own efforts do not seem to make much difference, they can make it easier for others to complete what we helped move forward.

Many have emphasized, correctly, that nuclear weapons cannot be disinvented. From this they conclude that we will have to live under the threat of nuclear weapons forever. But this conclusion is false. We can completely dismantle them and decide never to build them again. We can develop a *taboo* against their use and their construction, as we have developed many other taboos. We have not disinvented cannibalism, but we abhor that thought. Why can't we similarly abhor the idea of incinerating human beings with nuclear weapons?

Part II

Preventing War—Protecting People

7

War Prevention—A Political Task

War and Politics

War is an instrument of politics. Nothing else uses war as an instrument. Only politics uses war.

World War II raged in three continents. The war theaters were Central Europe, North Africa, and East Asia. At the end of the war the losers had lost everything, even their capacity to conduct politics, for they had relied on nothing more than their means to wage war and on war as an instrument of politics. The politics of the aggressors finally succumbed to its own instrument—in the hands of the victors. Unconditional surrender remained the only way out. This meant unconditional subordination to the war-making potential of the victors as their instrument of politics.

The politics of the victors ended that war. But it did not end war itself. It did not suppress the continuation of World War II by means of other wars. True, it has outlawed war. And it has banned war from the theaters of World War II, at least from Central Europe, by and large. But it has not prevented the expansion of war to new theaters in the Third World (See Fig. 3).

World War II was barely over when the "Third-World" war began. Despite the lesson from World War II that the use of war for political ends had completely deprived the losers of their political capacity, politicians were betting again on war to achieve political ends. Already at the end of the final year of World War II, four countries were involved in new wars; after that, never less than five. Often enough the victors of World War II had to realize that they were unable to achieve their political ends through war, no matter how superior their military means were.

The Third-World war goes on. The war theaters change. The parties change. The warlords change. The victors of World War II are often among them.

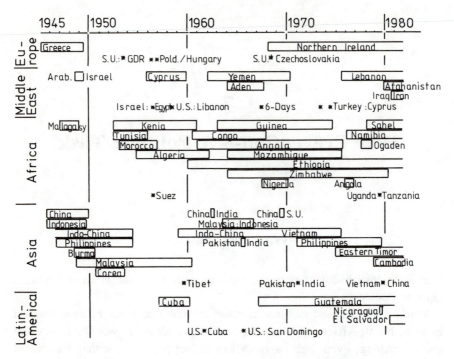

Figure 3. Derived from a graphic "Major Wars from 1945–1981" (Thompson 1981), this shows interstate wars, civil wars, guerilla wars, and interventions.

But they have not achieved any more victories. The only exception—the Falklands/Malvinas—cost the victor—Great Britain—dearly.

War is an overpowering instrument of politics. Often war alone seems to offer a way out of a belligerent policy. In war politics becomes even more constrained. Ultimately, war overshadows all politics, in war and in peace, especially in a peace that is dictated by the conditions of war. Nuclear peace in the shadow of nuclear armament is such a peace.

War has often led precisely to the loss of what politics wanted to achieve through war. Nevertheless, many believe they must prepare for war even in peace time to preserve the peace. They believe that the admonition of the Roman Renatus Vegetius, "*si vis pacem, para bellum,*" memorized from school days, contains a higher truth. Is it the latin text? Does the foreign language convert nonsense into sense? An "if . . . then" relation is postulated. If peace, then war. An idea, a contradiction, is captured into a formula and in this way is considered a mathematical truth. "War for peace" could be a first inversion. "The more war, the more peace" offers itself as a first derivation. "Peace is war" is the next inversion. "The more peaceful, the more warlike"—a word play with obsolete phrases?

Not at all. Nothing has been prepared more thoroughly by civilized nations than the means to wage war, in a vain attempt to render war impossible. In the process the attempt is made to convert nonsense into apparent sense. Stated in strategic latin: *Si vis* "war prevention," *para* "deterrence" is the present-day formula à la Vegetius. The more means of destruction, the better the chances for survival (every pharmacist knows better). The more catastrophic the threatened ending of humanity, the more reliably guaranteed is its ultimate (?) survival.

Achieve deterrence to prevent war. This is a matter of politics. Such politics employs war as a means. It uses war as a mental image. It deploys all the instruments for war in peace time. It anticipates war by imagining all kinds of destruction. It imagines "the extreme" (Clausewitz). It goes beyond the extreme by teaching to think "the unthinkable" (Kahn). It demands the most powerful weapons. It demands the most comprehensive strategies. It demands the most intransigent positions. It demands—war. It provokes the development that turns politics into an instrument of war.

Deterrence does not want to kill directly. But it wants to perfect the means to do so. War prevention through deterrence is a sort of perfection of Vegetius's formula. "Peace" is replaced by "war prevention," and "war" is replaced by "deterrence." War prevention is made the overarching notion of peace—because war, today, in Central Europe, nuclear, would not even preserve the word *peace*. Deterrence is made the overarching notion of war—because war, today, in Central Europe, nuclear, would not even preserve war in its traditional form. If deterrence fails, the fall from the roof is deeper and more destructive than the fall from ground level.

War is not a natural disaster. War is a consequence of political decisions. The more nonwar politics is inserted on the way toward war, the longer becomes the path to war. The less warlike politics is made, the less likely it is that politics will be overpowered by war. The less instruments of war support politics, the more room is created for peacemaking, for the peaceful prevention of war.

If war is an instrument exclusively of politics, politics alone can prevent war. It alone can renounce it. It alone can push it back, reduce its effect, ostracize it, end it.

The famous Clausewitz dictum, "War is a continuation of politics with the application of military means" is no longer valid at a time when war must be understood as a peril beyond the extreme. Clausewitz's statement must be modified to say, "War is the end of politics because of the application of military means" (Horst Afheldt 1976, 1985). To recognize this means to conclude: War prevention is the ceaseless application of nonmilitary means to politics.

Crisis—Conflict—War or Crisis—Conflict—Crisis?

The phenomenon of conflict and ways to overcome it are discussed in general terms in Part I. Here we focus more narrowly on military aspects of conflict. In this connection, the word sequences "crisis—conflict—war" and "crisis—conflict—crisis" represent time sequences. They indicate successive events. One follows the other. Each develops from the previous one.

The crisis may emerge during a time that can best be characterized as peace. Criticism is offered. It may be well intended. It may seek to promote peace. It is meant constructively. But it may be misinterpreted as endangering the peace. It can be misunderstood as destructive. Misinterpretation and misunderstanding produce countercriticism. It also may be meant to be constructive and misunderstood as destructive. The critics increase their criticism. The exchange of criticism develops into a sharp clash. There are critical moments. They become more frequent and lead to a crisis.

Robert Jervis (1976) has amply documented how misperceptions and misunderstandings can lead to a spiral of escalating hostilities. Each side is convinced that its own military preparations are only for defensive purposes, but that the other side's military preparations exceed what it needs for self-defense and reveal evil intentions. Observations that appear to confirm a preconceived image of the "enemy" are noticed and remembered. Observations that would signal friendly intentions are often either ignored or portrayed as a "trick" to lull us into complacency. In psychology, this phenomenon is known as *attribution theory*.

Criticism is natural in a free society, also at the international level. Free societies live and develop with criticism. Criticism is an instrument of society's development. Criticism is one part of operationalized freedom. A society without criticism is not free. The fact that criticism is permitted as a matter of course is a guarantee for the mastery of crises. A crisis need not lead to confrontation. A crisis can be overcome peacefully by means of freedom. The more pronounced the free exchange among the critics, the better is the chance that a crisis can be mastered. The less pronounced the free exchange among the critics, the slimmer is the chance that a crisis can be overcome peacefully.

The sooner one of the critics during a crisis resorts to confrontational arguments, insists on assertions instead of searching for proofs, allocates guilt instead of exploring reasons, demands subservience instead of seeking to gain partners, the sooner the crisis erupts into conflict. Conflict is confrontational. Confrontation makes partnership more difficult, blocks mutual understanding, inhibits the exchange of views. Confrontation hardens one-sided judgement. Confrontation leads to actions based on prejudice. Confrontation promotes stubbornness and false pride. Confrontation is not limited to criticism. Confrontation deals crushing blows. Confrontation hurts, hurts the partner, makes the partner an adversary. An adversarial relationship is conflict. Conflict is struggle at a lower level of intensity.

If crisis, figuratively speaking, is separation, confrontation, keeping a distance—then conflict, figuratively speaking, is collision, clash, entanglement. Crises may lead to complications. The problems of the crisis may become more complex, connected, interwoven. The problems of the conflict form an intricate, tight web. The situation of the conflict resembles that of a Gordian knot. Strands of incompatible interests are inextricably tangled in an interdependent system. Any attempt to resolve the tangle often tightens the knot further. Finally one of the parties strikes the first blow, and the entire system falls apart. In the worst case, completely. One of the parties may achieve a "victory," but at what price? At the price of war?

War as a way out of conflict so often appears to be the only feasible way. The means of war are ready. One blow, carried out with the instruments of war, leads to war itself. One surprise attack, one blitzkrieg, one first use, one first strike, leads to counterattack, to protracted war, to second use, to second strike. Today, in the nuclear age, it carries the risk of the destruction of the whole system, of omnicide.

Therefore, that one blow must not happen. That one blow must be averted.

Another way out of confrontation must be found. The entanglements must be dissolved. The other blows must be intercepted. The wounds must be cared for. The complications must be dissected. Ways out of the conflict back into the crisis must be opened. Criticism and freedom must take effect again. Development must be able to continue.

Therefore the sequence of crisis—conflict—war is no longer admissible. This sequence stands for growing inability for free development of society. This sequence has its counterpart in the word sequence: friend—adversary—enemy. It reflects from the outset the instruments of war. It implies, at the peak of confrontation in a conflict, military means must play the key role. It focuses from the outset on the military as the ultimate instrument of politics.

Therefore, the sequence must be: crisis—conflict—crisis, which symbolizes the ability to reduce a conflict to the level of crisis. This sequence has its counterpart in the word sequence of friend—adversary—friend, or the inclusive notion of partner. The sequence reflects politics from the outset. It implies that, at the peak of confrontation in a conflict, political means must play the key role. Among them may *also* be military means. But they must be only conventional and only defensive.

The sequence crisis—conflict—crisis . . . does not tend toward a peak, an endpoint, like war. Rather, it remains below the threshold of war. It averts the tendency toward war at the peak of confrontation and opens a new future for politics. It makes continuity possible. We can have crisis—conflict—crisis—conflict—crisis . . . an up and down instead of a "blow up" of people (Reagan 1985). An example: In 1984, the United States urged Egypt three times to go to war with Libya. Egypt refused the repeated requests each time and so was able to dampen the crisis three times.

Defense of Political Autonomy

By means of nuclear deterrence, humans want to control the "extreme." By preparing for the "extreme" to the extent of credible capacity and readiness, they want to prevent reliably the occurrence of this extreme, nuclear war. Only few arrogate this to themselves: that war prevention by means of nuclear deterrence will succeed forever. They must belong to those who deny the omnipresence of war.

Many, however, ask: what happens if deterrence fails? Many at least ask. Few know an answer. Often they prefer to conceal the answer. So that the terror in deterrence remains an unknown variable. Or they remain silent so that they need not render account of their conscious readiness for the extreme.

Suppose a policy exists that achieves this up and down between crisis and conflict. (Part I outlines numerous rules for such a policy.) But it would still be presumptuous to deny that such a policy might also fail; to deny that an opponent might nevertheless strike that one blow.

How then could it be appropriate to prepare oneself for nothing else but a counterattack, protracted war, first use, first strike, and second strike? How could it—in the face of the extreme political conflict, overburdened with military means—be appropriate to aggravate the conflict further with additional military means?

In this way politics is faded out, thrust aside. The primacy of politics is surrendered to the military. The question of the population's survival is replaced by the question of the capability of military forces to destroy the opponent. Surviving in a war is no longer a plausible option.

But as long as war cannot be reliably prevented, the aim *in* war must be primarily to protect the carrier of politics, the people—not only the politicians. The principal aim in case of war must be to preserve the political capacity of the entire (!) people. To this end, defense must be made plausible again, the defense of the community of citizens (in Greek: the inhabitants of the *polis*) as the political community.

Farewell to Deterrence?

For how long will what seems to work today continue to work tomorrow? This is the first question. How long will deterrence keep what it promises? How long will it be able to prevent war?

Nobody can answer that question with certainty. The future is largely unknown. Deterrence—a strategy of uncertainty—makes the future predictable. It keeps it in suspense.

The often-heard argument that deterrence alone has prevented war since 1945—at least in Europe—is on weak empirical ground, as mentioned in Chapter 5. Even in Europe, war is not an unknown phenomenon. And some European countries have repeatedly participated in wars outside of Europe (particularly those countries that maintain nuclear weapons for "deterrence"), inspite of Europe's painful experience during the world wars.

On various occasions internal problems have led to violent, warlike disputes, for example, the Basques' demand for autonomy. Since 1968 the civil war in Northern Ireland takes its bloody toll year after year. The civil war of 1974 in Cyprus between the NATO members Greece and Turkey still cannot be considered as "solved." The names of the Falklands/Malvinas, Afghanistan, Angola, Algeria, Suez, Indochina remind us of just a few of the many wars in which Europeans have fought. At present French troops are in Chad. Also the role of the multilateral forces of England, France, and Italy in Lebanon is ambiguous and could be interpreted as interference in the civil war there.

Western as well as Eastern European states have their specific share in the "Third-World" war: through arms exports, military advisors, troops, proxies. Especially via the latter the Soviet Union operates throughout the world. But it has also made Central Europe the theater of repeated "pacification" campaigns: Berlin, Hungary, Czechoslovakia are the most obvious cases. And European military bases in countries not directly involved have been used for military missions outside of Europe (e.g., in the 1986 bombing of Libya by the United States).

Forty years after World War II, Europe has not yet been weaned from war. Deterrence has not prevented war in these cases. Not even nuclear deterrence, if it had any bearing in this context (Huth/Russet 1984; Schmid 1985). Entirely different, nonmilitary efforts and relationships may have prevented war here, such as economic interdependence, the inner-German détente, the reconciliation with Poland in the framework of the "Ostpolitik," and more.

Also, the nonaligned and neutral nations can claim to have contributed more reliably to war prevention, and less to war, than many allied nations. They have not participated in wars inside or outside of Europe (except Yugoslavia and Albania in the Greek civil war of 1946, and Yugoslavia in several border clashes after 1945). Some of them—Finland, Yugoslavia, Austria, and Sweden (Buchbender/Bühl/Quaden 1983)—repeatedly supplied contingents to the U.N. peacekeeping forces to contain and reduce military conflicts in flash points around the world. They do this not to acquire territory or to gain power. Neither is the threatening situation in Central Europe caused in any way by the neutral and nonaligned. And nuclear deterrence is needed least of all against them; as nonnuclear states that don't threaten anyone.

They don't appear to be helpless, subject to arbitrary nuclear threats. They do not possess any nuclear potential to make counterthreats. Do they basically need any such potential? They have never been a target of nuclear threats or nuclear blackmail (Huth/Russet 1984; Schmid 1985). This does not mean that they have made no preparations against nuclear war. Many political decisions may have been made differently under the danger of nuclear war than they would have been made under a lesser danger. For they could always become victims of nuclear war. Already today they have to face the primary task of seeking to reduce, as a precaution, the unknown number of potential victims in case of a nuclear war.

Deterrence, particularly nuclear deterrence, is therefore not a part of the strategic mental image of the neutral and nonaligned states in Europe. But it is part of the mental image of NATO and the Warsaw Pact, for the collective defense of aligned states. These states either possess nuclear weapons themselves, or indirectly possess a share of nuclear might in the form of nuclear delivery vehicles, target planning, and nuclear operational and tactical concepts. They have not been accorded any right under international law to exert nuclear force during a nuclear war beyond the theater of war—for example, against neutral nonnuclear states. The use of nuclear might as a special—military!—instrument of politics, already during nuclear peace, exposes the tendency toward hegemonial thinking among the nuclear powers and their client states.

Yet it must be observed that the nuclear war between the antagonistic powers of capitalism-liberalism and communism-socialism, which we have been facing since 1945, has not yet been unleashed. Maybe deterrence has prevented it. But even this effect of deterrence is doubted in the relevant literature (Huth/Russet 1984; Catudal 1985).

Whoever considers to say farewell to deterrence must first make sure what deterrence is—what is to be given up.

Deterrence is a mental image. As a strategy it "rests entirely on the central idea of bringing to bear the existence of the weapons so skillfully that they never have to be used" (Beaufre 1966). Deterrence is unthinkable without weapons. They are the central element. Nuclear weapons make deterrence into what it is today: "Neither politics nor diplomacy, but an effective, even a most effective instrument in the service of politics, that is, a strategy."

Beaufre, a French general who has presented the first comprehensive theory of deterrence, subordinates deterrence to politics: "The solutions developed by the strategy of deterrence make sense only within the framework of a political goal" (1966). The goal is the prevention of war, especially nuclear war. Beaufre's work, in two books, is considered to lay a theoretical foundation. The theoretical construct erected on this foundation is in itself undisputed. Clearly, particular aspects have diminished in their actuality over nearly two decades. But the main arguments remain widely accepted to this day.

Barely twenty years later, another Frenchman speaks up, André Glucksman, once a young revolutionary and now rather conservative. With his earlier work, "*le discours de la guerre*" (1967), he had proven his military expertise during Beaufre's times. In 1984 he concluded his "Philosophy of Deterrence" with an answer to "the most serious and simplest question presented to us by banal reality." The question is: "Do we have the right to take women, children and children's children of an entire planet as hostages? May we threaten civilian populations, of whom we are part, with apocalypse? Does a culture deserve that name if, in order to survive, it consciously risks its extinction?" Glucksman's answer: "Whatever those with an overly tranquil conscience may say—yes."

Deterrence is—connecting the ideas of the two—strategy and risk. The risk of human extinction as a strategy with the ultimate weapons.

Deterrence is the mental image of the "unthinkable." It is possible to think of the ultimate weapons. In Beaufre's strategic construct one can even "calculate one's own risk" associated with their use "on the basis of material conditions" (Beaufre 1966). But the totality of their effect exceeds the imagination of humans. For "the extent of fear (instilled by deterrence via threats) depends on numerous factors of political, social and ethical nature, and on much else." And those "often escape material considerations" (Beaufre 1966).

Deterrence is more than merely a "mental image." It is the enormous multiplicity and variety of deliberations, plans, anticipated decisions for the conduct of war under nuclear conditions, planned battle engagements hoping for victory. Such thinking—originating in the East (Sokolowski 1969)—is becoming increasingly prevalent also in the West (Gray and Payne 1980; Clark 1982; Abt 1985).

Deterrence is finally—daily!—the use of nuclear weapons for politics, without igniting the fuses, without exploding them. Nuclear weapons are being developed and modernized, produced and deployed, flown around in the air, moved on land, submersed under sea and ice. They are tested in war games and trial launchings. They are aimed toward their targets. Only dropped on their targets and fired, this they are not. At least not yet as long as neither insanity nor human nor technical error release them. The risk of apocalypse rests entirely on human rationality and technical perfection. Deterrence is thus the hazardous enterprise of assuming that humanity has overcome its human weaknesses and has become master over coincidence. Deterrence is the pretension of the human to believe in superman and to imitate him. Those who hold this pretension and want to imitate superman may repeat Glucksmann's answer.

The president of the United States chose another way. Since 1983 he pursues an entirely different future vision: the defense of country and people against nuclear weapons. Reagan moves away from deterrence toward defense. He must know what deterrence is when it fails: Then deterrence is the release and ignition of nuclear weapons, the crossing of the nuclear threshold, being trapped ascending along the escalation ladder, without knowing whether one will ever be able to descend along it again and escape it. Deterrence is the certainty of risking human extinction.

The more Reagan's Strategic Defense Initiative (SDI) takes shape, the clearer it becomes: It will reinforce deterrence. It does not diminish the risk of human extinction at all.

Whoever does not want to take responsibility for that risk must say farewell to deterrence.

Farewell to Defense?

Defense has also gained ill repute. There is growing concern that it can no longer deliver what is expected from it. It seems that the danger of destruction increases with defense. Everyone expects that defense should repel (aggression), preserve (territorial integrity), protect (against the effects of weapons), and save (life). The concern that defense may no longer be "protective" but "destructive" pervades political decisions and actions. War, in whatever form, would be disastrous, so goes the argument in the political realm. Therefore any war should above all be prevented by any means. The most certain means of preventing war is said to be offered by nuclear deterrence, that strategy of uncertainty that we have called "playing with the extreme." Those who bet everything on deterence no longer trust in defense.

Those who make that argument often fail to distinguish between convention and nuclear war. They argue that a conventional war would be no less devastating than a nuclear war. The secondary effects resulting exclusively from nuclear war, discussed below, are often ignored. This is done from the narrow perspective of deterrence, with the short-sighted goal of seeking to prevent war at any price. (The goal is short-sighted because the price, if it means human extinction, is undoubtedly too high.)

Such argumentation is revealing. It exposes the depth of the conviction that if deterrence fails, defense would probably only destroy, even if carried out "only" with conventional weapons. It also shows that the nuclear threshold has long been crossed mentally, in advance. This applies from a conventional perspective. Conventional weapons have reached a destructive "quality"—or are about to reach it—that borders on nuclear weapons. "The new weapons technologies . . . can largely lead to a dissolution of the factual nuclear threshold" (Fesefeldt 1984).

But the nuclear threshold has also been mentally crossed in advance from a strategic perspective: the three types of forces—conventional, short- and medium-range nuclear, and strategic nuclear—have been linked (in NATO) into a unified "triad." It must be "uninterrupted." It is a "continuum." It enables NATO to escalate in a "controlled" manner, without any distinctive steps (Whitebook 1983, No. 272). The strategy of NATO, "flexible response," presupposes the crossing of thresholds. Strictly speaking, continuous escalation is not a stepping across thresholds but a sliding across: control is deliberately made difficult. For this reason, NATO—in its self-image—cannot renounce the option of first use. Otherwise it would rob itself of the possibility of self-initiated "deliberate escalation."

Like all the other deterrence options of NATO, first use also pursues the central aim preferably not to fight a war—in whatever form. A "potential war [should be] rapidly terminated" (Whitebook 1983, No. 273). The state of deterrence should rapidly be restored. Back to playing with "the extreme."

First of all, it is nuclear deterrence that has given defense the ill repute that it destroys rather than to save. Particularly the continuous entanglement of conventional and nuclear forces makes it difficult to imagine a war that is "only" conventional. Thus there is reason why every image of war in Central Europe involving NATO is linked to the nightmare of holocaust, the horror vision of apocalypse. For decades, nightmares and horror visions have strained our fantasies. Today, traditional fantasies pale before new revelations. Particularly the secondary effects of nuclear weapons, overlooked by the superficial arguments noted above, have been recognized as increasingly significant.

Most of the relevant studies are based on nearly identical scenarios of a nuclear war: approximately half the arsenal of nuclear weapons is ignited—along the path of escalation (IISS, Strategic Survey 1984/85, 25). They also expect that cities of both the United States and the Soviet Union and their allies suffer nuclear attacks. As the consequences of such a nuclear exchange, these studies describe numerous large-scale fires, developing huge amounts of smoke that spread across large areas of the globe, blocking sunlight and reducing temperatures. A dark nuclear winter sets in, followed by harvest failures, starvation, and mass death (of those who may have survived the nuclear war). Nonbelligerent nations are equally affected as the warring parties.

After the direct physical effects of nuclear war (flash: blinding/burning; blast: destruction; radiation: sickness/death), the indirect geological, meteorological, and climatological consequences have now also been explored. In this respect the politics of nuclear deterrence must be characterized as a game with the certain knowledge of the certain end of civilization. There remains another, perhaps decisive variable: the genetic consequences, the long-term damage to genes, the risk of mutations in plants, animals, and humans. This uncertainty does not instill faith into a defense that is inextricably linked with the "continuous, deliberate" escalation to the use of nuclear weapons.

Second, conventional defense itself has also contributed to the ill repute of defense. Just where protection from the effects of nuclear weapons was most important, where large populations should have been saved from the effects of attacks, conventional defense has often failed. The big cities—

Rotterdam, Coventry, Stalingrad, Hamburg, Dresden, Berlin, Tokyo, and many others (Irving 1982)—ended up destroyed. People were bombed and burnt. This impression from World War II finds its parallels in modern, "only" conventional wars in the "Third-World" war: Beirut, Hanoi, Kandahar (in Afghanistan) lay in ruins after being "defended." It should be stressed that usually these cities were not destroyed by the defenders themselves. But military defense proved incapable of offering the expected protection for people and cultural monuments.

This insight is not new. Because it is so obvious and important, it has found its way into international law, which prohibits military operations against so-called open cities (See Table 1) from which the defender has withdrawn all military assets (Hague Convention on Land Warfare of 1907, Article 25).

Table 1
Open Cities—Experience during World War II

City, year attacker	Formally declared an open city?*	Own military removed?	Ceased without defense?	Result: bombarded?
Brussels 1940 Germany	Yes	Yes	Yes	No
Reims 1940 Germany	Yes	Yes	Yes	No
Paris 1940 Germany	Yes	Yes	Yes	No
Constance 1945 France	No	Yes	Yes	No
Warsaw 1939 Germany	Yes	No	No	Yes
Rotterdam 1940 Germany	Yes	No	No	Yes
Rome 1943 Great Britain	Yes	Yes	Yes	Yes
Bologna 1944 Allied	Yes	Yes	Yes	No
Guernica 1937 Germany	Yes	No	No	Yes

*) This declaration is made according to the Hague Convention on Land Warfare, Article 25; the formal declaration is not a precondition for the obligation of the attacker to spare the populations of militarily undefended cities (Born 1978).

In this way the renunciation of military defense saved the lives of several million people during World War II. Brussels, Reims, Paris, Constance, Bologna—with their populations and streams of refugees—have survived the war (Born 1978).

Protection of the civilian population has therefore been a special, internationally acknowledged right for nearly a century. It seems appropriate to develop it into a legal obligation, even in conventional war of the traditional kind, but particularly under conditions of conventional war that approach in their effect the nuclear threshold, and most of all under conditions of nuclear armaments that "take into account annihilation" (Frei 1983).

Here a new idea can emerge. It can take root here because it connects to well-established thinking tested in war. Here it must set in, because a further erosion of confidence into defense can raise questions about its legitimacy. Loss of legitimacy of defense could lead to "surrender" before there is a new world war in and about Europe. Such a surrender would be equivalent to the subordination under the military means of a potential aggressor, used for political ends. It could mean the loss of any sovereign, autonomous, independent political capacity.

Those who want to preserve life and liberty, as long as war cannot be reliably prevented, must not say farewell to defense.

8

Defensive Thinking—Autonomous Protection

The Search for Alternatives

The way to defensive thinking, the search for a new orientation toward defense, is worth a brief excursion.

A starting point of the recent resurgence of interest in defensive concepts is an analysis of the consequences of war and methods of war prevention in Europe by von Weizsaecker (1976). Simultaneously, three conceptual studies reach the public: each of the three authors (Horst Afheldt 1976; Brossolet 1976; Spannocchi 1976) designs, with special reference to their own country, a structure of defense that is more oriented toward holding territory than mobile, far-reaching battlefield engagements: defense should counter the temptation to use nuclear weapons against the conventional superiority of the presumed aggressor, and conventional fighting should be made more effective. Nuclear weapons are relegated to the role of serving a purely deterrent function, in remote, sea-based locations.

After this first, triple push to new thinking, against the background of the dramatic studies on consequences of war by von Weizsaecker and other scientists, nothing further happens initially: years of silence. The great public strategy debate sought by the authors remains a matter of experts behind closed doors. Only the NATO double-decision of 1979, with the intention of deploying nuclear medium-range Pershing II and cruise missiles in Western Europe unless the Soviet Union stops and reverts its deployment of medium-range SS-20 missiles in Eastern Europe, confronts the public with the questions of the experts. More precisely: the public—finally shaken up—wrests these questions from the experts. A peace movement grows rapidly.

This movement, besides its protests against means of war prevention and defense that are in its view inadequate, also searches for alternatives to official strategy. A heated discussion sets in, rife with proposals of all kinds. The result so far is that the danger has increased, not diminished; the spectrum of options available to NATO has widened, not narrowed. This follows from the graphical representation below: if the range of conventional land operations (ignoring options for the air force) previously ended within territorial borders, they now reach farther in some of these new operational plans. If previously nuclear options reached their upper limit with a strategic nuclear exchange between continents, the tendency begun with SDI research now reaches beyond that space into orbit. NATO has increased its options. Have the alternative strategies, concentrating on defense, been ignored?

What are the goals of the "parties" in the strategy discussion?

Some of them are particularly concerned about the nuclear danger. They are looking for various ways to raise the nuclear threshold, which they view as clearly too low. No first use (Bundy et al. 1982), a freeze on nuclear armament (the freeze movement), nuclear weapon free zones (Palme Commission 1982) are central demands, but they have not yet been able to move NATO from its familiar track, even though highly respected personalities (such as Robert McNamara, Edward Kennedy, or Olof Palme) have given their active support.

Others expect to be able to strengthen deterrence by emphasizing the conventional component of NATO's defense. This line of argument was particularly supported by U.S. General Bernard Rogers, the former supreme commander of NATO forces in Europe. At the same time he has been preparing the way for a new operational conception for U.S. forces (AirLand-Battle) and for NATO (Follow-on Forces Attack/FOFA). Both conceptions foresee, to different degrees, an extension of the battlefield onto the territory of the opponent after his attack.

The INF Treaty, signed at the Washington summit in December 1987, in which the United States and the Soviet Union commit themselves to eliminate all SS-4, SS-5, SS-20, Pershing II, and land-based cruise missiles from Europe is a welcome first disarmament measure, which actually eliminates some nuclear weapons and does not just put ceilings on further increases. But the reduction will be less than 4 percent of the world's nuclear arsenal. And there are still plenty of airborne and short-range battlefield nuclear weapons in Europe and submarine-based nuclear ballistic and cruise missiles assigned to Europe. There is still plenty of overkill, and NATO's nuclear first use doctrine remains in place.

To the "hawks" of conventional deterrence, even AirLand Battle and FOFA don't go far enough. Some plead for counterattacks deep into the territory

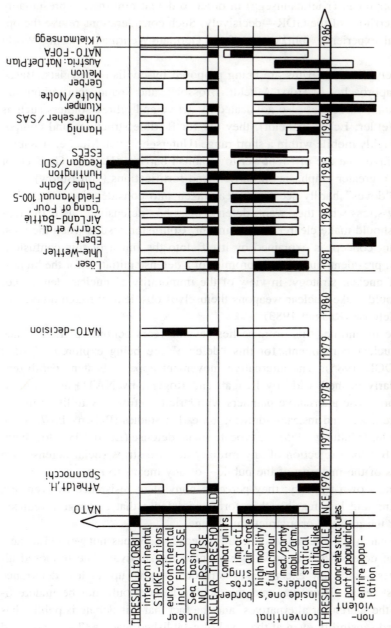

Figure 4. A decade of strategy discussion in NATO: flexible response—alternatives—expanded NATO options. The bars show the core of the strategies/alternatives. Dark shadows show the focal point of reform proposals. Proposals are assigned to the year in which they were published. No temporal sequence within years is indicated.

of the opponent (Kielmannsegg) in order to defeat him there—presumably on the territory of the GDR—decisively. Such considerations revive the operational experience (blitzkrieg) of the German Wehrmacht during World War II.

Entirely different paths are being proposed by civilian strategists. Based on the approaches of Horst Afheldt, Brossolet, and Spannocchi, emphasizing infantry forces (as also advocated by active and retired soldiers such as Uhle-Wettler, Eckart Afheldt), they opt for flexible structures and components, highly mobile within a short range (Unterseher, von Mueller, Canby). Others favor the use of firepower to establish barriers (Hannig, Gerber), or at least a greater emphasis on barriers and fortifications (von Bülow).

The "doves" hardly see their ideas taken into consideration. They desperately stress what they want: defense must be "defensive," as if the repetition should make clearer what is meant. Confusion results when the most important concept is explained by itself. Into the midst of this confusion, the U.S. president launches his promise of a defense initiative for the highest level of nuclear strategy: in view of the immorality of nuclear deterrence, SDI should make nuclear weapons themselves obsolete, through a conventional defense (Reagan 1983).

In the meantime, this promise lies several years behind us. Long since then, nuclear components for this "defense" are being explored (Gordon 1985; DOD 1985). The alternative movement appears beaten, paralyzed. Particularly pushed aside by Reagan and Rogers, by NATO and governments are those alternative planners who strictly refuse any military means to secure peace and instead—drawing on earlier studies (Roberts 1967; Sharp 1973, 1985; Galtung 1955)—advocate social defense (Ebert 1981; Jochheim 1984). But total rejection of any military defense strips social defense—in the eyes of the majority of the public—of any means to repel an aggressor from one's own territory: they perceive nonviolent resistance as even less promising and less feasible than forms of defense that envisage a reduced role for the military or a structural change.

The search for alternatives, begun a decade ago, has not yet led to new forms of defense that improve our chances for survival. The proposed alternatives—with few exceptions!—still do not give up nuclear deterrence as a last resort. However, and this achievement should not be underestimated, the search for alternatives, and the fact that this debate is public, has increased sensibility even at the level of established leaders. They have had to realize that a defense that means annihilation cannot be maintained much longer in a democracy.

Before the leaders of nations and alliances depart from democracy—and we need not fear that this is imminent—it should be possible to win them over to the defensive thinking developed over a decade.

The New Defensive Thinking of Soldiers

The call "Defense, not destruction" (Wernicke/Schoell 1985) appears on this background. Being at the center of the unfolding "process of delegitimization of the military in the nuclear age" (Vogt 1983; Barth 1985), the demand "defense, not destruction" becomes a question of identity for soldiers (Günther/Vollmer 1983; Bastian 1983; Generals for Peace and Disarmament 1983/85; Mechtersheimer 1984). They take an oath for defense, not for annihilation. With their oath, they accept the risk of their own death for the sake of the survival of people and state. Many have taken their oath under the premise that war is no longer an instrument of politics. They have been led by the desire that war ought no longer to be an instrument of politics. But when war is obviously (as shown above) an instrument of politics, then defense in war must again become what is expected of it.

This demand is completely misunderstood by those who insinuate that war should again be made possible. War *is* possible. Present reality demonstrates this. Such a demand does not want to unleash war, or make war more likely. It wants to make defense *in* war possible again. As a more credible defense, it wants to contribute more effectively to the prevention of war.

On the one hand, this demand originates in rather conservative, military thinking, insofar as the military sees its real task in preserving (*conservare*). All of the soldiers we know who plead for "alternative" security and defense (Brossolet 1976; Spannocchi 1976; Loeser 1981; Uhle-Wettler 1981; La Rocque/Tromp 1982; Bastian 1983; Guenther/Vollmer 1983; Klumper 1984; Wilhelm Nolte 1984; Generals for Peace and Disarmament 1985) neither want war, nor are they more willing to accept the risk of war. Instead, they do not want people to put their head in the sand and deny the possibility of war (Weizsaecker 1976), but *defend differently,* especially for the purpose of preventing war (see Table 2).

Many of these soldiers include in their search for alternatives nonmilitary, nonviolent approaches to defense, such as social defense (Bastian 1983; Klumper 1983; Nolte 1984; Generals for Peace and Disarmament 1985). In this respect they consider themselves to be progressive. But such progressive views already have a tradition in military thinking (King-Hall 1958; Liddel-Hart 1967). Also Clausewitz admits another than purely military defense.

"People's armament," is the topic of a separate chapter in the famous

Table 2.

Development/Promotion of Alternatives by Soldiers since World War II

Name	Rank	Country	Status	Alternative
Afheldt, Eckart	Lt.Col.	FRG	active	"light infantry" with techno-commandos
Barth, Peter	Capt.	FRG	retired	nuclear disarmament
Bastian, Gert*	Brig.Gen	FRG	act/ret	nuclear disarmament/defensive structure/ social defense
Brossolet, Guy	Mil.Att.	FRG	active	area defense
Christie, Johan*	Gen.	Norway	retired	nuclear disarmament/defensive structure/ social defense
Da Costa Gomes, F.*	Field.	Portugal	retired	nuclear disarmament/defensive structure/ social defense
De Lima, Rangel	Gen.	Portugal	retired	nuclear disarmament/defensive structure/ social defense
Farwick, Dieter**	Col.	FRG	active	dynamic forward defense
Gerber, Johannes	Maj.Gen.	FRG	retired	barriers with firepower (with Hannig)
Guenther, Ingo	Brig.Gen.	FRG	retired	transarmament/defensive structure
Hannig, Norbert	Lt.Col.	FRG	retired	barriers with firepower (with Gerber)
Harbottle Michael*	Gen.	GB	retired	nuclear disarmament/defensive structure/ social defense
Johnson, Leonard V.*	Gen.	Canada	retired	nuclear disarmament/defensive structure/ social defense
King-Hall, Steven	Adm.	GB	retired	social defense
Klumper, A. A.	Lt.Col.	Netherlands	active	subdefensive civilian defense/social defense

Name	Rank	Country	Status	Focus
Koumanakos, Georgios*	Gen.	Greece	retired	nuclear disarmament/defensive structure/ social defense
Liddel-Hart, Sir Basil	Gen.	GB	retired	civilian resistance (among others)
Loeser, Jochen	Maj.Gen.	FRG	retired	area defense
La Rocque, Gene R.	Adm.	USA	retired	nuclear disarmament
Mechtersheimer, Alfred	Lt.Col.	FRG	retired	nuclear disarmament/defensive structure
Papathanassiou, M.*	Gen.	Greece	retired	nuclear disarmament/defensive structure/ social defense
Pasti, Nino*	Gen.	Italy	retired	nuclear disarmament/defensive structure/ social defense
Sanguinetti, Antoine*	Adm.	France	retired	nuclear disarmament/defensive structure/ social defense
Spannocchi, Emil	Corps Cd	Austria	Act/ret	area defense
Tombopoulos, Mich.*	Gen.	Greece	retired	nuclear disarmament/defensive structure/ social defense
Uhle-Wettler, Franz	Col.	FRG	active	light infantry
Van Meyenfeldt, M. H.*	Gen.	Netherlands	retired	nuclear disarmament/defensive structure/ social defense
Vollmer, Günther*	Maj.Gen.	FRG	retired	transarmament/defensive structure/social defense
Von Acker, Alexander	Lt.Col.	FRG	active	artillery for technocommandos
Von Bonin, Bogislav	Col.	FRG	(active)	antitank barriers
Von Kielmannsegg**	Maj.Gen.	FRG	active	forward defense

Total: 31, of which 22 in the rank of general, 14 from the FRG, 14 include social defense.

* = Member of the group "Generals for Peace and Disarmament."

** = goal: offensive potential to raise the nuclear threshold.

military philosopher's work "On War" (1831). Here he writes: ". . . peo-ple's war must be envisaged in connection with a standing army" (p. 801), and later: "it should not smash the core [of the attacker], but only nibble at the surface" (p. 802). At many points in this chapter the reader is tempted to believe that Clausewitz describes nonviolent resistance or "social de-fense," perhaps here: "In our concept of people's war, it must—like mist or clouds—never coagulate into a firm, resistant body . . ." (p. 803). But Clausewitz means a defense that would rather be called guerilla today.

Guerilla is considered a proven and feared "strategy of the Third World" (Mao Zedong 1963/1966). It meets with great interest also in Europe and is—in a limited way—an element of Switzerland's "general defense" (Dach 1958; Schmid 1985). But guerilla results in a "war without frontiers" (Hahl-weg 1968) and in this way enters a dark zone of international law, in which the attacker gains a pretext for retributions against the civilian population. Even acts of sabotage will be used as welcome occasions for arbitrary ex-ecutions and for taking hostages. If defense is to protect the civilian pop-ulation, it must not resort to guerilla and partisan war. The latter puts the civilian population entirely at the mercy of the attacking troops, often at the mercy of the lowest level of command. The partisan war in Vietnam suc-ceeded, on the one hand, in forcing the United States, a superpower, to its knees; on the other hand it "allowed" the United States, under international law, to bomb the Vietnamese population. The bloodbath that U.S. soldiers created in My Lai had its roots *also* in the ruthless, perfidious partisan war.

The New Defensive Thinking of Citizens

The distrust in the official security policies of the allied and nonaligned states finds its immediate expression in the open criticism by politicians and scientists of rank and name (other examples, besides those noted in the first section in this chapter: Biedenkopf, Eppler, La Fontaine, Frei, Kennan). The peace movement has found articulate expression in a way that cannot be ignored. It has demonstrated that—all over Europe, in West and East, in the United States, Australia, Japan, New Zealand—more and more citizens want to solve the question of war or peace, of defense or destruction by themselves. They do no longer want to entrust that question exclusively to politicians, professional strategists, and the military. They increasingly care about it themselves, in writing, lectures, discussions, leaflets, individual and group initiatives, and mass demonstrations. Their imagination often seems unbounded, their optimism often promises to move mountains. By engaging themselves in these various ways, they mix politics "from below" into the militarily predetermined politics "from above."

Their defensive thinking is new in the sense that military thinking is originally foreign to them. Either they have newly acquired it, or they—now as before—reject it on principle and orient themselves—outside of military thought patterns—toward defense. Nevertheless, they are conservative, in the same sense as the soldiers searching for alternatives: they wish to "conserve" what they have, their liberty and their lives, as well as their neighbors' life and liberty. In this respect they think basically even more defensively than the soldiers.

They seek to realize their principles by refusing all violence that threatens human existence. Their refusal centers on armaments and the military. If politics followed their prescriptions exclusively, top priority would be given to the elimination of nuclear weapons, conventional armaments, and armed forces. Yet (for the most) they have no illusions that a region, demilitarized in this way, nevertheless needs some defense against outside military quests for power. They rather develop a form of defense that resists violence without violence. Based on the so far limited experience with past actions, often spontaneous, to preserve freedom nonviolently (Sharp 1973; Roberts 1967), they develop concepts to achieve above all one thing: to keep the population out of war, by seeking not to expose it to the effects of its own arms, and not to make it a militarily relevant target.

Their principled thinking is consistent and deliberately "radical": it goes to the *root*. It seeks the origins of conflict and war in society and wants to eliminate them at their root. This impedes the access of official security policy to the ideas of nonviolence (Thoreau, Gandhi, Sharp, Luther-King, Galtung). Similarly it inhibits nonviolent thinkers from approaching military thinking. The strategists of nonviolence who include some forms of military defense in their search for alternatives are few (Sharp 1970/1985; Ebert 1984; Galtung 1984; Roberts 1985/1986). Their number does not exceed that of soldiers who seek to integrate nonviolent methods into their proposals.

An old proverb says that two eyes see better than one. Another says: doubly sewn is stronger. The military likes to remember to march separately, strike jointly! In all these admonitions, two elements are at play.

Defense also must aim at two central elements: life and liberty. "Neither red nor dead." Territorial integrity and state sovereignty. What can two eyes see better with respect to defense? Military *and* social aspects? Doubly defended, with force *and* without? "Marching" separately—here military, there nonviolence—and repelling the aggressor jointly?

What are the new ideas of citizens *and* soldiers that could be fused into a new defense?

New Ideas: Life-and-Liberty and Autonomous Responsibility

Both the peaceloving citizens and the "alternative" soldiers are repeatedly being accused that they want to be "rather red than dead." This accusation is as infamous as it is stupid. The infamy lies in the insinuation of cowardice, of crawling to keep one's dear life, and in the false supposition that liberty is held in low esteem. The stupidity reveals itself in the attempt to play out the two values of life and liberty against each other. Rather, the two are preconditions of each other. Life must be allowed to be lived in liberty. Liberty must be experienced by those alive. If life and liberty are threatened, defense must protect both simultaneously, each for the sake of the other. Defense that results in "rather dead than red" fails in its objective. "Neither red nor dead" (Loeser 1981) is the right formula. Turned positively, it can be stated as "both free and alive!"

"Life and liberty" are the central terms. They are also the basic human rights anchored in constitutions. The great Declaration of Independence by the thirty-three-year-old Thomas Jefferson for the first thirteen "United States of America" in 1776 still forms the basis of the U.S. and every other democratic legal system. Among the "inalienable rights," it lists "life, liberty" in first place, in one breath. Other rights are added. Similarly, the U.N. Universal Declaration of Human Rights of December 10, 1948 specifies in Article 3: ". . . the right to life, liberty . . ." in first place, in one breath. Other rights are added.

If those two terms in a way form a unity, then they must not be torn apart in the context of defense. Instead, every effort must be made to translate these terms into concrete defense measures. Securing life and liberty must be the primary and determining principles of defense. Defense must reflect the unity of these twin principles. Defense must secure "life-and-liberty."

This opens numerous questions concerning the rights that are added and the duties associated with the exercise of these rights.

For example, the members of NATO and the Warsaw Treaty must realize that they share responsibility for the effects of the use of nuclear weapons, even if they do not possess nuclear weapons themselves. They entered these obligations at a time when the secondary effects of nuclear weapons were less well known than today. Could these new insights not lead the alliance members to a new, freely taken decision that they no longer want to share responsibility for the use of nuclear weapons, for the sake of life-and-liberty? Does sovereignty, which every alliance promises to defend, not permit national self-determination, particularly—or at least—with respect to the question of being free to refuse to share responsibility for global nuclear annihilation? Must this desire for sovereignty not be respected by every other freedom-loving alliance member (even if others use their sovereignty to *want* to share this responsibility)?

Some states are prepared to be responsible for risking global annihilation. Others are not. No one can be forced to accept such a responsibility. Nor can it be maintained forever as a historical burden if once accepted. If new insights emerge, this decision must be re-evaluated. Loyalty to a treaty cannot be the sole criterion. A treaty that seeks to defend life-and-liberty must allow for the freedom of choice to refuse responsibility for nuclear annihilation. It must allow its members to vote in favor of survival and to choose their own path to pursue that goal, a path for which they can accept responsibility.

Some want to possess nuclear weapons, develop and deploy them, aim them at enemy targets, use them to threaten and deter. If they wish to take that responsibility, they may do so, but *only within the realm of their sovereignty.* They may not do so in areas that are not subject to their sovereignty, even if they may consider them to lie within their sphere of influence and power.

This implies that nuclear weapons may be deployed *only* on a state's own territory. It implies that a nuclear power must limit the effects of nuclear explosions to its own territory, or to the territory of a country that has attacked it with nuclear weapons. This also means that the first use of nuclear weapons outside of one's own territory is prohibited by international law. This further raises the issue of what international legal norm, if any, permits the nuclear powers to limit the freedom of the seas they patrol with nuclear weapons, ignoring the wish of the nonnuclear powers to keep the seas nuclear weapons free.

Other alliance members will not want to possess nuclear weapons, not develop or deploy them, not aim them at targets in the territory of an opponent, not use them to threaten or deter. Within the realm of their freedom, their sovereign territory, they will prohibit any direct link (e.g., via nuclear weapons carriers) or indirect involvement (e.g., via participation in target planning). In this way they will also renounce the (supposed) protection of a "nuclear umbrella" before and during war. They do not shun all risk. Possibly they may be more vulnerable to nuclear blackmail or nuclear murder by an aggressor. But they refuse participation in an escalation that might lead to global annihilation.

Nonaligned countries have done so for decades as a matter of course. Even now they face the risk of secondary effects of nuclear war, and of nuclear blackmail. They have come to renounce nuclear weapons in various ways. Sweden, for example, has broken off an initial development toward becoming a nuclear power at an early stage. Finland and Austria have obtained their sovereignty by trading it for restrictions on their autarchy in weapons technology. Switzerland has never shown any particular interest in nuclear weapons. And Yugoslavia, as a moving force within the nonaligned movement, belongs to the advocates of nuclear weapons free zones.

There is one dark side, insofar as some of the neutrals appear to rely in a reticent, furtive way on the nuclear umbrella of at least one of the two superpowers. Some neutral and nonaligned seem to assume that the nuclear umbrella is extended also over them and spares them from nuclear attack or blackmail. Nevertheless, these and all other nuclear weapons free states can, beyond doubt, even today publicly assign full responsibility for nuclear annihilation to those states that bear the responsibility for nuclear weapons or (so far) still share it. Their identity would improve if they were more honest about this. Their contribution to security and the absence of war in Europe— for example, as buffer zones between East and West and their unwavering plea for nuclear weapons free zones—which is remarkable even today, would gain further in credibility and effectiveness.

"Marching" separately—securing life-and-liberty jointly; here the old military dictum obtains new meaning. On the one hand, a difference in the nuclear strategy of the alliance members removes the joint method of war prevention. On the other hand, it strengthens each alliance member in its determination to prevent nuclear war and reduces the danger of nuclear annihilation to the extent that each member is willing to help reduce the risk.

We characterize such decisions and action as *autonomous*. This is based on a meaning of "autonomy" that does not imply unlimited arbitrariness. Rather, it applies to—and derives from—a whole system. Autonomy of the members of an alliance system (or later of a collective security system, Lutz 1985) seems to be the basis for free, self-determined partnership. Superiority of only one partner and suppression of the autonomous aspirations of another degrades any affirmation of "equal partnership" to empty words.

Autonomy means "freedom, independence, as well as self-determination" (Bettelheim 1968/1979). Autonomy does not mean anarchy or autarchy. Anarchy undermines freedom. Autarchy denies interdependence on the good behavior of friends and adversaries. Anarchy makes blind, autarchy short-sighted. Autonomy, introduced in the context of security and defense, takes a long view toward the future of life-and-liberty of a world at the brink of its existence.

New Ideas: Life-and-Liberty and Autonomous Defense

Autonomy is possible at many levels, such as the level of civilians and military personnel who, at first individually, search for new forms of defense. Why should it not be possible, starting from the joint objective of securing life-and-liberty, to organize a form of defense in which various methods are combined? Why should it not be possible to combine force with nonviolence, military defense with civilian resistance? Why should it not be possible to overcome the mutual suspicions of the military and conscientious objectors and to accept that each wants to protect life-and-liberty, even if in different ways? Is it necessary that in a democratic society—according to the preference of a majority—a single solution must be developed that applies to everybody, for example, military defense and nothing else, with isolated exceptions? Should it not be possible in a democratic society to find a solution that takes into account the imaginations of several groups and builds consensus, where previously there was dissension, for example, military defense and nonviolent resistance and . . .?

We can and must learn to accept that more and more civilians will want to defend life-and-liberty in a different way from soldiers. Those civilians must learn to accept that the military—and for the time being still the vast majority in democracies—want to defend life-and-liberty militarily. Both must realize and admit that their own methods are less suited for certain purposes of defense than those of the others. Thus the military will no longer be able to claim cities as its battlefield. The risk of destroying life (and cultural monuments) is far greater here than in sparsely populated areas. On the other hand, the adherents of nonviolence must realize that they lack the strength to dislodge an aggressor from their own territory. The risk that nonviolent resistance is unable to prevent the loss of freedom is far greater if territorial integrity cannot be restored.

Conversely, it will be easier to organize and concentrate nonviolent resistance in cities than elsewhere. The cities must not fall into the hands of an aggressor without defense. But in sparsely populated areas, soldiers will be able to apply their (conventional) weapons. There they can detect an enemy advance early and bring it to a halt. Through heavy resistance and counterattack, they can liberate occupied territory.

In this way, the various methods of defense have their own sphere of action: soldiers in sparsely populated areas, civilians in cities. In their respective spheres, they defend autonomously, according to their own rules. They "march" separately, but they cooperate in the defense of life-and-liberty.

This indicates a blueprint. We call it autonomous protection, described in the following chapter.

9

Autonomous Protection—the Defense of Life-and-Liberty to Avert War

Autonomous protection comprises three central tasks of defense:

Area defense through military forces.
Urban resistance through civilian resistance forces.
Population protection through protection forces.

Armed forces, resistance forces, and protection forces together provide for defense in case of aggression. First of all, they serve the purpose of preventing aggression through a strategy of war prevention.

Population Protection—Increasing the Chance of Survival

All defense measures of autonomous protection have as their first objective the survival of the population. There are protection forces as they are generally envisaged within the framework of total defense plans in many countries. In current concepts, their assignment is to protect the civilian population from the effects of weaponry. Generally, this is done by preventively evacuating the population from combat areas before or during combat. Or, if the civilian population is surprised by bombardments and massive fires, as many as possible must be saved from the devastated, burning living quarters. Often, the population protection forces, inspite of their name, can do nothing more than care for the wounded and retrieve the dead from the ruins.

The countries of Europe have unequally prepared themselves for the protection of civilian populations and have reached very different standards (Kalckreuth 1985). With few exceptions, the conclusion appears justified that "independence from military blocks and therefore the awareness of the need to rely on one's own forces has significantly stimulated the will for strategic provision [in the area of civilian protection]" (Feldman 1984). Finland, Switzerland, and Sweden can be considered as examples among the neutrals—and not only among those. Here every or nearly every citizen finds a place in a solid or at least improvised shelter. These shelters provide adequate protection against the effects of conventional weapons, limited protection against massive fires (due to the danger of suffocation), and very restricted protection against the effects of nuclear weapons. Only the direct physical effects can be absorbed, and only partially. But the periods of survival in a shelter, no matter how constructed, are limited for a variety of reasons. And at the latest, after leaving the shelter during or after nuclear strikes, the citizen is fully exposed to the secondary effects of nuclear weapons.

Particularly poor provisions are found in those countries that have relied on nuclear deterrence, as the members of NATO, with the exception of Norway and Denmark. A glaring example is France, which has only one public shelter in a single city (Chartres). Decades of neglect have been catastrophic. The shortages have reached magnitudes that can no longer be bridged, at least not in the central part of NATO, not even in the Federal Republic of Germany, the "battlefield of Central Europe" (Zimmerman 1983). Whatever may have contributed to this deplorable state of affairs, it has deliberately imposed on the civilian population the function of being hostage to enhance the credibility of deterrence (Schwarz 1981). To our knowledge, no plebiscite (e.g., asking people "do you want to serve as hostage for nuclear deterrence and renounce population protection?") has been held anywhere.

Autonomous protection cannot compensate for this neglect either. But autonomous protection can help reduce the need for shelters, to a level that *can* be provided.

Without doubt, every form of defense is at least responsible to protect the civilian population from the effects of weapons that are employed by the

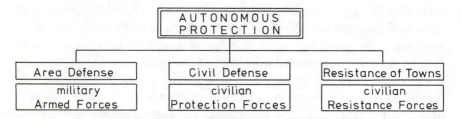

Figure 5. Autonomous protection—overall structure.

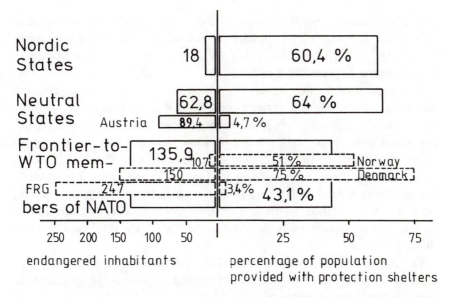

Figure 6. Population protection in Central and Northern Europe. The graph displays average values for the following groupings: Nordic countries—Norway, Finland, Sweden, Denmark; Neutral countries—Sweden, Finland, Switzerland (Austria's protection is not comparable); NATO—countries bordering on the Warsaw Pact—Norway, Denmark, Federal Republic of Germany. The values for individual countries differ enormously, as shown.

country's own armed forces. In autonomous protection, these are only conventional arms, not nuclear arms or other means of mass destruction. By limiting itself to conventional arms, autonomous protection is exempt from the political obligation to protect against the effects of nuclear arms. The latter form of protection can in any case not be provided reliably in the long run, both from a technical and organizational viewpoint. But consistent protection against conventional arms must be provided. For one's own use of conventional weapons attracts fire from the opponent, which may affect the civilian population as well.

Autonomous protection reduces the need for shelters by keeping concentrations of population and major cities free of weapons and by denying to an aggressor any pretext for attacks on or combat in cities and towns. According to the principle of open towns (Schilling 1981), autonomous protection withdraws, at the beginning of aggression or during mobilization in case of war, all its own military units and installations from these population centers. For example, during World War II in France, the interior minister declared all towns with over 20,000 inhabitants as open towns (Born 1978). Any shooting in such cities could only come from forces of the aggressor that might have entered. City dwellers could no longer be the victim of combat operations, only the victims of individual murder, acts of terror, or mass murder (the execution of hostages or nuclear annihilation, but see chapter 10 Strategy of War Prevention). Insofar as an occupier refrains from this, the population is protected (see Table 1).

This form of population protection, which can be achieved at no cost and which should also make it easier to provide people with supplies, suggests the evacuation of people from small nearby villages and towns into the major towns and cities. The civil defense planners need not worry about nightmares of refugee streams consisting of millions of city dwellers. Instead, thousands may stream from suburbs into the protecting cities. For example during World War II the city of Bologna, an important railroad junction, "doubled its population within a short time to about half a million people who sought protection from the troubles of war in the city" and found it (Born 1978).

The example of Bologna shows that big cities also have a great absorptive capacity for people seeking refuge. In Central European cities, thousands of apartments are vacant today.

For those people who cannot be evacuated, who have to remain in military combat zones, shelters must be provided. The way into a town may be too long or too dangerous. Farmers and doctors may need to continue their work. Other reasons may make it necessary to remain on the spot. Autonomous protection must provide shelter for these people. The Swiss standard should apply here: every remaining citizen should have room in a shelter that protects against conventional weapons, including essential reserves of food and other supplies.

It will also be necessary to have protection forces in these zones, as they already exist today in the form of fire squads, first aid squads, disaster relief organizations, and so on. Of course, such services will also be needed in towns, but no more than in peace time, except for supply and traffic control operations. Many other eventualities must be prepared for in advance. They include the supply of food and other necessities, and information services.

Urban Resistance—the Civilian Resistance Forces

Cities and towns, as indicated above, should not be defended militarily. Doing so would rather invite their own destruction. As open towns according to the Hague Convention, they are not permitted to be protected militarily. All troops and military installations, such as command posts, must be removed from them. It is not necessary to declare them officially as open towns. But such a declaration, made even before any conflict develops, can only help the purposes of autonomous protection. To be on the safe side, it is advisable to mark clearly the entry points to the city, preferably in the language of a potential aggressor. Then every enemy soldier can read it. Every soldier in every army in the world ought to be instructed in the laws of war. The prohibition to attack militarily undefended towns is one of the central provisions.

But one must be prepared that attacking troops will occupy the open cities. They invite this. For here an aggressor can hope to rest and to replenish supplies. He may wish to regroup his forces to continue the attack using the towns as staging points. Nobody in an open town is permitted to stop the enemy with armed force from doing so. To lead him into traps or to sabotage his plans by force in any other ways would only give him a pretext to terrorize the population.

Nevertheless, under the strategy of autonomous protection, an occupation force cannot seize a town without any resistance. It will not fall into his hands undefended. Rather, he has to face nonviolent resistance. Not every inhabitant of the city, not every refugee from surrounding areas, is willing and able to do this. Autonomous protection does not require that every citizen offers nonviolent resistance. Only the resistance fighters in the resistance forces are expected to do so.

Autonomous protection organizes resistance forces already in peace time. These forces are recruited among those who have confidence in their ability to resist nonviolently, or among those whose conscience does not permit them to bear arms: today's conscientious objectors. Women are also encouraged to undergo training and join nonviolent resistance forces, if they believe that here they can make a more effective contribution to autonomous protection than, for example, in medical service.

The training of the resistance forces, whose duration corresponds to that of the armed forces, has to be thoroughly planned and carefully executed. The resistance fighters must learn during their training what tasks they will be assigned if their country is attacked, where they will be located, what situations they may face, how they can influence the occupation forces, how they can establish and maintain contact with enemy soldiers, with what other resistance fighters they can cooperate, and where they can find support. They must be trained in various techniques of nonviolent resistance. Learning a foreign language, especially that of a potential aggressor, may also form part of their training, depending on the functions they are to perform. In this way the resistance fighters can address potential occupation forces, can engage them in dialogue, and can try to cast doubt into their mind whether the orders they receive are justified and whether their image of the "enemy" is accurate. But most importantly, the training must bring the resistance fighters to the limit of their psychological capacities. They must experience intensively what they are able to tolerate, and what types of violence they can stand without having to fear that they would become violent themselves.

The training must instill a feeling of self-confidence in the resistance fighters that enables them to defy armed forces without weapons again and again. They must make the aggressors think. Nonviolent resistance can—once an aggressor is inside a town—become "psychologically offensive" (King-Hall 1958). Through the way they appear, what they do and don't do, how they speak and remain silent, by staring and laughing, waiting and insisting they begin, together, to erode the morale of the occupying soldiers and bureaucrats. Their self-image disintegrates gradually. This disintegration leads the soldiers of the occupation force to a point where they either request to be transferred, or where the leadership of the occupation force stops sending soldiers into the cities, because the supposed rest from combat and recovery is illusory. It undermines their fighting morale.

The more the occupier has trained his forces in military behavior, forceful action, and obedience, the easier is the task of the resistance fighters, as the enemy will be all the more confused by the unrestrained behavior, individual freedom, and self-confidence that the resistance fighters demonstrate. The sooner the commander of the occupation forces, be it the administrator of a town or the boss in a factory "capitulates," the sooner the resistance forces have achieved their goal. The sooner the soldiers leave the city, the better are the chances of survival of the population, and the sooner the enemy soldiers have to face the armed resistance forces outside of the cities.

Nonviolent resistance must not be misunderstood as a random mix of uncoordinated actions. Rather, it must be planned and organized in painstaking detail. Cells of resistance must be established at as many places in the towns as possible. It is essential to form many small cells rather than a few large ones. The cells must also be dispersed over the entire city, so that an effort by the occupation force to eliminate them would be much harder than an operation against a centralized resistance force concentrated in a small area. A resistance cell pops up here, then there and there again, as in the popular fable of the hedgehog who challenged the rabbit to a race back and forth across a field. By having his wife hide at the other end of the field, the two hedgehogs fooled the rabbit, making him believe they were one and the same, constantly being ahead of him, shouting from the other end with a cunning smile, "I am already here!"

Forms of resistance as a component of autonomous protection can certainly be organized even better than the structure sketched below indicates. But this proposal can help clarify what is intended.

For example, we imagine: Resistance fighters work in pairs. Two such pairs form an active cell. At any time, only one of the two pairs offers "active" nonviolent resistance. The second pair remains in the background and offers moral support. Only in crisis situations does it step forth, trying to mediate. But the main task of the second pair is to observe the other pair's actions, so that it can serve as witness in court in case the other pair is arrested. It should also inform the public about successes and failures, and transmit information.

Such resistance pairs should be formed in areas where they have a fixed reference point, such as a common appartment. Here they know the other tenants and know whom they can trust. They must also familiarize themselves with escape paths and hiding places. Within their district, the resistance fighters can, among other things, speak to patrols of enemy soldiers and seek to engage them in prolonged conversations, alone or in groups. If these patrols keep changing, instead of being the old and familiar troops, this indicates already that the occupier does not trust the moral steadfastness of his subordinates. For it would clearly be simpler and more effective for him to assign patrols to an urban district once and for all and to have them patrol a known area repeatedly, instead of having them familiarize themselves constantly with new districts.

Similar principles, adapted to a different environment and different circumstances, also apply to public authorities and production units. Here, too, as many cells as possible should be formed, whether within firms, workshops, factories, or administrative offices. There will probably be less direct contact with the occupation forces. But go-slow tactics and working procedures according to the rule book can confuse the occupier and cause delays. Nothing that has to be produced or carried out for the occupier will be done without the most painstaking observation of issued decrees. The more decrees are issued by the occupier, the better this is for the resistance forces, because the more this delays what the occupier wants. As long as the occupier does not issue any decrees, everything happens in accordance with one's own rules. And if the occupier cancels all the rules, because he may not understand them, nothing can be completed at all. For how could a resistance fighter know how the occupier wants something accomplished if he does not describe the "how"?

These hints at the organization and tasks of the resistance fighters can be nothing more but sketches. There is an entire literature with a wide variety of concrete proposals. Even the training of resistance fighters need not break

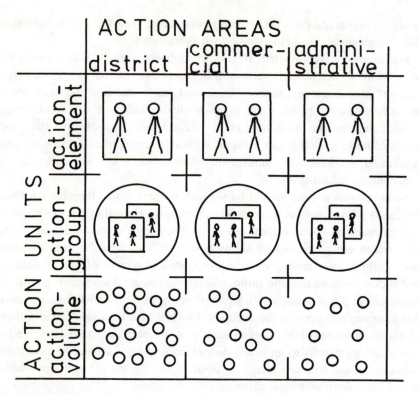

Figure 7. Resistance forces—proposed structure. A box symbolizes a house and protection. A circle symbolizes a head and resistance.

new ground. Here, too, beginnings have been made (Nolting 1981; Jochheim 1984). All that is required is to take them off the shelf.

Area Protection—the Armed Forces

The description of the forces of autonomous protection so far may give the impression that it is ultimately defenseless against an aggressor. Building shelters, occupied towns . . . is there nothing to stop attacking troops?

There is indeed! From the border of one's territory inward. For this purpose, armed forces are deployed, equipped, and trained. They are defensively structured, in every militarily sensible and politically feasible way (Mueller 1983; Lutz 1986). Their exclusive task is to defend. And they must be able to blend with the other forces of autonomous protection. Mutual structural compatibility is important, if one recognizes that the resistance forces and the armed forces have to cooperate to repel the aggressor's forces.

Despite the differences in their assigned territories and methods of struggle, they have to cooperate and accept each other emotionally. The best way to achieve this is through structural similarities.

The most immediate similarity is their readiness to make sacrifices. Whereas soldiers in the armed forces face death on the battlefield, resistance fighters face torture and execution. In light of this "ultimate" moral of resistance, both are individual fighters left to themselves, and in many respects—facing the aggressor or the occupation forces—they are, in extreme situations, individually "autonomous" (Bettelheim 1980). In order to find some backing, nevertheless, so as not to remain "lonely soldiers" (Bigler 1983), they are integrated into fighting units. For the resistance fighters, such units can be newly structured as described. For soldiers, the formation of combat units is an old tradition.

The tendency is to move toward smaller fighting units, because their effectiveness increases with greater autonomy and responsibility (Afheldt E. 1984, Afheldt H. 1983). It is increasingly recognized that success stems not from the concentration of massive forces in one place, but from the motivation and combat readiness of each individual, stemming from good education and training. An additional purpose is for the soldiers to seek to avoid enemy fire through dispersal and to enable them to use their own arms most effectively.

The rugged, hilly territory of Central Europe, but also the lakes, fiords, and high mountains of Northern Europe favor smaller units so that their heavy arms do not interfere with each other. They also should not offer concentrated targets for the opponent's heavy fire. Dispersal and contiguity are complementary requirements for military structures. They are best achieved through a structure based on small, highly autonomous units.

Nevertheless, to fight conventional battles against a superior aggressor, it is indispensable to concentrate one's own forces rapidly for short time-spans. Focal points of attack must be opposed with focal points of defense.

Therefore, there is a need for two basically different structures, which serve the two requirements of defense and can be incorporated into the overall concept of autonomous protection. For the Central European area, the structural model proposed by the *Studiengruppe Alternative Sicherheitspolitik* (Study group for Alternative Security policy) seems to us appropriate in its conventional components (SAS 1984). It generally does not foresee combat in cities or towns. But it brings together two different main forces for joint action in areas close to the border. On one hand, more static infantry troops, distributed in a network to cover the entire area, take advantage of the terrain to block and paralyze the enemy. On the other hand,

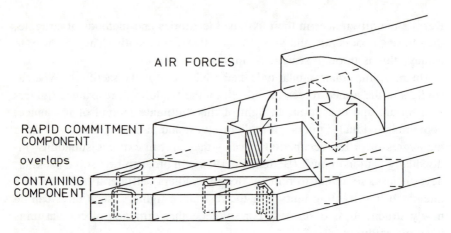

Figure 8. Armed forces and superposition. The defense is carried out in three areas: the stationary containing component (symbolized by position marks) is superimposed by the rapid commitment component (symbolized by arrows) and by the air defense of the air forces.

independent from the network yet in close coordination, very rapid, highly mobile mechanized forces keep attacking the aggressor from the flanks and the rear, in constantly new locations.

Even superior forces are drawn in this way into a sort of blind alley (Nolte H. 1984) or "shrinking tube" (Unterseher 1983) and, in analogy to the operational concept of Hannibal in the battle of Cannae, they are attacked from two sides simultaneously and smashed. In a series of many small skirmishes, through a constant, persistent struggle, the aggressor can be repelled from one's own territory.

The aggressor may vainly try to break the resistance in towns. Maybe he will surround them with troops to starve or to intimidate the inhabitants. Maybe the aggressor, reckoning in military terms, will expect to find the weakest point of autonomous protection at the juncture between armed forces and resistance forces, and will seek to break it. He won't succeed in this. For he would first of all be widely exposed from the back to the armed forces of autonomous protection. Second, and this is decisive, the connection between urban resistance and area defense is weak only in appearance. The absence of defense forces between towns and rural areas is deliberate. For the connection between urban resistance and area defense is not of military but of a political nature. This intermediate zone is not guarded by any military forces. It is virulent only in a political sense, as a zone for the exchange of mutual motivation.

The detailed structure of military forces may have to be different in other European countries. Norway's high mountains, Sweden's fiords, Finland's

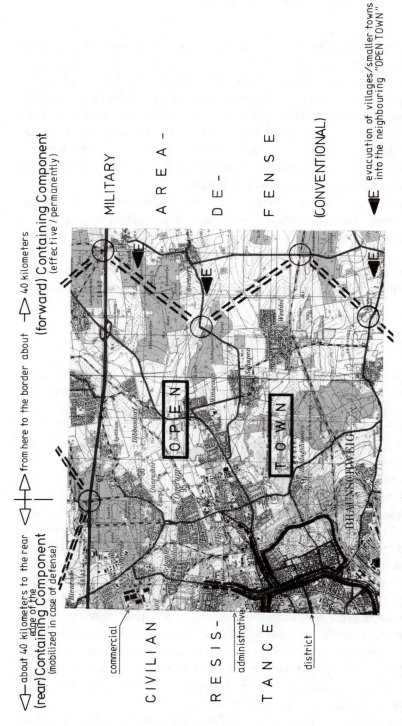

Figure 9. Resistance forces in towns—armed forces in rural areas. The figure shows a town close to the border. The borderline of the open town follows marked features in the landscape. In the living quarters and urban districts, resistance is organized—only indicated here. The town shown here happens to lie on the boundary between the rear containing component, which is mobilized only in case of aggression, and the permanent forward containing component.

lakes, Denmark's coasts, Germany's rivers and hills, to mention only a few differences, require different force compositions. Also, the hardly comparable geostrategic conditions need to be considered. Even brief characteristics make this obvious: Norway is on NATO's northern flank, partially bordering on the Soviet Union; Sweden and Finland, grouped around the North Sea, form a dual buffer between NATO and the Warsaw Pact; Denmark blocks access to the North Sea and forms a bridge between NATO's northern flank and the potential main battlefield; and Germany *is* potentially the main battlefield in a future war in Europe.

But all have one thing in common: they have populations that don't want war, and who should survive in case of war. The majority of their people live in cities and towns and can find protection there. Nevertheless, these towns, presumably the most important strategic goals, must not fall into enemy hands undefended. The best form of defense here seems to be the one with the greatest promise to spare the population, nonviolent resistance.

Recruitment of the Forces

Protection forces, resistance forces, armed forces—from where should the personnel for all these formations come? Even today the armed forces of many European countries suffer from a shortage of personnel. The invention of birth control pills a generation ago shows its effects (Alford 1984). Further, isn't it necessary for every citizen to participate in nonviolent resistance so that there is no more room to recruit soldiers?

Concerning the protection forces, it was noted earlier that their size corresponds to what is foreseen in the countries of Europe today. Therefore, in principle no special consideration is required with regard to their personnel. Yet for another significant reason (the legal basis for recruitment), the protection forces must be included in a calculation of personnel requirements for autonomous protection.

Autonomous protection requires, as far as can be foreseen today, a uniform duty for all three services. The reason is that all three should be able to cooperate in protection and in the strategy of war prevention, using their respective methods in their own areas, on an equal legal basis, as equivalent partners. Although autonomous in their operation, they serve the joint function of prevention of war and protection in war. This cannot work if the soldiers consider the resistance forces as outsiders, or if the protection forces find themselves legally subordinate to the soldiers.

Legal equality among the forces makes it possible to implement a basic principle of democracy: the free choice of the preferred service. Every conscript should be able to decide freely what type of service he or she believes to be able to perform best, and in what capacity they expect to be able to make the greatest individual contribution to their country's protection. This makes unnecessary the still widely practiced (and criticized) investigations into the consciences of those who are still called conscientious objectors today. On the other hand, it can be expected that precisely the latter will participate enthusiastically in the resistance forces, since they will perceive their prospective loss of freedom more vividly than many soldiers, who need not pass a test of their conscience today.

The free choice of the type of service implies at the same time general conscription. *One* of these three services *must* be selected. Dispensation can be granted only for medical reasons. Even then, it is recommended to require a compensatory tax, as it is levied in Switzerland. During a transition period, it may be necessary to have some regulations to avoid excesses or shortages of personnel in the various services. For the moment, there has to be no concern that nobody would wish to become a soldier anymore. The majority of citizens still find it easier to confront an armed aggressor with armed force. But in the long run, a free choice of the type of service does not preclude a gradual process of social change that may lead a country to adopt nonviolent resistance as the only form of defense.

Even before such futuristic considerations, the introduction of general conscription with a free choice of service can bring closer a solution to the problem of women's participation in defense. If they are included in general conscription—and not only in civil protection as in many countries today— they can increase the reserve of personnel for the resistance forces, and possibly even the armed forces. This can advance the cause of complete social equality between genders.

Each of the three services is equivalent. None can function without the other two. Each is equally important and depends in its function on the other two. Autonomous protection only works if the three equivalent components cooperate.

With the inclusion of groups that are marginal today—such as the conscientious objectors—and the inclusion of women, the personnel basis for recruitment obviously increases. Recalling that the protection forces stay at the same level as today, those on duty can be estimated at 1 percent of the total population.

In surveying the size of the armed forces in these selected countries, we find an average of nearly 1 percent of the total population. In the model mentioned (SAS 1983), the armed forces of the Federal Republic of Germany are calculated as about 350,000 soldiers in peace time and about 750,000 (1.2 percent of the population) in case of war. This is considerably less than

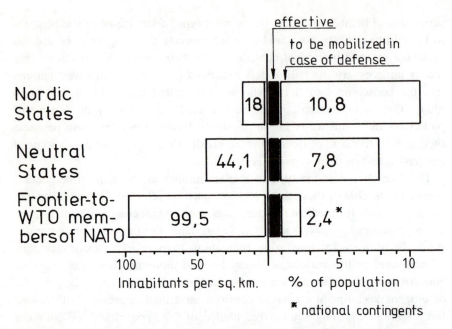

Figure 10. Participation rates of the population in defense. The figure shows significant differences in reliance on mobilized defense potentials. It also illustrates that the more populous countries of Europe still retain considerable reserves of personnel. The graph shows average values. The following are included in the various groupings: Nordic countries—Norway, Sweden, Finland, Denmark; neutral countries—Sweden, Finland, Switzerland, Austria, Yugoslavia, Albania; NATO countries with frontier to Warsaw Pact—Norway, Denmark, Federal Republic of Germany, Italy (as easternmost barrier between the Alps and Greece), Greece, Turkey.

the increase that NATO expects from the Bundeswehr today (about 1.3 million troops or 2 percent of the population). Based on first investigations for the Federal Republic, the resistance forces also require about 1 percent of the population. Thus the total for armed forces and resistance forces is about 2 percent, or with inclusion of the protection forces about 3 percent in case of war. This percentage is comparable to the personnel requirements for the armed forces and civilian protection today, if one considers the larger basis for recruitment. It is still far below the participation rates in the armed forces for 1981 in Switzerland (9.9 percent) and Sweden (6.8 percent), which are essentially still the same today.

These estimates only intend to show that irrespective of different assumptions about the current availability of personnel for defense, there is apparently still much leeway. On this basis it can be expected that the recruitment of the forces for autonomous protection will not pose any insurmountable problems.

Table 3

Nonviolent Actions (Selection)*

1	Public speeches
6	Group or mass petitions
12	Skywriting and earthwriting
17	Mock elections
30	Rude gestures
34	Vigils
37	Singing
42	Motorcades
46	Homage at burial places
50	Teach-ins
54	Turning one's back
55	Social boycott
64	Withdrawal from social institutions
70	Protest emigration
77	International consumers' boycott
79	Producers' boycott
80	Suppliers' and handlers' boycott
85	Merchants' "general strike"
87	Refusal to pay fees, dues, etc.
96	International trade embargo
98	Quickie walkout
100	Farm workers' strike
104	Professional strike
107	Sympathetic strike
115	Selective strike
117	General strike
119	Economic shutdown
122	Literature and speeches advocating resistance
132	Refusal to accept appointed officials
135	Popular nonobedience
136	Disguised disobedience
141	Civil disobedience against "illegitimate" laws
148	Mutiny
150	Noncooperation
161	Nonviolent harrassment
180	Alternative communication
192	Alternative economic institutions
197	Work-on without collaboration
198	Dual sovereignty and parallel government

*These selections are from *The Politics of Nonviolent Action* (1973), in which Gene Sharp describes 198 distinct actions of nonviolent resistance. (Numbers refer to Sharp's counting).

10

A Strategy to Avert War

At the end of the section on area defense in chapter 9, it was noted that cities are "seemingly" important (in fact, unimportant) strategic objectives. This contradicts century-old experience and practice in war. Indeed even today cities are strategically important—as long as they are defended militarily. As long as they are militarily undefended—as Bologna in 1944 (Born 1978), they can be passed by. Attack and counterattack will proceed without tying forces to cities. They are then militarily insignificant. Stalingrad gained enormous military significance during Worl War II almost exclusively because each of the changing occupiers was unwilling to give up one inch of territory once seized. Long since leveled to the ground and useless as a railway junction or anything else, it was nothing more than an object of prestige of the opposing powers. If it had never been defended with troops, the war might have taken a different course.

From this one must not conclude that it is best not to offer any military defense. That would imply to accept a foreign occupation and to renounce the means by which to restore territorial integrity. But it must never happen that military considerations stifle political considerations, that political aims are guided by military-strategic aims. The strategy of nuclear deterrence prepares the conditions for such a development in war under the cloak of the nuclear umbrella. For nuclear weapons have the tendency to become the decisive elements of security policy for war prevention and "defense" in case of war. If deterrence fails, politics in the form of deterrence should be restored by force. Politics then is to be based again on the same instruments of war prevention that have just proven to be inadequate for that purpose.

The strategy to avert war creates no such dilemma. For:

- It opposes the military-political nuclear weapons of the opponent primarily with a political potential: STATE RESISTANCE.

- It opposes the conventional military forces of an aggressor primarily with a political potential: COMBINATION OF FORCES.
- Military forces are combined *together* with other forces: ARMED FORCES.

Here it must be explained how autonomous protection confronts nuclear force.

Excursion: State Resistance Against Nuclear Force

As is well known, an attack with nuclear weapons is militarily feasible, but defense is not. The U.S. president's 1983 vision that produced the Strategic Defense Initiative (SDI, or star wars) promises nothing but the wish to make such defense feasible and to make nuclear weapons obsolete, to disinvent them, so to speak. It has led to research, but has not yet created any defense. Instead, nuclear options are included in the defense from the outset (Gordon 1985; DOD 1985). As was explained in Chapter 5, SDI as currently envisioned would increase, not reduce, the risk of nuclear war. If in a distant future—inspite of widespread skepticism (e.g., OTA 1985)—defense against a nuclear attack should nevertheless become possible, then an entirely different strategy would have to be developed anyway. From this angle, recent proposals for a de-emphasis of nuclear arms and greater emphasis on conventional war fighting capacity (Rogers 1982ff; Nunn 1982) point in a different direction (Altenburg 1986). But they point in the opposite direction from autonomous protection, which seeks to achieve a reduction also of conventional forces.

If all speculation about SDI is set aside, we still have the fact that military defense against a nuclear attack is impossible for the foreseeable future. Only a nonmilitary, political form of "defense" is possible. Autonomous protection draws the consequence and opts for nonviolent resistance by the state as the legitimate representative of the entire population.

Through the president or chief of state, the state declares, in front of the entire world, its determination to use nonviolent resistance against any form of nuclear force. Any attempt at nuclear blackmail is immediately transmitted worldwide through all accessible information channels, without any regard for the blackmailer. Any blackmailer is immediately exposed and branded as ready to commit mass murder. For a nuclear attack on militarily undefended villages, towns, cities, and regions is, from the viewpoint of autonomous protection, given all of the associated risks, nothing less than genocide. Nuclear threats are treated as intention to commit murder, nuclear attacks as murder.

On the other hand, autonomous protection categorically refuses any offer by third parties to make nuclear counterthreats or counterattacks. For it wants to have no part in the responsibility for risking global annihilation.

If the blackmailer implements his threat, despite public exposure, and launches a nuclear attack on a capital city, he gains nothing from a military-strategic viewpoint. Rather, such an act of murder has the effect of rousing the survivors against himself. A nuclear attack will only strengthen the determination for common defense against the outlaw. A murderous aggressor cannot credibly promise freedom. Rather, more murder can be expected.

It is unlikely that any aggressor would resort to an unprovoked nuclear attack. Winds would carry nuclear fallout ultimately also into the territory of the attacker. Nuclear winter could lead to widespread famines. Moreover, why would an aggressor wish to destroy the presumed objects of conquest—economic assets and industrial areas—with nuclear weapons?

Nonviolent state resistance against nuclear force forms the sociopolitical bond that unites the defense forces. It cannot be grasped from a purely military viewpoint. Such a free, self-confident, autonomous decision for a responsible option to survive must fascinate and simultaneously confuse a state whose citizens enjoy less freedom. The risk taken here by autonomous protection is far less—from the standpoint of the entire world—than any share, no matter how modest, how furtive, in the responsibility for risking global annihilation.

Could a would-be aggressor succeed with a conventional attack?

Before a conventional attack, any potential aggressor faces the political union of urban resistance, area defense, and population protection. The mere prospect of the mobilization of organized, capable resistance in cities and towns will make a totalitarian government think twice. In this way, autonomous protection deliberately challenges a potential aggressor to reflect before attacking. It does not frighten him, but it does raise questions: How would the latent, clandestine domestic resistance react? Would it be necessary to secure the success of the aggression through additional forces posted at home? Will resistance emerge, get organized, rise up—in the back of the attacking troops? Will it put into question the government's grip on power in its traditional domain? Is it worth risking the collapse of the internal system in an effort to extend power abroad? A global power that intends to win the world for its own political philosophy can hardly afford to ignore world opinion.

Even if a great power were able to enter foreign territory with military forces, this does not mean that it would be able to hold that territory permanently. If the Soviet Union were to attempt to occupy Western Europe, it would risk losing control over Eastern Europe, where popular uprisings would likely occur if Soviet troops were deployed elsewhere. Even the United States experienced sharp internal protests and divisions during the Vietnam War. President Nixon refrained from the use of nuclear weapons in Vietnam, partly out of fear of domestic unrest.

The potential aggressor will, in our estimate, *refrain* from aggression. He will do so on his own. He, as subject, will decide against aggression, against war. He will not be "deterred"—as if he was an object. Rather, he will pause for reflection and will autonomously desist from aggression. He himself will avert war.

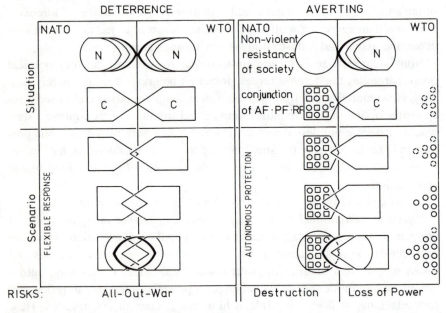

Figure 11. Strategy to avert war compared with deterrence. The graph shows in simple symbols the nuclear (N) and Conventional (C) potentials that NATO and the Warsaw Pact pit against each other. That is the present situation. Autonomous protection, in the strategy to avert war, deploys other, political potentials: state resistance against nuclear force and the combination of conventional military forces (C) with nonviolent resistance (small circles symbolizing heads) and population protection (small squares symbolizing houses). The dotted "heads" in the realm of the Warsaw Pact indicate latent resistance. In the part of the graph marked Scenario, in the case of deterrence, one side attacks, meets resistance, reinforces the attack, risks nuclear strikes, and retaliates against them: the consequence is escalation—the risk of all-out war. In the strategy to avert war the same side attacks, encounters the united forces of autonomous protection, reinforces the attack, risks the eruption of resistance in its back, may launch a nuclear attack, and will finally withdraw to stay in power within its own domain: destruction may result—but there is not escalation—all-out war is averted.

Despite the authors' conviction, even efforts to avert war, since they can't be superhuman, can fail.

So, if the Warsaw Pact were to let its troops attack, it would never achieve victory. For "capitulation" is impossible, since the military area defense, as only one of the three elements of autonomous protection, can never "capitulate" in the name of all three elements. Let us assume for a moment that the aggressor should succeed in defeating all military defense forces, although the military structure of the SAS model need not give rise to any such fear (Huber & Hofmann 1984). Even then, the cities would continue to offer resistance. Autonomous protection would continue to survive in them. If the aggressor should succeed in breaking the resistance in the cities and towns, the will to resist would continue in the area defense and population protection.

The component forces of autonomous protection can mutually encourage each other. If a town falls, the area surrounding it is not yet lost. If the countryside falls, the towns and cities continue to resist. This opens up entirely new options of political resistance, employing political means, which can dispose of military as well as other political means. All sorts of mixtures are feasible. In an army that is strictly trained in military subordination, such a strategy will sow confusion.

11

Autonomous Protection—a Future for the Europe of Neutral and Allied States

No matter from which side one looks at Europe, our idea of a unit is different. Europe is divided geographically. In the south, peninsula after peninsula, with islands in front, extends into the Mediterranean: Iberia, Appennin, the Balkans. There are islands in the north, too, and ridges extending into the eastern Atlantic, forming the North and Baltic seas: Iceland, Ireland, England, the Caledonian Mountains and the Baltic Shield, and the splintered Danish peninsula that protrudes between the North and Baltic seas. All of these territories extending into the sea seem only harbingers of a continental land mass. They seem attached to a space that extends eastward via Central Europe.

But here, where land areas finally "hang together" (what is meant by "continent") and vast planes open that stretch to the Urals, Europe is torn apart politically. The actual European land mass belongs politically to the East and is the heartland of socialism. If one drew a borderline between East and West Europe by connecting with broad strokes the major cities from Helsinki to Stockholm, Copenhagen, Hamburg, (Berlin as a prepositioned island), Munich, Vienna, Belgrade, Istanbul, it appears as if the East were protruding into the West.

What remains of Europe in the geographically splintered West is no less divided politically. There are the neutral states: Sweden and Finland in the far north, connected through the sparsely populated area known as Lapland and the Gulf of Bothnia; Switzerland and Austria, attached to the Alps, reinforcing politically the natural barrier of the mountains; finally, facing Italy on the eastern side of the Adriatic, bordering on the members of the Warsaw Treaty, estranged from it, yet close in a sense, experienced in partisan war, Yugoslavia. Many small and a few larger states share the re-

Figure 12. The dual barrier in Europe. Black circles = NATO, white circles = neutrals, black squares = Warsaw Treaty. Two lines are drawn schematically. The broken line connects the neutral and nonaligned and includes Berlin, which in a sense is "neutralized" through the Allied occupation. The solid line connects the easternmost cities with over a million inhabitants in NATO countries. It is assumed that the defense of these cities is of special significance. This gives at least the appearance of a dual, widely extended barrier against the East's drive toward the West. The East, on its part, can interpret this as a dual Western encirclement in its flanks. This interpretation is reinforced if the East includes Norway and Turkey in its considerations. It may perceive the need for a strong defense in all directions.

maining space and have formed the NATO alliance to defend themselves against the East's drive for power. (Some mini-states lie sprinkled along mountain slopes in no danger).

But even these states, joined in an alliance, do not give a united picture: the one with the largest area, Spain, has joined NATO only recently. The next largest, France, has withdrawn from the military arm of the alliance decades ago, but remains a member of the political arm. Nuclear autonomy was the driving force behind De Gaulle's decision to leave, the national

Table 4
Autonomy of Selected NATO Countries

Member state	Characteristics
USA	The commander of US forces in Europe is identical with the Supreme Allied Commander for Europe (SACEUR); national sovereignty regarding nuclear weapons within the alliance; dominant power in the alliance.
France	Militarily disengaged; autonomous in the nuclear field.
Great Britain	Nuclear power besides United States; autonomous concerning theater operations.
Norway	Prohibition of the deployment of troops from other NATO members; demilitarized zone near the Soviet border; prohibition of the deployment of nuclear weapons.
Denmark	Prohibition of the deployment of nuclear weapons.
Iceland	Permission to station NATO troops as condition for membership; no troops of its own.
Netherlands	Restrictive nuclear policy.
Belgium	Restrictive nuclear policy.
Fed. Rep. of Germany	Renunciation of national supreme command; complete renunciation of autonomy.
Greece	Left and rejoined the alliance; democratic institutions interrupted by military regime in the past.
Turkey	Significant use of outside economic and military assistance; "friendly cooperation" with the Soviet Union (1978); democratic institutions repeatedly interrupted by military regimes.
Spain	Special U.S. rights to station troops. Demanded withdrawal of U.S. tactical air wing from base near Madrid.
Italy	Agreed to accept U.S. air wing removed from Spain. Little autonomy within NATO.

"force de frappe" was the visible result. The former global power, Great Britain, having lost its colonial empire like France, is the only European nuclear power committed to the treaty. Besides Great Britain only countries closer to the East-West dividing line have nuclear weapons stationed on their soil: Italy, Greece, Turkey, Belgium and, the Federal Republic of Germany. "Central Europe" is the battlefield: the Federal Republic of Germany. Most endangered, it is most densely packed with troops and arms, nuclear and conventional. As legal successor to the loser of World War II in Europe, the Federal Republic is most willing to increase the density of weapons and troops even further. To many, the economically very strong republic seems politically to be a faithful vassal. Smaller states often exhibit more self-confidence and autonomy. Belgium, for example, delayed the deployment of cruise missiles; the Netherlands accepted new nuclear tasks only on the condition of withdrawing from earlier ones; Denmark rejects nuclear deployments entirely; Norway does not even permit the permanent stationing of conventional NATO troops on its territory; Iceland does not have a single soldier. On the other hand, Greece and Turkey, although both are members of NATO, have a conflict over Cyprus that flares up intermittently.

The common element of the alliance is thus primarily its disunity. This characterizes Europe and gives it its unique strength, which appears threatening to the East. All NATO members are committed to democracy. And just the manifold forms of expression, which seem to delay all efforts at European unification, confirm the firm grounding in a system-political way of thinking that promises greater freedom than other political systems. They wish this form of state structure and no other. They want to keep it. They want to defend it against others. The defense efforts may differ, in expenditures, troop strengths, armaments, and strategic concepts. It may also be possible to discern qualitative gradations in the motivation for defense. Only the will for defense is beyond doubt; it is a European characteristic.

There are also the diverse national roots of the European states, stemming from the geographical separation into islands and peninsulas. All lie somewhere on the edge, all paths to others are far. If one spends vacations in a distant country, one flies over those in between or rapidly passes through them by road or rail. Intermediate countries are recognized by different road signs and police uniforms, but they are hardly recognized as different countries. This way they can remain "who" they are: unique, original, willful, naturally self-confident, politically more or less autonomous.

Autonomy is nothing radically new in Europe. A striving for autonomy is, so to speak, a seal of quality of Western European nations. It can be felt also in Eastern Europe, but the West has the better starting position. Not least of all, it is based on the West's economic prosperity. It is also largely based on a common culture that transcends nations. Before this background, as developed further in the next chapter, only those who misinterpret its common cultural heritage can see a danger in Europe's striving for autonomy.

Autonomy, applied to the special, unique security problems of Europe, between two superpowers, between two poles of power, between two nuclear giants, between the Eurasian land mass and the Atlantic, between socialism and capitalism, facing the East-West conflict, recognizing the risk of global annihilation, for Europe, autonomy must mean:

- Departure from nuclear force.
- Departure from deterrence.
- Departure from the military as the primary means of politics.
- Departure from conflict resolution with violent means.
- Orientation toward crisis-conflict-crisis mechanisms.
- Orientation toward nonviolence as a means of politics.
- Orientation toward averting war.
- Orientation toward nonviolent resistance against nuclear force.
- Decision for autonomous protection—both for alliance members and neutral countries.

Orientation toward nonviolent resistance in politics is less obvious than autonomy. But Europe also has experience in nonviolent resistance, particularly Northern Europe: Germans, Danes, Dutch, French, Norwegians. A number of rough historical accounts have been prepared (Roberts 1967; Sharp 1970/85, 1975, 1979, 1985; Galtung 1967, 1980, 1984; Ebert 1981; Nolte, H.-H. 1984). The next step is to translate these approaches into strategic and operational concepts (Klumper 1985, Mellon 1985, Ebert 1984, Nolte & Nolte 1984). Criticism of nonviolent resistance as the exclusive form of defense (Hueber 1985; Frei 1983; Vetschera 1983) is an additional argument for combining it with protective military defense, since it might fail by itself.

Autonomous protection pushes this effort further. In few regions are the strategic conditions for this purpose as opportune as in Europe. On one hand, neutrals like Sweden, Switzerland, and Yugoslavia have already developed similar forms of defense (Schmid 1985; Fischer 1982). In addition, countries like Norway (Mez 1976) and Denmark (Nolte & Nolte 1984, Ebert 1981) have gained relevant experience, which can form the basis of a tradition. There is also growing official interest among Western governments in an integration of the potential of nonviolent resistance as an element of war prevention (Mellon et al. 1985) or as an element of total defense (Oesterreichisches Bundeskanzleramt 1985). Or parties that are so far still in the opposition opt for such combinations (Alternative Defense Commission 1983; Die Grünen 1983).

On the other hand, the resistance movements against hegemony in the East that flare up repeatedly (Gati 1985; Zielonka 1985) should encourage the autonomous countries in the West, which enjoy greater freedom, to use their freedom with more self-confidence. Finally, one should expect that the leading power of the West will show sufficient understanding to integrate nonviolent resistance as a supplementary instrument of politics and not to obstruct it. To our knowledge, the United States is the first country in the world that celebrates each year a national holiday in honor of a nonviolent resistance fighter—Martin Luther King, Jr.

Precisely this official U.S. orientation toward resistance against the institutions of its own state power can dispel concerns that the organization and training of resistance forces could endanger the internal stability of the state.

The model of autonomous protection offers an opportunity and a challenge. It offers a new strategic-political potential, which can replace nuclear potential and can avert war. It offers a defense potential that gives again greater emphasis to political means in politics than the military means permit today. It offers a model of social consensus on security and defense that can integrate marginal groups, without forcing them to deny their identity.

The challenge lies in the idea to give nonviolent resistance a first chance as a means of politics and to push military approaches into the background. The challenge lies in the idea not only to preach nonviolence, but to make it politically usable, to make oneself available for political ends, as a preacher of nonviolence, and to participate personally—in the extreme prepared to give up the ultimate. "Death is the ultimate limit of everything," writes Horatius (Bettelheim 1979).

The challenge lies also in realizing more nonviolence in the world by using less violence. For the sake of the world. To secure life-and-liberty.

Part III

Changing Our Ways of Thinking

12

What on Earth Are We Talking About?

In the 1940s Albert Einstein, described the situation we are in today, and he did it with remarkable precision: "Our world faces a crisis as yet unperceived by those possessing the power to make decisions for good or evil. The unleashed power of the atom has changed everything save our modes of thinking and thus we drift toward unparalleled catastrophe."

In this statement Einstein makes reference to our whole world, the crisis we are facing, the "everything" that changed, and to catastrophe. In other words, he emphasizes *the existential perspective of the problem confronting us*.

Further, he points out that the change is unperceived by those in power and that our mode of thinking has not changed. That is, as a civilization and as individuals we have not changed our world views, our basic perception of things; we have hardly really understood what happened when the first atomic bomb exploded on July 16, 1945 at Alamagordo in the deserts of New Mexico. This attention to "ways of thinking" we shall call the *cosmological perspective*.

Finally Einstein emphasizes that there is physical power and there is human power. What should concern us is, essentially, the choice between good and evil. The force we have created is overwhelming and we have to change our ways of thinking—also those pertaining to good and evil, to norms, values, and perspectives on the earth. This we shall call the *ethical perspective of our time and situation*.

In what follows, we call these perspectives or objects of our attention premise 1, 2, and 3. We take them to be fundamentals in *any* discussion of contemporary international politics, defense, security, and peace.

But it is worth noticing that in this statement Einstein does not address the issue of what to do. Neither does the statement point in the direction of problem solving—apart from emphasizing the immaterial "way of thinking" that must change if we are to avoid the catastrophe.

Confronting us is, therefore, the problem of *alternatives*—in thinking and action—and of *strategy*, that is, how to set in motion change toward a more peaceful global development, avert the crisis, and much more than that.

This is no small agenda. But it happens to be ours—that of humankind approaching the twenty-first century on a spaceship Earth probably bound on a fate similar to that of the *Challenger* space shuttle in 1986—unless we stop to think, re-think, change our ways of thinking.

We need alternatives, visions, hopes. Shortly before he died, philosopher Jean-Paul Sartre said that hope was the only concept through which he could envisage the future. We tend to believe that a long-term peace policy and the human commitment to carry it constitute arguments for visions or "eutopias" (the place that is desirable and realizable) rather than for building on permanent fear, crisis management, and critical work against that which we don't want in the future (dystopia).

Human potential may be mobilized for protest for a certain time. But if we take for granted that a peaceful and humane, just and ecologically balanced world is not around the next corner, we assert that constructivism in thinking and action, "imaging the future" seminars by historian and peace researcher Elise Boulding, and "future workshops" by futurist Robert Jungk and dialogues about strategies for change are, in the long run, better mobilizers.

This is a psycho-political consideration. But there is more to it. We all know people who say yes, you are right, the world is dangerous, I would also rather live without nuclear weapons and militarization—but what are the alternatives? What would they look like and how should we act to achieve them?" And then follow numerous arguments against changing toward such a deeply desired world, for instance, that the change itself could "rock the boat," that there are those who would not like to see change come about, or that—since many are employed in military industries—it is difficult to convert economy and technology for peaceful purposes.

It all amounts to saying that change for a peaceful wold is a little more dangerous than continuing the arms race, this arms race, which according to all member states of the United Nations is dangerous and stands in the way of human betterment worldwide. Stop the arms race or the human race. This is, to say the least, a bleak prospect.

If this should really be the best we can come up with, we certainly live in a dark time (Humphrey & Lifton 1984) and almost certainly in a prewar— or rather preomnicide—age.

But it tells us probably something much more important. Namely that if only more "alternative futures" could become part of the imagination and political consciousness of all of us, there is hope. Most people adhere, we think, to the present course because they are kept from seeing that there are alternatives. They are told by power elites and the media that, by and large, this is the best world possible. That their leaders "could not do anything else." And authorities are being trusted ad absurdum in this world. It is particularly easy when many feel powerless, overwhelmed, filled with images of death, destruction, nuclear winters, and the like.

As researchers working with these problems for a time, we have come across very few fellow citizens who say: "Yes, I believe the nuclear arms race and overall militarization of economies and politics are alright, and I don't see any need for thinking differently." Many politicians, diplomats, grass-roots, experts, officers, professional groups such as engineers, physicians, priests, and teachers are deeply concerned. Many more are concerned than are enthusiastic about global developments.

The basic reason under these circumstances for adhering to the system is either personal privileges or lack of a vision and of a way out. We are inclined to think that only very few people in top positions are so mad, so ignorant, or so immoral that the present world system is the only possible or desirable one in their view.

Constructive perspectives are the most important long-term mobilizers. However, we should not ignore that people are also, in very concrete but limited ways, motivated by catastrophes. Three Mile Island, Bhopal, Chernobyl are catchwords here. It is, indeed, a moral problem whether and to which degree one finds such accidents "helpful" in raising the consciousness about what we do on earth and about the deep interconnectedness of every society and about the delicate and fragile balance with "Mother Nature."

Again, we are tampering with powers here in which we are not deciding about the existence of *us* but about the existence of everything, in principle, and—particularly—the existence of a future at all. Accidents that officially "simply cannot happen" have happened and shocked us. Are we really not apt to change our security policies before they also happen with nuclear *weapons* and thousands, perhaps millions, are killed and even more harmed? Are Hiroshima and Nagasaki a dangerous experience in conveying the— false—image of survival today, should the catastrophe happen?

Personally we hold the principle of Martin Luther dear that we want to plant a tree today even though the world should go under tomorrow. Likewise, as researchers we embark on analyses and arguments in the belief that humankind is sensible enough, that we have time to change our ways of thinking and save the world. And although the world may see a nuclear catastrophe (by accident or planning) tomorrow, we carry on our tasks.

If for no other reason than this: to remain human, to preserve our hopes and visions, to bid defiance to anyone who wants us to be fearful or despairing. By writing we want to care, be responsible, and plant—not a whole tree but perhaps a seed or two, The "even if . . ." is our ethical foundation. And it is compatible with the three premises and the six alternative security principles we now set out to work on.

13

Premise Number 1: We Face An Existential Choice

The problem of war and peace in the nuclear age is not only unique in terms of intellectual complexity. It is also an exceedingly emotional issue touching us in our innermost individual existence as well as on our role as a tiny subject within humankind.

There are approaches aiming primarily at intellectual modes of understanding to be found in strategic literature, military-political analyses, defense debates, and in much of modern society's attitude to technology as such. There are approaches focusing on the "softer" aspects, driving forces, and consequences from a variety of angles, be they psychology, psychiatry, history, culture, or anthropology.

Likewise there are approaches that take their point of departure in the individual (how do we cope with the world situation and what can we do?) and there are those who start out from the global perspective, from the totality, East/West perspective, from the need for world order restructuring and survival values.

Criss-crossing these dimensions are basic assumptions concerning scientific modes of understanding "the problems" and our lives in general as compared to philosophical, cultural, and other "science plus" ways of understanding the world. They may be hidden or explicitly stated, but they are always there, and they may see science and other approaches as compatible or incompatible, desirable or troublesome, relevant or irrelevant.

Ours is an existential approach. What do we mean by that?

First, we take it to be necessary to conceive of our global situation as part and parcel of our own individual existence as human beings, not only as role players such as computer scientist, soldier, or peace researcher. Each human being has a particular capacity and background. That is what makes us unique and different. At the same time we are alike: facing an existential challenge created by us in 1945.

In other words, we do not accept that one science or one approach should be dominant, neither do we hold it likely that there is only one single solution to be found. We see the micro-life of each and the macro-life of all as basically one.

Second, since any deeper attitude to the totality, to life on earth, to death and the question of why we are here and now cannot be derived exclusively by one science or by all sciences together, but must be interwoven with much larger fields such as philosophy, religiosity, the arts and elements of value systems, myths, music, literature, basic world views or cosmologies, imagination, dreams, and the like—we should permit ourselves to use scientific modes of understanding where necessary but *not* further any (self)-deception that in doing so we have exhausted the issues with which we are confronted.

Thus it goes against the existential premise to perceive of the nuclear policies and problems (not to speak of the general militarization of civilian society's economy, technology, research and development, social relations, and ways of thinking) as if they were just like any other researchable, academic, expert territory to be explored and controlled.

Living in the nuclear age does not pose problems in the ordinary sense of the words—it "changes everything" and it does so constantly. One may see nuclearism as a "problem" to be solved (by more or less rational means) like any other, that is, as something objectivized in relation to ourselves and something we can simply choose to live with or choose to take away. But this is the mechanical perspective. What we are trying to say here, although in almost improperly short terms, is that *the existence of the human being, of humankind and of nature under nuclear conditions is the problem.*

Much of what goes for good science and brilliant research or analysis in the fields of security, defense, military and peace research may well be so on its own narrower premises, but remains an example of Einstein's point—everything save our mode of thinking has changed.

Karl Jaspers pointed out in his seminal book, *The Atom Bomb and the Future of Man* (1958), that "departmental thinking" leads us to view our own limited activity as absolute, to carry it out regardless of the whole "until, despite formal mutual acknowledgement of the departments, it grows like a tumor in the living body, harmful to the spirit of the whole."

But isn't it dangerous or naive or immodest or arrogant to attempt such an all-integrating (holistic) approach? We would answer along the following lines: yes, but only if you carry the illusion that you succeed once and for all. We never do.

Jaspers points out that in the nuclear bomb issue today each type of expert merely states his or her case and then declares him- or herself incompetent outside the specialized field. This may be true in regard to specialized knowledge or skills, but it becomes untrue, he says, if applied to concepts or decisions that concern the issue as a whole and thus the whole human being and all human beings.

The nuclear issue is not an expert issue, one question among many others. Its shadow falls on whatever we think and do. It is, Jaspers maintains, the one issue: To be or not to be. Therefore its solution lies at the depth of human existence. As a matter of fact it requires us to commit ourselves all through life to cope with it, in peacetime by our entire manner of living and in crisis by courage and sacrifice.

Thus as authors we would rather maintain that the sheer choice of *an existential perspective is incompatible with compartmental thinking*. The value of the existential-holistic approach is to be aware of one's unique responsibility vis-a-vis existence—existent as both human being and researcher. We must avoid the creation of the tumors Jaspers talks about and *dare* approach the big issues. If research is of any deeper value it leads to change—inner or outer or both. Our assumption is that departmental thinking, dividing the reality constantly into subject and objects, is not very likely to change our overall modes of thinking. It aims predominantly at outer change to a list of all the arms control and disarmament measures, for instance, we would like *others* to work for. Existential points of departure lead more in the direction, as pointed out by Jaspers, of inner change, reflections on the meaning of life, and to original thinking, self-awareness, and, one might hope, to sharing with others a new general-universal consciousness that *embodies* change rather than *appeals* to change.

However, these distinctions should not be seen as inseparable.

Perhaps, after all, change comes about when we do not try to force it upon ourselves or others. According to Jaspers we can never avoid essential questions such as: What will I be? How will I live in awareness of my humanity and our common peril? "What makes life worth living," he states, "has consequences in action and in the conduct of life, but it cannot be willed—for it is the source of our will . . ." (1963).

What is important is that solutions, proposals, plans, and institutions issue from the entirety of human life and experience. If they all do so and work together and support each other, then a "new politics" will be created that could help us out and bring peace.

In other words, there is more in existence than meets the scientist's eye. As the nuclear physicists who contemplated the meaning of life and the meaning of their role as scientists when they experienced the first nuclear explosion in 1945 seriously came to reflect on the nature of the scientific enterpise as such, *we* who face the present and the future in the light of their work must take responsibility and question *our* modes of doing science, whether in security, defense, foreign policy, or peace.

Many of us are concerned that the military-industrial complexes absorb such a huge proportion of all resources and personnel available for research and development. Most place the blame on the military and the political establishments and say that they are "just carrying out a profession," "must have a job and care for their families," and such.

But we should also ask ourselves this question: What is it about modern science that has made it so attractive to and compatible with power, offensiveness, and ultimately extermination? How did we, as scientists, researchers, experts and the like, *rationalize* the fact of nuclear weapons being stockpiled to absurdity under the pretense of developing "national security" and "survival?"

What does it mean for us, then acting as researchers, that much of this absurdity is considered "natural" or unavoidably given? And does it have something to do with departmental, nonexistential modes of dualistic understanding, that is, with *employing the scientific role as a shield* between ourselves and an almost unbearable reality in suppressed collective anxiety?

Psychologist Abraham Maslow (1966) pointed out that the scientific enterprise is *also* a defense mechanism. "It can be primarily a safety philosophy, a security system, a compilated way of avoiding anxiety and upsetting problems. In the extreme instance it can be a way of avoiding life, a kind of self-cloistering."

We feel that we have to take into accoutn the possibility that contemporary research in defense, security, and peace may be a case of what pshychiatrist Robert Jay Lifton (1979) has termed "psychic numbing" and "doing business as usual," seeking one's own security in narrow perspectives that become absolute because understandable? Or could it be that the "rationalizing" of the very existence of the mass-killing instruments of extermination into scientifically acceptable, logical theories, concepts, and paradigms, and into the sociability of scientists' conference culture, book publishing, and so on are just elements of what he calls *nuclearism*? By that he means the "passionate embrace of nuclear weapons as a solution to death anxiety and a way of restoring a lost sense of immortality. Nuclearism is a secular religion, a total ideology in which "grace" and even "salvation"—the mastery of death and evil—are achieved through the power of a new technological deity."

Lifton (1979) continues the argument by saying that the "deity is seen as capable not only of apocalyptic destruction but also of unlimited creation. And the nuclear believer or "nuclearist" allies himself with that power and feels compelled to expound on the virtues of his deity. He may come to depend on the weapons to keep the world going."

The bomb as a destroyer or killer, yes, but the bomb as a creator, savior, a godlike thing? This point brought forward so eloquently by Lifton may turn everything upon its head, take you by surprise. Lifton seeks support mainly in the deep considerations and statements of those who witnessed the first nuclear explosion. Perhaps there are other, more contemporary themes that lend support to the thesis?

We have all heard others say things like, "No, I don't like nuclear weapons, but what else can we do than continue developing them?" Or, "I don't really think we can get rid of them; they have come into the world and cannot be "dis-invented" again" Or, "I believe they have preserved peace." Or, "The bomb is so overwhelming and the consequences of its use so horrible that we would really never dare use this weapon." Or, "They are here *not* to be used, but to deter, to punish."

In other words, many have infused positive values into the very existence of "the bomb." We cannot do without it, it is indispensable for peace. And like God it is very powerful, it is above each of us, it cannot be seen physically, or touched (except by those few who operate the worldwide nuclear systems day and night). The bomb carries a secret since we don't really know exactly what its "action" would lead to. And its very existence carries both a hope of salvation (preserving peace) and the deep threat to all of us— being punished if we don't live with it in respect and follow "its" logic.

All of us must recognize the fact that our basic attitude toward "the Bomb" is a matter of fundamental beliefs and values, whether "pro" or "con." The question "Does it exist?" is not relevant here; the bombs exist and proliferate. The question is: "Will it act and, if so, what will *we* be?"

What else, we may ask, can account for the self-righteous, take-it-for-granted attitude of nuclear powerholders worldwide but their deep conviction that *they* have the "Bomb on their side," that they are out to check and potentially eradicate evil, that they are doing good, that their world-destroying instruments are—potentially—creators of the Good? Thus, by infusing the Bomb with godlike imagery and integrating it in what is a consistent belief system bordering on deep religiosity, people can play God themselves, become the Maker and the Destroyer, create an eternal future (nuclear energy as a nonexhaustible resource) *or* punish—themselves and/or others. What Lifton calls the "passionate embrace of nuclear weapons as a solution to death anxiety and a way of restoring a lost sense of immortality" could be, we think, one of the least thought of explanations of the fascination held by many vis-a-vis nuclear power.

In this perspective much of what strategists, defense and security researchers have done during the last decades comes close to what theologians do. And government experts, spokespeople, and a good many journalists and commentators resemble, in their social roles, that of the priesthood, the interpreters, and intermediaries, the missionaries, and messengers.

There is no need to carry this point further. It has been clearly illustrated that the role of scientist is not without deep problems in this field. We are saying that from time to time it is important—indeed vital—to step back and reflect not only on the problems of the world but on larger meaning systems, immaterial issues such as imagery and belief systems, *and* to look, introspectively, at one's own role of a scientist in the world as it is here and now. Thus we would assert that one advantage of the existential approach is that it "forces" upon us to free our activity from narrower material and "realpolitik" consideration and from an exclusive empirical-positivist attitude to our daily work.

Third, by the existential approach we mean that research in this field cannot avoid the issue of life and death, the existential *choice* between being and nothingness. The nuclear age is unprecedented in human history not the least because it implies that, for the first time, we are able to kill (probably) all human beings and destroy most of the remainder of the biosphere. It is a power of our own making; there is nobody else to blame. Only we can feel and be guilty.

Individual death, the fact that we are aware all through life that we shall die has occupied every thinking human being throughout history. We are more or less consciously occupied with this fact of life, that death is part of our life, of our project, that it is (or represents) an end to existence. And that we shall have to face it individually. We are weak, life is precarious, our heart can stop beating, and seconds later we are gone. Where to and what for—we simply don't know. It is all in our imagination, dreams, or belief systems.

The way out can be resignation, it can be neglect and psychological repression, it can be religiosity, and—when conscious about it—death anxiety. If the individual does not "accept" this, it may strive for immortality—creating a life or a "result" of some kind (e.g., great literature or having children) that will offer a sense of immortality and thereby, continuity. When the person is no longer there, he or she will leave memories, artifacts, or impressions on others' lives, and thus be present. Suicide can, of course, be seen in the same perspective, creating a life more worth living through death, become oneself, take responsibility, decide the end by will.

The nuclear image is naturally filled with allusions to death and dying. Think of words like "mass destruction," "hunter-killer," megadeath, Trident, Tomahawk, Lance, Harpoon, decapitation, death blow, deep strike (in the heart of the enemy).

Symbolically speaking, there are interesting parallels betwen nuclear issues and the life/death theme. The search for the smallest unit of life led to the atom, which is also the seed of utter destruction. The test in Alamagordo was code-named Trinity, and it was discussed among the scientists whether it would be a "boy" or a "girl"—a success or a failure, that is. It took place in Jornada del Muerto, Death Tract, and Robert Oppenheimer associated it with the Bhagavad Gitā's words about the thousand suns, the Mighty One: "I am become Death, the shatterer of the world" (Jungk 1956/1982; Easlea 1983; Szasz 1984; Lifton 1979; Lifton and Falk 1982).

In getting close to the Beginning *and* the End, we discovered the power of the secret. There is the secret of the universe, of the bomb, and the consequences of its eventual use; there is the element of forbidden knowledge (like the eating of the apple in the Garden of Eden), the immense power, and the feeling of guilt and shame that follows. Lifton finds that:

> The myth of the "bomb secret" is integral to the entire structure of illusion and deception around security. It enables a small group of bomb managers to assume a priestlike stance as exclusive possessors of secrets too arcane and too sacred to be made available to the rest of us (Lifton & Falk 1982).

Could one argue that nuclear death is more attractive or more acceptable than individual, natural death? If it is, as Tom Lehrer sang in the early 1960s, that "we'll all go together when we go, every Hottentot and every Eskimo"—true in the imagery of people that that is what it will be like—then one may hypothesize, *my* own death becomes somewhat easier to think of. I am relieved of the pain and fear in meeting death alone, and I can take some comfort in the image that we are facing the last moment collectively, almost in solidarity. And since somebody else is pushing the button, *I* am not responsible. I am victimized and don't have to feel guilty about it.

Reference is often made to suicide. The mutual assured destruction on which classical deterrene theory builds is said to imply suicide if breaking down: "Nobody would start war because they know it would be a suicidal act." Literally speaking this is nonsense, of course. A's mass destructive means are not fired against A's population, but agains B's, and it is B's weapons that will kill A's population. Symbolically speaking, however, the expression seems to carry some validity.

Suicide may be committed for a variety of reasons. Foremost among them are guilt, depression, a more conscious making up the account by which the person comes to the answer that it is better to kill oneself and thereby throw oneself into the unknown (or as the existentialist would probably state it, recreate authentic existence). As is known from, for example, Alice Miller's studies (1981, 1983, 1986), guilt, self-effacing thoughts, and self-punishment (created partly at least by not having had an outlet for rage and anger with others during childhood) may be other, very central motives leading to self-destruction.

Within a psychological frame of reference it is hardly far-fetched to ask: Is the often-heard talk of (nuclear) suicide a way of tampering with the possibility of suicide at the collective and global, more or less subconscious level? Is it, in that case, a "cry for help" or something that people allied with the technological deity from before feel attracted to?

We do not try to answer such a question here, but it deserves to be raised and discussed, if for no other reason than this: *If* there are *any* signs to the effect that our civilization and our time are suicidal, it is the first time in humankind's history that we *are* also able to carry out the decision and exterminate ourselves. Having created a total weapon that may be used for global suicide, we must somehow have convinced ourselves that we are able, as a race, to withstand the impulse, the urge to kill ourselves.

A final theme pertaining to death should be mentioned here—that of Christian eschatology, the doctrine of the last things, especially in Judaism and Christianity, concerning beliefs about the end of history, resurrection of the dead, the Last Judgment, apocalypticism, and messianism. (Apocalypticism means end-time views about a sudden intervention of God in history, the judgment of all, the salvation of the faithful elect, and being with God in a renewed heaven and earth).

Western eschatology is historical, whereas Eastern eschatology is more mythical. We are used to perceiving of time as linear, building up to a "bliss" point towards fulfillment/growth and such or degrading step-by-step in order to be dissolved into catastrophe, crisis, breakdown, after which something new begins, a New Age, "a novum." History, permanence, continuity, all crushed, but for some there is salvation in the New World. History is ended and fulfilled. The promise of the Kingdom of God, after some kind of purification (catharsis), is a comprehensible image within our civilization.

These are, of course, extremely complex issues. They cannot be understood literally or "tested" empirically. They are parts of cosmologies, imagery, of the "program" of Occidental civilization. What questions do they pose for us here?

One may ask, first, whether the word *God* in the above quotations could be substituted with something like "humans in the nuclear age"? Few in the contemporary world would see nuclear war and annihilation as the "punishment of God"; rather, they would acknowledge it as a human deed (or as a failure of manmade technology and control systems). In this sense humans would be "playing God" since they set in motion the catastrophe.

The question is whether those who are responsible for developing the nuclear (and other mass destructive) arsenals and doctrines in peacetime can do so without, somehow and sometimes, reflecting over this question: Are we already playing God today by just possessing the instruments and planning their potential use? Is it that the sheer potentiality of their use, that is, their coming into the world and existing there, which is a fact that we have "learned to live with," implies a view of ourselves as super human, almost as standing above ourselves in the belief that we are omnipotent? Omnipotent both in tems of controlling the nonuse of the weapons and the use of them if necessary.

Does this make any sense, we may ask? If "we shall all go together when we go," who is there to shape the new world? Isn't it just a fantasy, a game? The only reasonable answer we can see is this: Nuclear weapons are a positive thing in the eyes of those whom we have entrusted with the control over them because *their* omnipotent belief is that (1) they are doing right, (2) they are in the capacity to control the deity because they are part of it, (3) if war comes it will be a catharsis eradicating evil and solving our crisis, and (4) they themselves will be that minority that is chosen to survive into "the Kingdom of God," the Millennium, the New Postnuclear World.

Those who believe that they are both in control of the "deity" and find nuclear war "thinkable" and even plan for it are likely in their imagery to have a vision of being chosen, achieving salvation. By having been faithful. This is where the absolute positive about nuclearism is basically to be found. It seems to be the intellectual as well as emotional "credo" of nuclear deterrence advocates.

It is true that there *is* a suicidal impulse that negates this vision. It would hold it that all of us will be gone, even the "I" who pushes the button. But there is also the interpretation that huge underground bomb-resistant shelters built for elites in the nuclear powers and the consistent talk of "winning war" and "gaining victory" are indicative of visions that have to do with survival, catharsis, with being chosen to build the new and better future "from scratch" so to speak. This is also a kind of sensed immortality, the very few surviving almost all other living creatures and creating life by genetic engineering in the postnuclear reborn world.

One can hardly help referring to Adolf Hitler when in *Mein Kampf* he wrote: "I believe that I am acting in accordance with the will of the Almighty Creator: By defending myself against the Jew, I am fighting for the work of the Lord" (Lifton 1979). The ultimate destroyer probably always will have to see him- or herself as a creator assisting the Creator in building a better future via destruction.

What about the rest of us? We who are not in control and not physically or politically near to or allied with the nuclear deity? We are playing the role of victims. In peace time we are held hostages in the mutually assured destruction game of deterrence, and in war time we are supposed to be exterminated as battlefield or by global "collateral damage." We are the non-chosen ones.

Is there any promise in this? Can it in any way be seen as part of a positive imagery? The thought may be appalling to us.

Victimizing generation after generation, never knowing whether we'll be gone thirty minutes from now, not having the human right to know that there will be a future for us and coming generations, living in ever deeper crisis, contaminated by the effects of still more local nuclear accidents and environmental degradation, and so on; all of this can further the attitude of "Let's get it over, done, finished, once and for all. I don't care!"

Furthermore, scientists and large parts of the public seem to be interested in knowing "what would a nuclear war be like, can we survive it, what would the postnuclear world be like" (Galtung 1984)? Thus we have the studies of nuclear winter, X city or country after the bomb, analyses of the medical, social, environmental, effects of various types of nuclear uses, and we have the keen interest in films from Hiroshima and *The Day After*, and a trend in film-making and science fiction dealing with survival (although a very individualized one focusing on "me making my own way through a dangerous world").

Most of these "war scenarios" are, of course, so appalling and horrifying that most of us would prefer (that is, if there were a choice) to die instantly and not survive into such a postnuclear existence where the living, as Khrushchev said, would envy the dead.

And then again, there is this little paradoxical reflection left. It is well known that even in the most hopeless of situations, in concentration camps and during natural catastrophes, for instance, many people never loose their hopes of surviving. In the nuclear age it can be hypothesized that at least the nuclear planners relate their more or less conscious death anxiety to the image and perception of *the enemy*.

Lifton (1979) expresses this through "what may be the most fundamental of all definitions of an enemy: a person who must die, so that one may oneself transcend death." We are not only the victims of our own leaders and their policies, but also—and psychologically even more strongly so—of the behavior of the official enemy. We may seek through war to eliminate evil ("the Empire of Evil") and personify that with an enemy, the existence of whom embodies this evil. So did the Jews to Hitler and Nazi world views.

Jean-Paul Sartre pointed out that the anti-Semite is one who is afraid, not of Jews but of himself, his consciousness, liberty, and ability to cope with the human condition. The one who victimizes others seeks public confirmation, according to Lifton, of the absolute distinction between his own immortality and the victim's death taint, as he expresses it.

Thus nuclear policies and doctrines, the "super power game," becomes a public theater for the reassertion of the only true path to immortality, defined on the background of the wrong path, that of the enemy.

This is where the paradoxical hope enters and makes a war just a little bit less horrifying. If only the enemy were killed and I/we survived . . .

Nobody *knows* for sure that we will actually all go if there is a war. It *could* be limited somehow and that means limited to harm mostly or exclusively the "enemy"—that is, the person who must die to let the victimizer gain a sense of immortality; that is, transcendence in the sense of surviving into a harmonious enemy-free future world reborn.

When associating victimization not with "the Bomb" as such or with our own nuclear managers but with the existence of a (nuclear-armed) enemy, *there appears to be something attractive about nuclearization even from the view of the potential victims.* Either in the sense of contributing (perhaps by severe personal losses and sacrifices) to an enemy-free world (it would not be really enemy-free, but it can be imagined so) or in the sense that the Romanian-French dramatist of the theater of the absurd Eugéne Ionesco expressed it so eloquently in his "Journal" of 1966:

> I must kill my visible enemy, the one who is determined to take my life, because I am dimly aware that in killing him, I have killed death. My enemy's death cannot be held against me, it is no longer a source of anguish, if I kill him with the approval of society: That is the purpose of war. Killing is a way of relieving one's feelings, of warding off one's own death (Humphrey & Lifton 1984).

So enemies are convenient for us—in legitimating the ongoing war planning with all its unbelievable resources and in giving us hope in the nuclear age. Either they personify death and I can attempt to kill it by killing the enemy and even reach a harmonious "enemy-free" and reborn world *or* I can take comfort in the "dystopia" that that war will be so horrifying anyhow that I'd rather die instantly. Or both.

Somehow we are drawn to the perspective that there is something positive and hopeful *both* in being annihilated and in surviving, *dead or alive*, physically or in our minds and imagery.

Confused? Hopefully so. Who could honestly state that he or she is not overwhelmed by these perspectives? Others have done much more consistent work in these fields, many of whom we have relied on (see Øberg 1986). The point here is to bring them into an exposition that also addresses more concrete and political issues. We have taken the liberty to raise difficult issues and issues to which there are no clearcut answers—in order to avoid compartmentalization of our minds. If stimulating the minds so much the better since we believe that the most interesting and important aspects of human existence are those about which there can only be a dialogue and no proof or one right "answer."

14

Premise Number 2: The Ways We Think Must Become Conscious to Permit Change

We have all heard it time and again, that we must think differently, change our attitudes to war and peace, realize that in the nuclear age war is no longer possible, that we must understand our enemy and ourselves better and learn to solve conflicts in more humane ways than constantly threatening each other with annihilation.

But what does all this mean? It is no solution just to "be nice" to each other. We must ask what is really meant by the "way we think" (Nakamura 1964).

It means at least two things, namely the ways we think consciously and determinedly when we make up our minds and decide what to do in various situation *and* the ways we think unconsciously, the images, world views, the unproblematized world-taken-for-granted. Thus there is a way of thinking, a set of reasonably clear variables based on our consciously raising questions, and there is a set of values or variables that we usually do not question. Naturally, this last type is, the most difficult to pull up to the surface. It is our "collective mind," it is what it implies to identify a "Westerner" (in our case), it is our "program" or what Galtung calls "cosmology." As in psychiatry, trying to raise the consciousness about the individual's hidden structures and more or less suppressed thoughts, only a dialogue can make our cosmology more transparent to us as social beings, members of the collectivity. It takes a certain amount of introspection and had perhaps better be done by analysts from other cultures than our own. However, we believe it is worth—again without the illusion of solving problems once and for all—to focus on these issues.

The moment we start out, we are tangled up in webs of conceptualization and methodological problems. Thinking, for instance, cannot be clearly distinguished from feeling, sensing, and the use of intuition, metaphors, fantasies, dreams, visions. Second, making cosmology our subject forces us into issues such as what is consciousness—individually and collectively; what does it mean to *be* conscious of "the world" and one's own thinking about it? How do we create, live with, and hand over the elements that make up our consciousness? How do we experience the world and make "sense" of it? How do we conceptualize the micro-level ("I") and the macro-level ("You"/"the world"/"the Universe"/Existence/Being/etc.) and the relations between the two? How do we at all speak about such immaterial things, in what sense do we "know" about consciousness and cosmology, how can we select some "components" of it to give it substance, make it intelligible to the reader, visualize it?

And what on earth you may ask, with many a good reason, has this second premise to do with defense, security, and peace?

Let's start out from the assumption that we are all mapmakers. Each one of us lives a life different from any other in the sense that we perceive it as "my life." Kenneth Boulding, economist, peace and future researcher, helps us get into this fascinating world when he writes that

> the most creative kind of conversation, especially among those who differ or are threatened by each other and are hostile toward each other, might also be described as "image tourism." Each human mind is a vast world of it own, a great landscape of memories, experiences, beliefs, propositions, and so on. In similar aspects, it can be tested by experience, which changes our minds . . . The testing of larger systems, however, and especially of the unfamiliar, is much more difficult. One of the ways in which we do this is to explore the images of larger systems in other people's minds. And where their images differ from ours, we may not change ours, but at least they are challenged (Boulding 1985).

In order to bring some order, meaning, and guidelines into our individual life, we construct "maps" of the landscape. We make representations of what is called "reality," we are constantly letting experiences, event, memories, human encounters, happy or sad, settle in the deep layers of our mind. Over time this "sedimentation of meaning" (Valle & von Eckartsberg 1982) becomes more and more solid, gives us much of our identity, offers security, in the sense of being a tool for interpretation of what goes on around us, establishes a personal "world view," and serves as a reservoir of things good and bad. You may also conceive of it as a sorting device, a scheme for classification of what is meaningful and what is meaningless. Like a computer program we use this mind-mapmaking mechanism to be given messages such as "go ahead" or "stop/start again/wrong."

Thus we are simply open to the world in many ways and are constantly receiving messages from it, filtering them into our consciousness, which develops on the basis of this ongoing sedimentation. And we act vis-a-vis the world (other human beings, nature, ourselves) according to the "stop" and "go" signals so that we do not only see "our" world as reasonably meaningful but also become able to act meaningfully.

In this sense we relate to the world by means of subjective images of that world. Human meaning connects the micro and macrolevels. But it must be emphasized that this process is basically social. It is tested, as Boulding (1985) says, through "image tourism," through perceiving openly and acting *into* the world, by being receptive and active. If our "inner world" (our map) is wrong in some sense of the word, we are likely to get the message from the world, because we act counterproductively.

Reality is a difficult concept here, of course. But it is reasonable to state that it is socially-collectively constructed (Berger & Luckman 1969) in the sense that it is "the product" of the actions, encounters, and interplay of all other human beings. And they, like you and me, also have their minds, their individual maps, or consciousness about the world at large on the basis of which they act.

All this, unfortunately, has to be expressed basically in terms of metaphors. We are approaching issues that, at least at some stage, go "beyond words" and far beyond scientific language and may actually better be expressed in poetry, music, meditation, and the like. However, to clarify the terminology so far, there is in each of us some kind of *mind* or deep interpretative structure that helps us create individual meaning in our own life, a personal map. This mind is very broad and very deep, it stretches, in principle, "up" to conceptions of transcendence, the (universal) mind, the one, peak experiences, "highest meaning of life," and so on. Some of the sediments in the mind may be shared with others and found similar in others' minds; some of it is deeply individual, something we would not or could not share with our fellow human beings, and in some cases not even with ourselves (subconscious).

But this does not explain how reality is socially constructed. To communicate, to be "image tourists," to act into the world there must be some collectively shared meaning structures, some "collective maps." By means of them we *understand ourselves as a totality, as a community—or larger: civilization*—through dynamic interaction and "civilizational image tourism." Galtung has called these "programs" *cosmologies* which, literally speaking, means ways of understanding the structure of the universe (kosmos) by ultimate priciples.

The cosmology we want to expound a bit on here is *social* cosmology, that is, general world views as they are shaped by cultural habits and history. Thus social cosmology is a concept that is more narrow than the individual mind or the universal mind; it is placed somewhere "in between" these spheres as basically *a tool for collective self-understanding*. But as we shall see, it may encompass images or "maps" of what goes on in the micro-mind as well as in the macro-mind.

Peace researchers Galtung, Rudeng, and Heiestad approach social cosmology in the following manner:

> It is conceived of here as "deep ideology," a set of usually unquestioned assumptions about all kinds of things and how they relate to each other; implicit rather than explicit. The metaphor of *social grammar* may be useful here: the idea that there are basic rules defining elements, their relations and transformation . . . Social cosmology is seen as something located inside the only concrete social actors there are, individual human beings. One may postulate that human beings have an inborn capacity for a number of social grammars, and that their experiences with the outside world activate and build up one such grammar, partially activating and building some others (the less dominant, the less manifest ones).
>
> Each impression from the outside of how things concrete or abstract, are organized will serve as raw materials building up the grammar. Identical patterns (isomorphisms) are recognized, sedimented unto the deeper recesses of human consciousness, then gradually serving as a cognitive filter rejecting patterns that are different as "unnatural," "abnormal," thereby sliding into a more normative concept . . .
>
> Thus, social cosmology becomes like a program, not unlike the program of a computer; accepting inputs in some forms, rejecting or changing other forms, capable of carrying out some routines and delivering some kinds of output, to the exclusion or partial exclusion of other possibilities.
>
> But then there is the basic dissimilarity between human beings and computers: it is given to man to arrive at a certain level of consciousness about how he is programmed, including biological programming, and it is even given to man, probably under very special circumstances, to make changes in his program" (in Burke 1979).

This is an excellent approximation of what we are trying to get at here. What should be particularly observed is the distinction between dominant/manifest cosmology and subordinate/latent cosmology. When in what follows we use the term "Westernness" or "Western civilization," is designates the dominant-manifest cosmology. It is very important constantly to avoid black-white imagery or to attempt placing all phenomena in one and the same category. Neither the "landscapes" nor the "maps" *are* like that.

Let us next turn to the question: What are the components we should look for in order to construct the program? What does it "consist" of? How do we build the program?

As in so many other conceptualizations of these immaterial issues, we shall work with layers—from the most evident and material objects to the most immaterial and "invisible" parts, that is, along a high-low dimension.

The modern classical sociologist-philosopher Pitirim Sorokin maintains that all *socio-cultural* phenomena consist of three components, namely (1) immaterial, spaceless and timeless ideas and meanings, (2) material objects that give substance in the physical world to the ideas and meanings, and (3) human actors who use and operate the meanings with the help of the objects around them (Sorokin as quoted by Darnton 1973).

This categorization into ideas or meanings, material objects, and human actors needs refinement but makes a good beginning. We suggest the following "ranking" of levels of understanding at the bottom of which (high-low, shallow-deep, again) we mention cosmology, thus:

- Actors, events, and things
- Organization
- Structure
- Concepts and (scientific) theories about the above
- Paradigms
- Value systems, ideas, images
- Cosmology (dominant/manifest, subordinate/latent): twelve building blocks or "indicators"

Now, how to pinpoint such layers, their relations, and place in a hierarchy is not a "logical"-rational enterprise. Ours is developed out of intuition, various ideas from thinking, dialogue, and reading of specialized literature in the field, and from imagination. The dimensions built into it are outlined at the left-hand side of Figure 13, and to the right-hand side we have attempted to illustrate what we mean by each of the layers by making reference to a concrete case, central to people engaged in security policy debates and research.

Why a pyramid? To illustrate the horizontal dimension, that of time. The dots at the top are here-and-now flashes of events that compare to, let us say, the news in today's broadcast. This is the surface, the top soil of the social world, and we can dig our way down as sociological archaeologists. At the top things change quickly, whereas at the bottom—indicated by longer lines—things change much less rapidly. At the bottom we are facing the "grand waves," epochs, the cosmology, or world views that change only very slowly.

What are we trying to illustrate with the high-low indication of the time dimension? That what happens here and now are manifestations of deep-lying patterns. That what happens today in terms of actors, events, and things we take to be the same as the "real world" are "products" of the "raw materials" in the bottom of our civilization. They are *variations on a theme. And that theme (in our case) is the dominant cosmology of Westernness.* We assume that there is some kind of correspondence from the top to the bottom, and vice versa. The similarity with an "iceberg theory" is no coincidence.

But *time* as such, is not an easy category, either.

In a highly interesting analysis of "maps of the mind," Rolf von Eckartsberg deals with the time-dimension of the existential experience in the following manner: There are of course the three classical time zones—the past, the present, and the future. The past has to do with historical being, memories, personal "stories"; the future is the present in becoming, it is what we anticipate, plan, and project into.

But according to von Eckartsberg this does not exhaust the possibilities. There is a time zone further ahead and one further back. Each of us is able to move beyond the projected future and imagine things, develop visions, free ourselves from existential limitations (for example, in dreams). Our fantasy is personal and unlimited—and may go beyond what we usually call the future.

Similarly, he maintains, we can also go beyond our remembrances and "into the never-never land of missed opportunities, of regrets, of guilt and wishes, recasting our fate and ask "what if . . .?"

We think it is important to show the richness in combining personal and collective time zones with such a "wild"—but very common and "unscientific"—dimension as fantasy of the human mind. It ought to be quite natural to include such a perspective in discussions about the future and our ways of perceiving it (as well as the past). But somehow it is seldom taken into account in intellectual or academic projects. How else should we be able to "image the future," choose futures and participate in future workshops and ordinary brainstorms—not to mention genuine future research?

Thus appears Figure 13. But by now you may rightly wonder what we

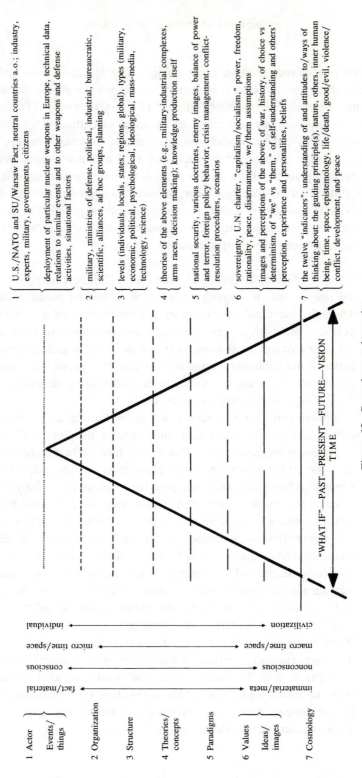

Figure 13. Cosmology and security.

mean by twelve indicators of a cosmology. The question is of major importance since those twelve points make up the bottom of the whole pyramid; they are somehow the root "causes" of everyday events. To approach an answer, imagine that you arrive at a society or culture in which everything seems different from what you know of and in which you don't seem to understand the language or the social habits. And since you are interested in the overall qualities of this culture, you don't investigate details like what the inhabitants eat or what they wear; instead you approach the macro question: "What is this society about? How does it understand itself?" To pursue these questions means to explore imaginations and value judgments, in a new series of questions about questions.

1. What is the collectively held image of a "highest authority"? Here we maybe able to identify at least the following possible answers. There is one God, two or more, or no images of a god (mono-, poly-, or atheistic patterns). Next, it will be important to understand the nature of the relationship between the faithful and the god(s) and between the nonbelievers and their image of wisdom (e.g., the council of elders). What, according to the inhabitants, do(es) the god(s) "look like", is it female or male, etc?

   Is there some kind of pact in which the faithful are promised protection and survival (salvation) in return for obedience? Can one or more truths be permitted? Is there any idea of being chosen? How does the civilization relate to belief systems outside itself? Is it missionary or receptive-assimilating in its religious cosmology?

2. What is the image of nature? We may think here of three basic categories—humans standing in wonder and humility "below" nature, in "partnership" with nature, or "above", omnipotent, dominating, and controlling nature. Furthermore, is there a basically mystic, rationalistic-mechanistic or organic view of nature? Is the human-nature relationship dualistic—split in rather independent subject ("I/we") and object ("it") terms? Is nature related to sex, as in "Mother Nature," and what imagery does it lead to?

3. What images do we find about other human beings and cultures? Are they fundamentally vertical or horizontal (what imagery is built into concepts of a first, second, third, and fourth world, for instance)? How do human and social categories such as races, generations, and gender appear in the world views of the inhabitants? And what are the dominant organizational modes?

4. What is the image of inner and outer human beings? What "solutions" to the soul-body problem can one identify? How occupied is the culture with "visible" versus "invisible" aspects of existence? In which fields does it particularly develop a knowledge or wisdom about human life? What is its concept of health? How is normality defined and how are the "less normal" looked upon? Is there any deeper consciousness relating the individual to a "community of souls" and a vivid image of transcendence? Is there an essential one-ness with the universe in the self-perception or a more personal-individualized perception?

5. What is the image of time like? Is there a short- or long-time perspective behind what people do? Is it part of their sense of history to see time as circular or linear, mechanical (quantitative), or organic (qualitative)? How does the collective time encompass birth (creation), life and death in relation to each other? What role does time play in comparison with other important resources in people's minds? How intimate is the connection between biography and history? What images of the future—and "beyond" in the visioning and wishful thinking—can we identify? Can we understand the culture as one of hope (just begun, great future) or one of despair and crisis ("we are approaching the end")?

6. What is the image of space? Does the culture comprise of (or in everyday life "take interest in") the entire world, does it look upon itself as part of a micro or a macro space? As a center of everything or basically as periphery? Is its self-image essentially one of being involved in the "space" of others and, if so, for what reasons?

   Does it see itself as elevated as a "kingdom in the middle" high above the "barbarians," or as "bigger and better" with a mission to control the world? Is it outwardly or inwardly oriented as a civilization? Are the people "go-getters," grasping things and knowledge, or more of the meditative kind, open and receptive, "stay-recipients"? Does it conceptualize overall development in terms of smaller or larger units, in a limited or unlimited way? Does it define when enough-is-enough, or not? Is it basically self- or other-reliant?

7. What is the image of the construction and relevance of knowledge and wisdom? How does the collective arrive at the conclusion that it "knows" something about itself and the world at large? What modes of understanding are dominant—"primitive," scientific or wise-meditative-intuitive modes? What does it take to arrive at expert status in

that civilization? What do the institutions of knowledge-production look like? What is considered relevant, reliable, and "good" knowledge? What paradigms in the (re)search for understanding and meaning of life do we find, and how do things like values, theories, and facts relate to each other?

Does the image of "right" thinking imply fragmentation or holism? Is knowledge for understanding or manipulation of the environment? Is there a dominant belief that everything, more or less, can be understood in terms of cause-effect relationships? Is there a part of life that the inhabitants believe they cannot "reach" by systematic investigation, but, rather, must be "reached" through intuition, "seeing," wisdom?

8. What are the images of life and death? This point, of course, is about the existential dimensions, the meanings of life at large, which we have dealt with at some length under premise number 1.

9. The image of good and evil? The central distinction pertains here to whether the world (and its smaller units, like human beings) are *either* good *or* evil or can be *both* good *and* evil. In general, of course, there is the task of finding out how important ethics is at all in the particular civilization and in the minds of the people? Is there a right to life built into the consciousness? What basic norms such as rationality, utilitarianism, means end logic can we identify?

Is ethics and the set of moral rules aimed at realizing an ethical life "passive" or "active" in daily thinking and acting? What inconsistencies can we find ("It is, of course, wrong to harm or kill, but . . .")? What basic ethical role is assigned to humans vis-à-vis the greater existence of the totality? On what criteria is punishment for immoral behavior meeted out? (Since we deal more extensively with ethics under premise number 3, we do not go further into illustrating what we mean by this point here.)

10. The image of conflict, conflict-resolution, and violence. Are conflicts as such viewed as good or bad, by what means should they be solved—fights, war, courts, arbitration, bargaining, sports? Do people tend to participate in conflict resolution themselves or do they hand it over to "professionals"? Does resolution imply that one must be winner and one loser, or is the image of good conflict resolution one of the actors being a little of both?

We may also ask what constitutes a conflict. In some cultures certain features are considered compatible, whereas in others they are incompatible and, therefore, conflict-creating. What openness is there toward "foreign" elements? Compromise, accommodation, learning to handle and live with conflicting views, the relations between rights and conflicts—all these are indicative of what type of cosmology we are investigating. Particularly important is the collective training in harmonizing opposites, whether or not the people are able and willing to see them as parts of a larger unity; to mold "foreign" influences, being open to "both/and" rather than "either/or" images of the surrounding world and its problems.

Closely related is the image of violence. We know that most cultures tend to consider violence bad or unacceptable, but then comes the problem of creating and maintaining some kind of order. What, therefore, are considered appropriate reasons for employing violence? Which types—direct/structural, material/nonmaterial, individual/collective, bodily/psychologically, visible/invisible—are the most common? We might also explore what kinds of heroes and violent "entertainment," symbolic acting-out methods are vivid in the social habits and in people's imagination. What, for instance, does it mean to have power or be powerful, who are selected to be in power, and to which degree is the imagery of power related to strength, courage, authority, violence, destruction, etc?

11. The image of development. What does the culture perceive as its raison d'être, its real mission? Human fulfillment, welfare, inner perfection before meeting God, cultural maturity, sheer material growth, imperial power, conquering the world—or something else?

Is development conceived of as taking place in stages according to an established "program"—or is it more voluntaristic in people's consciousness? What kinds of metaphors is the general development thinking built on—eternal progress, cycles of genesis, growth, decay, and breakdown? Paradise-fall-darkness-enlightenment-progress-crisis-catharsis-Paradise reborn . . .? Is the civilization seeking optimization or maximization of its goals? Historian and sociologist Robert Nisbet (1969) distinguishes between change as natural, as permanent, as continuous, as directional, as necessary, as differentiating, and as uniforming. What basic image of change and stability do the inhabitants cherish?

12. The image of peace. What kinds of thought associations do the people get when they hear the word peace? Life? Death? Activity? Passivity? Something we create ourselves through our manipulating the environment (for instance, stopping wars and arms races) or as something the world can only prepare for, each of us, and receive deep down

in our minds? Is the culture as such at all concerned about peace—
compared with other "missions"? Is it earthly or heavenly? We know
that the conceptualizations of peace differ from culture to culture, in
time and space (see chapter 15).

It is time to recapitulate.

First we described how we think that everyday events make up only the
tip of the iceberg. Down through a number of layers, we imagine—or believe—that there is some kind of very important, rather solid but immaterial
cultural-civilizational program with which we constantly interact. Appear-
ances may differ quickly from day to day, but collectively we share with
each other this base of a social grammar—a world taken for granted. Something that stretches far beyond the lifetime of the single human being. In
this sense we live our social lives, our lives as a civilization together with
everybody else who shares this program.

Next, we have tried to enumerate at least some of the components of this
program or cosmology. Imagine it as a kind of checklist, a tool you may
use when you try to get to the collective consciousness of your culture. They
are the building blocks of our collective identity, what we find "natural" as
Westerners. Each of the twelve components have a number of dimensions
and we have gone through some of them. So, imagine that you carry out
an analysis of such a civilization (our own to the degree possible) with the
aim of finding out what it means to be a living human being in the Occidental world.

You may find that, for example, we are a monotheistic civilization, relying on vertical god relations, not particularly humble in our dealings with
nature and its resources. We tend to care more about the body and what can
be measured and quantified than about the soul and that which is invisible,
and so on. You may go on yourself according to your experience and opinion and analytical capacity. There is no single "right answer."

When we have gone through the twelve indicators and their numerous
dimensions, we may end up with a *"profile,"* one that will be indicative of
what it means to be a Westerner toward the end of the twentieth century as
we share it collectively. Then we know a little more about the ways we are
programmed ourselves. This profile will be different in various aspects from
what somebody looking at the Orient (or Hindu culture "in between") or
Africa would come out with.

Why is all this important, indeed essential?

*Our fundamental assumption is that the social cosmology, the "program,"
is basic in shaping the ways we think.* And, no less important, it is so in-

timately connected with our perceptions and action at the "top" of the pyramid that it is *reasonable to assume that it determines (as a program) whether or not we are ending up in war or in creating peace.*

This is the fundamental importance in the idea of social cosmology. By analyzing our deep collective consciousness as a culture, that is, by taking a deliberate macro perspective, we arrive at the "roots" of what we call ways of thinking.

It is therefore crucial to be aware of the "go-between" function of this program, particularly if we support the Einstein thesis that we *must* change our ways of thinking. When we state that we *must* it implies that we have the suspicion—or, rather, fear—*that the specific and general Western cosmology is so constructed that it will, sooner or later, end in catastrophe.*

This demands a serious study and dialogue of what is really the content of this program. Mind you, so far we have exclusively outlined the framework, the "map of the map," and the indicators. It remains to fill it in, to give it substance. Thus we use the words *suspicion* and *fear*.

What this leads up to is a tentative conclusion that the most important military problems—so central in mainstream debates about defense, security, and peace—are not essentially military, but products of the purely civilian program on which we operate. We have also said that although empirical, solid scientific investigation is necessary, it is not a sufficient tool in identifying the dangers that we fear are built into the program.

One year we talk about intermediate-range nuclear weapons in Europe, the next about the MX, chemical warfare, deep strike, star wars, and we talk continuously about arms control and disarmament. We tend to believe that each new "problem" is just a manifestation of, a variation on a deep theme, that of our Westernness. We shall hardly ever really be capable of changing the ways we think unless we become aware of the tremendous collective consciousness-program on which these day-to-day problems rest.

True, in the West there have always been countercultures. There are "pockets" or subprograms, peripheral, "softer" components in the Western cosmology. We think here of the ecological stream, the monastery tradition, the grass-rooting, the artistic dynamism, the "good" sides of technology for humane purposes, popular participation in many respects as well as the practice of nonviolence. One other element stands out and brings more hope than any other: Feminine countercosmology.

We don't want to exclude those aspects. The world is still rich and reductionism is a much larger sin in research than factual errors. But we have tried to outline the general version of the general West, and that culture *is* rather "either-or" programmed instead of "both-and" programmed.

What may bring additional hope here is, of course, that a cosmology pertaining to human and social matters, to existence itself, does not change all in one. It changes slowly up and down through the pyramid. Water drops hollow out even the hardest stone over time.

All in all this exposition is an analytical one. It deals with what we think the socio-culturally sensitive person may gain from listening carefully to what this collectively programmed "we" think. The illustration is two-dimensional indicating layers of thinking over time together with the component parts of the cosmology. But there is also an "I," a third dimension expanding into the page, something that gives the intellectual space explored so far a depth and connects *my* individual existence (being) with the existence of it *all* (Being) (see Fig. 14).

There is such a richness throughout history on these matters and minds that it would be presumptuous to try to cover even a fraction of it. The whole field is now being reactivized in discussions of the intelligibility of the universe, world views, paradigms, turning point, holographic imaging, in the East as well as the West. There is a revival of books on the philosophy of life, on death, on mystic traditions, on total ecological and feminine aspects,

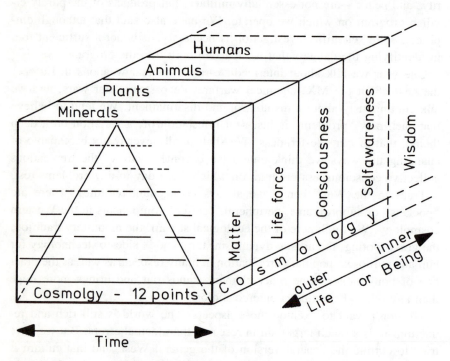

Figure 14. Cosmology and levels of being.

and so on. Fortunately enough we would say, much of it also raises critical questions about the meaningfulness of modern Western science as it is traditionally applied (excellent examples are Bohm 1980, Capra 1982, Keller 1985, Merchant 1980, Pirsig 1974, Prigogine & Stengers 1984, Sperry 1983, Valle & von Eckartsberg 1981; Wilber 1977).

One of those we have found particularly illuminating and comprehensible for a wider audience is E. F. Schumacher's *A Guide for the Perplexed,* published in 1977, the year he died. It seems to be as overlooked as his *Small Is Beautiful* is world-famed. Perhaps it is indicative that his thoughts on Buddhist *economics* turned out a bestseller, whereas the book on the *life* philosophy and *wisdom* he devoted himself to and based the book on was, by and large, repelled by the "program" of the Western world, even the grass-roots and the alternativists.

Schumacher starts out precisely with the limitation he finds in the modern West and its self-understanding when he says that

> The maps of real knowledge, designed for real life, did not show anything except things that allegedly could be proved to exist. The first principle of the philosophical map-makers seemed to be "If in doubt, leave it out" or put it into a museum . . . Would it not be wiser to turn the principle into its opposite and say "If in doubt, show it prominently"? After all, matters that are beyond doubt are, in a sense, dead; they do not constitute a challenge to the living . . .
> The maps produced by modern materialistic scientism leave all the questions that really matter unanswered. More than that: they do not even show a way to a possible answer: they deny the validity of the questions" (Schumacher 1977).

We are now so clever, he says poetically, that we cannot do without *wisdom.* The seeking for wisdom starts out with wonder, and the most important part of any inquiry is its beginning. When we reduce existence, research, and the meaning of life to only-what-can-be-scientifically-understood, to "nothing-but-ness," then, maintains Schumacher, we shall never arrive at any deeper understanding. We can only agree since we have stated the importance of starting out with an existential perspective on the nuclear age.

Schumacher approaches the great Chain of Being in a verticalized fashion, sharing the type of structure with which we have treated cosmology, but remember we are now progressing into the third dimension of Figure 14. Life at the lowest level begins with minerals; then come the plants, which have a "life force," that is, the difference between a living and dead plant.

Third comes the animal, at which "consciousness" appears. And then on top come humans, whose "mysterious power" compared with the other levels is self-awareness, being conscious of the conscious. So, humans can be written "minerals + life force + consciousness + self-awareness."

The universe is a great hierarchic structure of markedly different Levels of Being. There is *no* continuity from one level to the next. At each level we therefore need special resources to understand life, or as Schumacher expresses it:

> To say that life is nothing but a property of certain peculiar combinations of atoms is like saying that Shakespeare's "Hamlet" is nothing but a property of a peculiar combination of letters . . . The extraordinary thing about the modern "life sciences" is that they hardly ever deal with *life as such* (Schumacher 1977, 28–29).

Humans are thus *not* just a combination of life forces and consciousness, not just somewhat "higher." Self-awareness is their unique, distinctive mark. But it doesn't stop there, of course. Throughout humankind's existence, those we consider the wisest or greatest have almost all been of the opinion—or "seen"—that the Chain of Being extends beyond the human. Through self-awareness we can reach higher, which, according to Schumacher, is to progress into inner space to gain Wisdom, unity. Higher always means "more inner." Human beings are capable of bringing the whole universe into their experience. But—and there is a but—it presupposes that we accept a priori that life is not only external, material, and thus visible and limited, but also internal, spiritual, and thus invisible and infinite. Beyond the human "level" there is no ceiling. There are limits to quantity and material life and scientism, but not to quality, spiritual seeking, and wisdom.

This is, indeed, a fascinating definition of reality and expands tremendously what ought be called "realistic" in our day-to-day existence. We are approaching a complementarity in modes of understanding—intelligence supplemented with faith, truth-seeking. Intelligence has to do, basically, with scientific-rational modes (striving for control and manipulation of the visible world), whereas faith has to do with wisdom. When we start out analyzing an aspect of life we *always* choose a perspective, "an approach"; we limit ourselves. This is what most of the training at schools and universities helps us to do. Schumacher emphasizes that the choice of level of investigation is always a matter of faith. It is not a matter of intelligence. I choose my methodology and value sets and approches on the basis of deeply held images of what *my* Life is about, the richness of my Level of Being.

Thus there is the brain, but there is also the heart. Faith, he maintains, is *not* in conflict with reason; nor is it a substitute for reason. "Faith chooses the grade of significance or Level of Being at which the search for knowledge and understanding is to aim" (Schumacher 1977).

Scientific investigation may yield knowledge, thinking may yield opinions, but using all guided by the heart leads to insight. The "eye" must be in the heart.

Wisdom is "science for understanding." It does no harm. It does not seek to convince, prove, or manipulate. It frees the mind up through the stages to make it ever more open so it can *receive*.

Here we find one of the basic reasons why we need this third dimension in Figure 14. Cosmology tends to be shared collectively, whereas wisdom need not be shared. Science as practiced today is good if it *works,* one criterion being that it must have general validity and reliability. In this sense it must be publicly, "democratically" shared; another scientist would be able to arrive at the same result as the first given identical circumstances. Objectivity means intersubjectivity. However, wisdom—science for pure understanding of life—cannot be transmitted in the same way; it is not available to anyone unless he or she trains and seeks. Individually, that is.

In this distinction between science and wisdom, based on the four Levels of Being with the self-awareness reaching potentially limitless heights of wisdom, a central "cause" why so much of contemporary science is part of our existential problems (employed so easily for destructive purposes)? Because it is good at describing a very limited field of reality monopolizing it as the totality and because it is good in its countermode (alternativist, critical science) at criticizing and pointing out dangers, but is so *desperately deficient in coming up with images of the "good society"*? If what Schumacher calls striving for wisdom is excluded from the (re)search process, how could it be otherwise?

Imagine this thought applied to mainstream research on defense, security, and particularly to nuclear problems, and you have an excellent explanation of why we insist on this piece of peace research starting out from an existential premise. We consider it an integrated part of *our* (present) level of being in a world so torn and threatened by manmade problems.

Finally, one more reason why we feel we need something of the kind Schumacher develops in order to enrich our model is expressed by him, almost as though he had dealt with the social cosmology we have elaborated on:

. . . at the human Level of Being, the *"invisibilia"* are of infinitely greater power and significance than the *"visibilia."* To teach this basic truth has traditionally been the function of religion, and since religion has been abandoned by Western civilization nothing remains to provide this teaching. Western civilization consequently, has become incapable of dealing with the real problems of life at the human Level of Being. Its competence at the lower levels is breathtakingly powerful; but when it comes to the essentially human concerns it is both ignorant and incompetent . . .

Without self-awareness man acts, speaks, studies, reacts mechanically, like a machine: on the basis of "programmes" acquired accidentally, unintentionally, mechanically. He is not aware that he is acting in accordance with programmes; it is therefore not difficult to re-programme him—to make him think and do quite different things from those he had thought and done before— provided only that the new programme does not wake him up. When he is awake, no one can programme him: he programmes himself" (Schumacher 1977).

We are close to seeing a combination here of our two dimensions, which has been one basic reason to choose Schumacher (apart from his own unique merits as a thinker and pedagogue). Furthermore, the last sentences of the quotation could just as well have been written by an existentialist, worded in something like "life acquires meaning when we choose it freely, when we accept facticity and enter into existence authentically." So, there is even the fascinating perspective here of seeing connections between a Westerner inspired strongly by Oriental thinking and the existential (although not necessarily existentialist) perspective we have chosen.

From such a connection may emanate, genuine intercultural dialogues in book form (Marsella et al. 1985; Katz 1983; Welwood 1983; Toynbee & Ikeda 1976) or in projects and networks such as the U.N. University's "Goals, Processes and Indicators or Development (GPID)," the World Order Models Project (WOMP), the International Foundation for Development Alternatives (IFDA) with its IFDA Dossiers, the World Future Studies Federation (WFSF), and—so we hope—the Transnational Foundation for Peace and Future Research (TFF).

To change our way of thinking is a matter of "awakening the programmer" in each of us and to change the social program on which we fear we are bound for unparalleled catastrophe. Awareness of this need can come only from some combination of research *and* wisdom, from inner development, from deeply personal convictions and responsibility. It cannot come from "science" or only from the "scientist."

At the same time as we intensify the search, we detach ourselves from the collectively accepted/acceptable program. That means also to detach oneself from power and manipulation, from what is "realistic" in narrow political terms. The terrible fact is that such a search not only for what we can know (epistemology) but also for what there really exists at various levels (ontology, religiosity) is considered a luxury these days. How can you withdraw into yourself when the world is approaching deep crisis? How can you take your time when we need your research results urgently? Why don't you care about the world, why are you not busy? Don't you care? Or as Schumacher maintains:

> Anyone who openly goes on a "journey into the interior" who withdraws from the ceaseless agitation of everyday life and pursues the kind of training . . . without which genuine self-knowledge cannot be obtained, is accused of selfishness and of turning his back on his social duties.
>
> Meanwhile, world crises multiply and everybody deplores the shortage or even total lack of "wise" men or women, unselfish leaders, trustworthy counsellors, etc. It is hardly rational to expect such high qualities from people who have never done any *inner work,* and who would not even understand what was meant by these words (Schumacher 1977, 100).

When lecturing and in other settings, among friends and foes, we often get questions like: What do you think we—or I—can do? Where do we start? How can we work for peace? (See also Chapter 25.)

The above approach is one among many guidelines, but certainly one that has left impressions on ourselves: *Start investigating the ways we think and the programs they build upon and "know yourself" in order to break out from that program and become your own programmer!* That is, become human, free, ever-searching in all of reality. Choose the existential responsibility and care for the world. That may be peace! Remember Gandhi's argument that there is no road *to* peace, peace *is* the road. The process, the striving, the becoming, being, reaching wisdom is for the individual as well as for the common good. No harm can be done by that. It means to care, to use our unique faculties as human beings, and constantly be aware that there is something beyond ourselves.

These are also catchwords for the third premise to which we now turn.

15

Premise Number 3: Take care—
Ethics Matter!

Ours is a civilization and a time that does not care. Many individuals, of course, do care, particularly about the long-term consequences of what we have done and do today in terms of overall and incremental environmental decay and in terms of the risks of sudden nuclear catastrophe.

It is no problem to imagine that *had* we built the Western civilization throughout preceding decades and centuries on an ethics of care, of respect for other human beings, life-supporting systems of a natural and artifactual kind, and of nature as such—in responsibility for future generation—then the world *would* have looked differently.

Neither does it take much reading or listening to mass media to be convinced that ethics as such is simply "no argument." What counts is what is "economic" or profitable, politically "realistic," or otherwise related to the one basic argument underlying our crisis-ridden growth and progress "cosmology": You can't stop the development!

Our time perspective has become shorter and shorter compared to the powerful technological means available for creating long-term consequences of human actions. At the same time, our space (perception) has widened constantly, we are now all members of a "global village" interconnected by all kinds of economic and technological exchanges, and each of us shares a welfare built on "somebody else" out there. The names of the game are unequal exchange, expansion, dominance, and so on.

It was summarized to the point in the midst of the Vietnam War by a professor of international law, Richard Falk, in saying that "moral decay is evident whenever a society loses belief in itself to the extent of abandoning its own proudest traditions without even an awareness of what is happening" (Falk et al. 1971, 7). When society faces increasing problems, it turns to technicians, economists, and other "hardware," factual expertise, not to wise old men and women, philosophers, independent thinkers, or fellow citizens of high cultural or moral standing. Thus a vicious circle develops between de-moralization and anti- or a-moral tendencies.

It would be unfair, however, to maintain that there is *no* interest whatsoever in ethics and moral conduct. Many people may act because of deep convictions, but publicly they justify it in the fashion that appears more *comme il faut,* namely to argue in political rather than moral terms. No one wants deliberately to be ridiculed in public. So, there is probably a quite strong undercurrent of informal, deeply personalized ethical motives, but the public sphere is virtually devoid of ethical, explicitly stated norms about what is good and what is bad.

Turning the argument around, it could also be stated that ethics as such has come to a turning point, that much of what used to be relevant norms of good conduct is no longer that relevant. The framework has changed fundamentally.

One of the thought-provoking analyses and arguments in favor of a new ethical responsibility adapted to our times and circumstances is that of philosopher Hans Jonas in *The Imperative of Responsibility. In Search of an Ethics for the Technological Age* (1984). He argues that our task is not to go into theories of the "best life" or the essence of human beings. Rather, he says, "for the moment, all work on the "true" man must stand back behind the bare saving of its precondition, namely the *existence* of mankind in sufficient natural environment."

Today the ever open question of what humans are or ought to be is less important compared to the "first commandment tacitly underlying it, but never before in need of enunciation: That they should be—indeed as human beings." Our first task is to care and secure that the world and humankind at all exist in the future! To develop an ethics around that, we must transcend the old neighbor-ethics on which we have operated so far, according to Jonas.

It may be relevant to ask whether it is "worth" discussing an issue so exotic as ethics in a world that does not publicly care about it, a world in which high-level decision making usually does not integrate ethics.

First, ethics counts anyhow. All the solemn speeches and ceremonies in which ethical dimensions are touched on, all the public legitimation of "wrong," violent, human rights-violating policies in terms of the "good" aims they further, all is evidence of the fact that even the im- or a-moral agents know that ethics counts (at least with their voters or soldiers).

Second, as authors we would be in error if we neglected the ethical dimension of our problematique just because it is not appealing to "realpolitik." We believe it to be inseparable from the existential and cosmological premises we already have dealt with.

Third, by taking up ethical issues one may reveal a little more of the global madness and contribute to reconstructing a more decent public dialogue, expand on the issue of security and peace in contrast to immorality. Well aware that the international community does not have a law-enforcing procedure and machinery, neither a "tribunal" for ethical conduct, the purpose of what follows is a completely different one:

> The importance of the criminal concept is to reinforce a boundary to paint the limiting condition of state behaviour in bold colors—not to provide a foundation for punishment and retribution. . . . The importance, then, if the inquiry into war crimes is to discover the erosion of the criminal boundaries and the need to restore their claims upon our actions . . . We also need to reorient our sense of citizenship towards the position that it is disloyal for citizens to abet the crimes of their government. As well, we have to make our governments sensitive to the criminal boundaries that restrict the exercize of political power (Falk et al. 1971).

Thus we work with ethical issues first of all because they matter to ourselves, *we restore the boundaries of good and evil upon our own action— and thinking.* If we did not we would, intellectually and "morally," automatically have become co-opted into the immoral power game.

Fourth, there are so many substantive reasons. Dealing with nuclearism is to deal with killing. Thus ethics is immediately involved. It is to deal with our relations to nature and other living creatures, and ethics is immediately involved. It is to deal with responsibility, that of ourselves and that of others, and ethics is immediately involved. It is to deal with the next child being born—or not being born because the father or mother was killed— and ethics is immediately involved. How could it possibly escape us?

Fortunately, there is an increasing awareness of the existence of ethical problems surrounding the nuclear policies and nuclearism in general (see Fox and Groarke 1985; Blake and Pole 1983, 1984; Jonas 1984; Lifton & Falk 1982; Lackey 1984; Gay 1985; Hardin et al. 1985; Cohen & Lee 1986; Schell 1982). Philosophers here deal with the nuclear aspects of modern life, or we find intellectuals and security experts approaching moral issues. In a few cases, a discussion of ethics is used to justify preconceived positions, but in most there is a genuine will to ask difficult questions and rethink our situation.

Points of departure vary, of course. There are those who simply state that any probability of nuclear war/use of nuclear mass-destructive weapons greater than zero is unacceptable. There are philosophers taking off from conceptual analysis of principles such as "the right to life," "the right to a life worth living," "the sanctity of life," and argue back and forth as to what is reasonable and unreasonable—arguments in which the nuclear issue is one "problem" along with others such as killing, abortion, suicide, and other classical themes (Glover 1977).

There is Ramsey, quoted by Walzer (1977), who states that "whatever is wrong to do is wrong to threaten, if the latter means 'mean to do' . . ." And there are those who start out from the facts of modern politics, war-fighting strategies, and the like and ask whether there is, after all, good moral support behind nuclear policies. Could it be, for instance, that threatening mass destruction is acceptable if it can be proved that it prevents the weapons from ever being used? Can some of the arsenals and the war planning be ethical in the sense of raising the probability that a war, should it start, will be terminated quicker than would otherwise be the case?

Fifth, and last, there is a very urgent motivation for discussing ethics and restoring it in our consciousness, politics, and personal action. It is that our time is one in which the existential threat is so clear and potentially so all-encompassing that a sense of a-morality may gain momentum. Why care about the future if we can be gone in a while? Why not "give a damn" in higher principles when there is so little I can do? Why should I care, be responsible, try to be fair when this gross injustice of victimizing and killing millions just as well can hit me? The world *is not* moral, leaders *are not* responsible, ethics *do not* play a role in world affairs. Why, then, should I not enjoy the time it seems we have left and fulfill my own interests egoistically?

Such ponderings may come in different forms, not the least with the youth, but they are quite conspicuously with us toward the end of the twentieth century. And, we might add, for good reasons. The overwhelmingly bleak perspective around ecological and political disasters does not automatically further the restoration of values, ethics, and norms in personal, neither in global, activity.

However, we believe that the ethical reflection is an integral part of being and acting human. No matter the overall perspective. Ethical decay is not stopped (neither its consequences) by giving up the ethical dimension just because we are relatively powerless. If anything it calls for civil courage and "provocatively" ethical arguments.

Isn't it all too difficult, isn't it a theme more or less only for professional philosophers? Absolutely not! Our basic "philosophy" here is that no one has to be an expert in humaneness. If ethics *is* an integral part of existence, in becoming a human being, it is for each of us to ponder. Likewise, you don't have to be a theologian to live a religious life. And, you may add, few of the philosophers by profession have adressed the nuclear problems, and much of it is far too academic to be of here-and-now relevance for us. It is precisely for this reason that it is promising to witness such an upsurge of literature in the field. Lackey summarizes much of it when, in his *Moral Principles and Nuclear Weapons* (1984) he outlines three basic elements of *moral criticism,* namely:

> "To criticize a national policy morally, then, is to do something different from saying that it is unwise, or contrary to the national interest. But what *is* a moral criticism? Here we will assume that a moral criticism is one of three things.
> (a) It is moral criticism to say that a policy is contrary to the interests of humanity;
> (b) It is a moral criticism to say that a policy violates human rights; or
> (c) It is a moral criticism to say that a policy is unfair or unjust.
> In short, we will assume that there are three basic moral concepts: The common good, human rights, and fairness, and that there are three elementary moral principles: Do good, Respect rights, Be fair."

It is not the purpose here to involve ourselves in a variety of deeply philosophical issues. We pick two issues to elaborate on without any aim of reaching clarity or drawing conclusions. The following stems from a wish to approach two issues that we find a little more exciting than most other philosophical issues pertaining to nuclear weapons and their function as deterrents. They are:

1. Michael Zimmerman's discussion of Martin Heidegger and the concept of "anthropocentric humanism."
2. Hans Jonas' analysis of the need for an ethics of the future, a new way of conceiving ethics in the technological age.

In earlier days, says Jonas, himself a student of Heidegger, ethics was basically "neighbor ethics." Traditional ethics is anthropocentric, that is, it centers everything in human beings and all dealing with the nonhuman world was perceived as ethically neutral. Good and evil were close to the human act in both time and space; the long run of consequences were considered in the realm of fate or left to chance. In all the well-known maxims like "Thou shalt not kill," "Do unto others as you wish them to do unto you," "Subordinate your individual good to the common good," there is an immediate, close relation. The actor and the "other" share a common present and a foreseeable future.

With modern technology and power, all this has changed. Of course, the "neighbor ethics" still exists—"but this sphere is overshadowed by a growing realm of collective action where doer, deed, and effect are no longer the same as they were in the proximate sphere, and which by the enormity of its powers forces upon ethics a new dimension of responsibility never dreamed of before," says Jonas. The trends underlying this change are, among others, the following.

Nature is critically vulnerable to human action and our technological power; the science of ecology alters our conception of ourselves from being just a causal agency in a larger scheme to becoming responsible. Thus nature—indeed, the whole biosphere—must be seen as a human responsibility, which is a "novum" in ethical theory. We are responsible for the whole system, that it, much more than the human part, because we extend our power over it. Preservation of nature and acknowledgement of the cumulative effects of our doings over time become obligations, a moral priority.

The gap between the ability to foretell the consequences of our actions and the technological-instrumental power to act, which humankind has today, creates a novel moral problem. We must, Jonas argues, take upon us a *stewardship* of things beyond ourselves. We are used to, in our dealings with nature (the entire biosphere), thinking of its conservation for *our* own ulterior sake. Now, since we seem to be able to destroy it all, we must strive to preserve it for its own sake, too. It has a right to exist of its own. The "good life" is unthinkable, actually, without seeking what is good also for things extra-human.

Unfortunately, however, the scientific view of nature denies us all conceptual means to think of nature as something to be honored; "having reduced it of any dignity of ends," as Jonas expresses it.

In other words, in our human hands technology and modern political power assume a completely new ethical significance. Jonas argues that the expansion of human powers is accompanied by a contraction of the human concept of self and of being. We have become used to see ourselves as evermore the maker of what is all around us and the preparer of everything we plan to do and achieve. We seek omnipotence and, as Lifton saw it, we have allied ourselves with the imagery of a deity in more than one sense.

What do these—admittedly not very easy—considerations—lead to? Jonas's reasoning only unfolds step-by-step, and we have to follow on a little further. There is the question: Who is to be responsible?

The almost paradoxical thing is that it is not the individual "he" or "she." It is the aggregate, it is the "all of us and everything around us." If we can create and destroy everything once and for all, our ethical responsibility must reach into the indefinite future. We cannot say that this or that is okay to do if it does not harm other people or nature within, say, five or ten years when we know that its cumulative effects are devastating over time. And we cannot plan wars and push buttons in the limited "here" in X city or Y country when our act may have worldwide consequences. The changed nature of human action changes the very idea of politics.

And it changes ethics, of course. Who else can carry a moral order now and in the future but human beings—us? Thus for ethical considerations to be relevant we must secure that there is an "us" in the future, that is, that we and coming generations exist. Otherwise, there is no moral order or universe possible unless we acknowledge the fact that our obligation, first and beyond everything, is to ensure existence of the world in the indefinite future. That is the meaning of Jonas's idea of "stewardship." You will surely also notice that this type of ethical consideration is deeply present—although implicitly—in the earlier parts on protective defense in this book.

It is not enough, anymore, to say with the 18th century German philosopher Immanuel Kant: "Act so that you *can* will that the maxim of your action be made the principle of a universal law" since this statement takes the *existence* of a community of human actors as a *given*. We must say, instead, something like: *"Act so that the effects of your action are compatible with the permanence of genuine human life"* or *"In your present choices, include the future wholeness of humanity among the objects of your will." We may risk our own lives, but never the survival of humanity.*

This is a completely new collective thinking and public policy, still addressing personal conduct but caring for total, long-term consequences. Jonas points out with emphasis that it is *not* a hypothetical "*if* everybody acted like that . . ." in an indefinite future. The new imperative of responsibility orients itself at a concrete real future, a predictable, total situation brought about by our own actions.

Faced with the gigantic powers of modern technology and with the risks of rather total destruction through the use of nuclear weapons, faced with scientific developments and the prospects of genetic engineering and the extension of life itself, and faced with numerous other trends of our own making under the pretext of "progress," we are in dire need of a new ethics of long-range responsibility, corresponding to the range and impact of our power. That is, according to Jonas, a new kind of humility.

This type of contemporary humility is not like the age-old one through which human beings felt humble before God and acknowledged their smallness vis-a-vis life and the universe. It is a humility *owed to the excess of our power to act over our power to foresee and judge about the consequences of our actions*. "Ignorance of the ultimate implications becomes itself a reason for responsible restraint," states Jonas.

What, then, is the content of an "ethics of the future"?

First of all, it embodies a new kind of future-oriented knowledge, futurology, anticipation, or imagination. Before acting we must try to identify the possible and potential truths about predictable future(s). Much of it will come forth if we let our deep concerns and fear out. In a way, Jonas argues, we need threats in order to know what to care for and preserve. "We know the thing at stake only when we know that it is at stake."

Working at anticipating all possible consequences in the long run of what we do here and now is one element in ethical action. Secondly comes something that is perhaps more difficult: summoning up a feeling appropriate to the future-oriented views. We must learn to live with uncertainty in a new way, and that is another argument for constant restraint and humility. But more important is that "we must educate our soul to a willingness to *let* itself be affected by the mere fortunes and calamities of future generations," Jonas says.

It's a deep empathy, taking the place, so to speak, of coming generations; look deeply at what *their* future will be like if *we* do this and that now. It is not just idle curiosity or idle pessimism; it is an attempt to prepare ourselves emotionally *before* we act. This is why we need future thinking, imagination, visions. (We pointed out this need under premise 2, and here it appears from another angle.)

Again, we see why this, if realized in a deep sense, would lead to a new kind of politics. Today decision making is a matter of limiting choice a priori and employs a short time and small space perspective, and what we need to act responsibly is precisely the opposite.

A third element in the ethics of the future is this: "Never must the existence or the essence of man as a whole be made a stake in the hazards of action." We *have to*, for reasons given above, forbid ourselves to incur the risk of nothingness for any purpose whatsoever. This principled argument also states that we should never even allow the mere possibility of nothingness (utter destruction of everything) among the options of our choice. And this is not meant as advice, but as a commandment, provided we accept responsibility. Thus caution and care become the heart of the matter. No argument of the highest good (even peace) can justify the existence of situations in which total risk is inherent. We have a duty—unconditionally—to exist.

But why is that so? Here comes the fourth element.

Logically, you may say, only what exists can claim a right to existence. I cannot say that I have a right to exist unless I already exist. But although this seems simple enough, Jonas argues that such a principle is utterly insufficient because duties and rights usually assume reciprocity—my right responds to your duty. In modern life, we cannot apply such an idea of rights and duties only to what already exists. It must stretch into the indefinite future and encompass the not-yet-existent, that which cannot claim any rights and that of which we cannot claim reciprocity.

A question like "What did the future ever do for me?" is meaningless. Therefore, included in the idea of humankind's stewardship ethics is that we must take upon ourselves a number of nonreciprocal responsibilities. It is very much like the responsibility we take upon ourselves vis-a-vis our children, those we care for and who would perhaps perish if we didn't. We would, of course, never dream of setting up rights and duty relations with them.

The mother naturally does everything to *care* for her baby, out of love. It is absurd to expect her to constantly threaten the very life and right to the future existence of the child. She takes for granted that it is her duty to secure the future existence of the child, and as long as it is dependent upon her the reciprocity of right and duty is meaningless. This is where we feel that Jonas comes close to what is elsewhere called female or feminist ethics and maternal thinking, and we return to it shortly.

Jonas raises, of course, a conspicuous problem himself. What about the life of those who seem to be doomed? Is life "worth" preserving under all circumstances? Is a nonhumane life possibility desirable at any price? And he gives the answer that what we deal with here is not the wishes of our successors, which—since we don't know them—can only be products of our imagination. What is in focus is "the ought above both of us." The gigantic crime would be to make it impossible for coming generations to strive for what *they* (think they) ought to be. It is thus not a question of their right to be happy but their right to be and be human in the sense of taking the stewardship upon them (and become happy, if possible) that is at stake.

What is the use of such an exercise? We want to see it as just one element under premise 3, and thus as one component in a larger philosophy that we deal with not as philosophers but as human beings interested in defense, security, and peace.

A deep and very complex argument like Hans Jonas's ought not be fit nicely into some other purpose or into a fine-looking intellectual scheme or argument. Our point is simply that we have been inspired by his argument and find it an important source of inspiration in our own thinking. We are not out to conquer, twist, or adapt it neatly into defense or peace thinking as such.

However, we feel that it is an excellent example of how "soft," elusive, even metaphysical arguments and ethical norms are valuable, as valuable as purely empirical analysis or politicized arguments like "this is not realistic," "this is not relevant," "nuclear weapons are counterproductive," and the like.

We could not have argued so well for the idea that there ought to be something in the future rather than nothing. And it is convincing enough to stand independently on its own feet. And be remembered while you read— and hopefully afterward!

It deserves repetition that there is something "beyond" human beings, that we are not the center of everything. It is an age-old insight from greater thinkers. Basing a new ethics on the recognition that we must depart from the ruthless material and anthropocentric thinking of the Hellenic-Judaic-Christian tradition is so important and forceful as an argument that it bears repeating also in this connection.

It is obvious from this discussion of an ethics of responsibility that *feminist philosophy* is a valuable source. One may say that whereas it hardly carries such an elaborated and, from time to time, rather abstract theory-building system, writers on female ethics have drawn by and large the same conclusion but on the basis of a different approach.

Harvard professor of education Carol Gilligan (1982) draws extensively on women literature and on her own research in outlining a critique of male psychology and theorizing on morality and an alternative to it. Studying children's development (although a limited population), she argues that, in general, girls are trained in empathy more than legalism, attachment more than separation, inner activity more than adventure, in a morality of responsibility, intimacy, caretaking, and basic relations in smaller units more than in a morality of rights, success, and goal-oriented organizations. Girls and women more than boys and men are socialized into maintaining relations in spite of conflicts focusing on and accepting the limitations of any solution, whereas, from a male perspective, a morality of responsibility appears inconclusive and diffuse. Women may be more apt to see "the other side" of success than men are.

She cites examples of boys and girls solving dilemmas and notices that girls respond contextually and boys more categorically, "according to the rules." To women, Gilligan argues, a life cycle is always involved in the "recognition of the continuing importance of attachment." This life cycle comes, as a principle, very close to what we describe in Chapter 14 as the "security cycle." Female ethics may be based much more on acting because someone is depending on you, regardless of one's own needs, whereas male ethics seems to relate to doing or not doing anything because rules, ideals, or "high" principles so demand. And she concludes at one point by saying that "the experiences of inequality and interconnection, inherent in the relation of parent and child, then give rise to the ethics of justice and care, the ideals of human relationship—the vision that self and other will be treated as of equal worth, that despite differences in power, things will be fair, the vision that everybody will be responded to and included, that no one will be left alone or hurt."

Philosopher Jean Grimshaw (1986) at Bristol deals explicitly with female ethics as part of philosophy, and she offers the following recurring themes underlying it:

1. A critique of "abstraction" and the belief that female thinking *is* (and moral thinking in general *should be*) more contextualized, less bound by abstract rules, more "concrete."
2. A stress on the values of empathy, nurturance, or caring, which, again, are seen as qualities that women both value more and tend more commonly to display.
3. A critique of the idea that *notions of choice* or *will* are central to morality, and of a sharp distinction between fact and value; a stress, instead, on the idea of the *demands* of a situation, which are discovered through a proces of *attention* to it and require an appropriate response.

Particularly useful for our purpose is her discussion of what it means to *care*. She does not, as Jonas, go into any "grand theories" but applies the idea of care to everyday situations. Care has connotations of anxiety, of taking on a burden and a responsibility for something or someone; of desire, of wanting to be with and care for another person; and it has connotations of carefulness, of appreciating the situation of "the other." She relies on Noddings's (1984) definition that care means "apprehending the reality of the other" and involves the "engrossment in another, a putting aside of self and entering into the experience of another as far as possible."

There is both a psychological and a political misuse of the idea of care ("Texaco cares"!)—mixing self-interests with altruistic care concerns publicly, and such. Grimshaw is certainly correct in pointing out that mere appeals to "caring" are rather useless and that each single situation deserves careful interpretation rather than strict adherence to large-scale goals and principles. She finds that the idea of an ethics of care helps us to be flexible, not to accept any kind of quantification of suffering. Each individual case matters; for each suffering or in need of our care our action matters—no matter how many millions are also suffering. We should never be "numbed" because of the magnitude.

Second, she says, it help us clarify the relationship of means to ends and a very pointed critique of any sharp distinction between a private and a public morality.

There is no doubt that Grimshaw and Gilligan on the one hand and Jonas on the other, in their different ways of conceptualizating, theorizing, arguing, and writing, are representative of the best in the male and the female approach. Jonas's high principles can be supplemented with the feminine element, and Gilligan's and Grimshaw's can be supplemented with a thinking that goes beyond the close and interpersonal relations. None of the theories offers us clearcut answers to exactly how we ought to act in concrete situations. It's up to each of us to judge, wonder, care, and be responsible.

Thus there is ample opportunity to combine, identify compatibilities in a common male-female search for an ethics of the future. The seeds are already there, a way of thinking that can easily stimulate our general thinking about peace and our specific interest in short- and mid-term goals of defense, security, and survival.

There is hardly any doubt that feminine thinking on *power* is also much more compatible with defensiveness, protection, nonthreatening, and non-controlling principles such as those built into Parts I and II of this book.

Would more feminine approaches in security doctrine, defense, and strategic discussions help us even further toward a more humane future? Would their contributions to self-reflection in fields such as ethics, political science, security, and peace research be helpful in developing the subjects and relate them to existential issues? We are not in doubt and would love to see even more coming forth than those excellent ones we already have, such as Halkes 1977; Henderson 1984; Pietilä 1985; Enloe 1983; Jones 1983; McAllister 1982; Reardon 1985, Baker Miller 1976; Brock-Utne 1985; Keller 1985, Pietilä and Jackson in Friberg & Galtung 1986; Sülle 1981 and, of course,

Easlea 1981, 1983. Some of these contributions are dealt with in some more detail in Øberg 1986.

In other words, we need a comprehensive approach to ethics in the nuclear age. It could help us redefine power, security, and defense. It would probably demand that male researchers (and others) would become less scared and more open toward feminine understanding of life, and that women would, generally speaking, be less scared about defense issues.

Therefore we find it rather futile when questions come up like: Do you think women should participate in the military forces? The relevant question is, instead: Can we develop a model of defense and security and such visions about peace that build on the best of both male and female approaches and cosmologies and, thereby, make it acceptable and even attractive for both men and women to participate in the defense of their community, country, region, and the world?

Perhaps there is a vast intellectual, intuitional, and political potential to be developed and exploited here. It is readily seen that the feminist approaches above *do* care about limitations; that is, they are less "anthropocentric" (human-centered) and build on an understanding of the whole, the interconnectedness, the situation, and the need for attending to social relations not being broken because of conflict. But what does anthropocentric actually mean?

Let us look into it on the basis of Michael Zimmerman's analysis of the concept and its relation to the arms race, appearing in Fox and Groarke (1985). It is an exposition that relies to a considerable extent on German philosopher Martin Heidegger.

The anthropocentric perspective involves, naturally, a placing of the human being in focus of everything. In and of itself that is good, of course. But the dark side of it is, as Zimmerman states, "an arrogant human centeredness that reduces the non-human world to the status of commodity whose only value lies in its usefulness for human purposes."

It allows us to convince ourselves that we are *omnipotent* and that we are the purpose of everything. We adopt a false sense of superiority that undermines every chance of understanding the universe as an integrated totality. With a basically anthropocentric "cosmology," we are barred from experiencing our own (limited) place in the big order of things as well as the oneness of the whole.

Could it be, he asks, that such an anthropocentric perception and image of ourselves is an element in the underlying disorder of which armaments and nuclearism form a dangerous symptom?

The anthropocentric view gained momentum the moment Europe freed itself from the medieval authority. Reason, enlightenment, and knowledge gained superiority over religion, superstition, and folk wisdom. But, says Zimmerman, although insisting that there is no supernatural world, no metaphysics, but only a natural one, anthropocentric humanists smuggled in another god: the human being, self-worship. Through science and technology we expanded human powers over the entire environment, wanting to exploit and dominate, appropriate and control, be missionary, and adopt a systematically instrumental view of everything else than ourselves, but even of other peoples and races, too.

The more we succeeded, the more we have tended to see ourselves as the source of all values, meaning, and purpose. Power means to assert oneself over the environment; it is, in the contemporary world, even to manipulate life and be able to cause technological mega-death.

But, again, that has a dark side to it. Humans become lonely. Appropriation, control, expansion are accompanied by inner dissatisfaction, emptiness, insecurity. This is where the "meaning" of destruction itself and images of destruction enter reality with force. Zimmerman refers here to Hannah Arendt who states that destruction is a means to deny an enemy what we want to gain control over ourselves. Property and insecurity, control and enemy-images relate closely to each other:

> Property by itself . . . is subject to consumption and therefore diminishes constantly. The most radical and only secure form of possession is destruction, for only what we have destroyed is safely and forever ours. (Zimmerman, in Fox and Groarke 1985)

Bringing potentially everything under control, in the name of humanism whether in the Western capitalist version or the Western socialist version, leads naturally to controlling also what "the other" is able to get control over. Security is related to controlling the environment, Nature and "the other" in order to avoid the disadvantages (insecurity) incurred from their actions upon us and what is ours. Is it, in this perspective, so strange that it has become natural to so many that "security implies the ability to retaliate," threaten mass destruction, and—mind you—includes the risk of being destroyed ("committing mutual suicide" as it is euphemistically termed sometimes)?

Lifton (1979) makes the point that the term *security* is derived from Latin *sē* (without) and *cūra* (care, concern), that is, security literally means "feeling no care or apprehension." To threaten nothingness, to even plan for "creating" nothingness and declaring oneself willing to set in motion utter destruction of "all" has, in the final end, to build on a premise of no care.

In our attempt to anthropocentrically control all and everything, particularly by means of mega-machines in the civilian and military spheres alike, we have become godlike and able to create life and terminate it *as an instrumental action*. The only thing we have lost control of is the limitation of our own powers, of the "power over power." As everybody knows, nobody would be able to control the tremendous machine of destruction, consisting of the world's 60,000 nuclear warheads and millions of conventional warheads, should it be set in motion (Bracken 1983).

As so often before when facing complex social issues, we have to strive for holism, seeing the linkages between ideas, concepts, words, and acts, rather than dissecting them separately. If, for the moment, we accept the Arendt-Heidegger thinking about the deep relation between *insecurity and destruction* on the one hand and *the permanent ambition to exert power over and control people, things, and nature* on the other, it is perhaps not so strange that—in the name of security and freedom—we have accepted as perfectly normal the possibility of total *destruction as a means* to achieve peace. Heidegger says that:

> "What is deadly is not the much-discussed atomic bomb as this particular death-dealing machine. What has long since been threatening man with death, and indeed with the death of his own nature, is the unconditional character of *the mere willing* in the sense of purposeful *self-assertion in everything*" (Fox & Groarke 1985, 139).

In other words, we have forgotten that there must be limits. Instead of being, being in an existential sense of revealing ourselves through an inner "becoming" or maturity, we strive relentlessly to present, assert, force, and project ourselves upon the "something" out there. We are the subjects, the center of everything, objectifying the world. We see ourselves as the makers—Homo Faber—of the world, standing above it. Thus we are separate, lonely. We rely on a Western subject-object dualism (the subject being, in principle, both individuals and nation-states) preventing us from acknowledging that harming others by the mentioned permanent self-assertive struggle amounts only, in the long run, to harming ourselves.

What is needed, instead?

> A profounder humanism would acknowledge our uniqueness but would also reveal that the aim of human life is not to dominate all beings, but in some sense serve them by letting them be manifest as what they are.

Such service can be understood as tolerance and love. We serve others by respecting them, which means in part giving them the freedom to act as they see fit for themselves, so long as they respect this freedom in other people as well . . .

According to Heidegger, our highest possibility is not to dominate things, but instead to care for them and to let them be. For action-oriented humanists, such talk of "letting things be" seems frivolous, especially when so much remains to be done to alleviate human suffering. By "letting things be," however, Heidegger does not mean to imply passive acceptance of evil and destructiveness. He urges us to do what we can to improve the world within the limits of the existing humanistic paradigm. Letting things be entails loving behaviour guided by profound awareness of what beings are. I cannot let a plant *be* a plant, that is, help provide the conditions needed for it to grow and flourish, if I am ignorant of its need for water and sunlight. Letting something be can involve decisive action and speech, but such action and speech must be rooted in an understanding of what the thing is to begin with (Zimmerman, in Fox and Groarke 1985).

By this, we have come a full circle and return back to a contemporary reconceptualization of ethics, toward caring, being responsible, for maintenance, preservation, literally speaking, defense of the existence of earth. It seems that the enemy is us—not "we," not "them"—but us, playing an illusionary omnipotent godlike game with ourselves as major losers.

But, it may be argued, saying all this is nice and good. But where does it take us? Politically we think that on the basis of this type of ethics a strong case can be made in favor of the Nuremberg principles, which, among others, Falk has repeatedly and persuasively done. They state, inter alia, that:

Any person who commits an act which constitutes a crime under international law is responsible therefor and liable to punishment.

The fact that internal law does not impose a penalty for an act which constitutes a crime under international law does not relieve the person who committed the act from responsibility under international law.

The fact that a person who committed an act which constitutes a crime under international law acted as Head of State or responsible government official does not relieve him from responsibility under international law.

The fact that a person acted pursuant to order of his Government or of a superior does not relieve him from responsibility under international law, provided a moral choice was in fact possible to him."

These are the four first principles—fully consistent with the unanimous opinion of the members of the United Nations that they represent a desirable development in international law as of 1946. Since then they have certainly not diminished in importance. Making reference to them here does *not* imply a view that present international law and its law-enforcing machinery, such as the Security Council, is a sufficient framework for embodying the ethical principles of humility and responsibility discussed above. The point we make is that there *is* already a legal framework that catches the spirit of responsibility, deeply rooted in the individual. Responsibility vis-a-vis greater existence cannot be laid down in a legal framework. Individuals, human beings—*we* are the only ones who can take upon us the task of being responsible and humble—vis-a-vis ourselves, fellow human beings, and nature. That characteristic, that single dominant ability, cannot be transferred to organizations, structures, or "systems." The basis of responsibility remains us. And, as we have maintained, there already exists a legal framework pointing in that very direction.

In summary, we should take care and be aware that ethics matter. Instead of immediately engaging ourselves in what types of weapons systems should be placed where and doing what and when, we should begin our search by defining a defense philosophy, ethically desirable and humane. Humane because it does not aim at destruction but at preservation and care.

The ethical perspective may—may, we say—help us redefine our task and redefine what we mean by defense, security, and peace.

Security could be changed from a framework of NO CARE to WE DO CARE.

Defense could be changed from meaning destruction of the opponent to implying preservation of ourselves and care for the totality. Further, it would imply a switch from offensiveness, other-destruction, and assertiveness (control and deterrence) toward defensiveness, self-preservation, respect, and "letting things be," that is, permitting ourselves the type of freedoms we would also accept others to have vis-a-vis us.

Power would change from meaning control and external dominance ("bullying the world") to being a struggle for self-discipline, control over oneself and the future, being resistant in the face of external challenges, and self-reliant to the highest possible level. It would be much more feminine (caring) than today's power, which is exercized in the masculine mode.

Limits would be respected. We would become aware that there are limits to quantity—but not to quality—of the ideas, cosmologies, actions, and policies we work with. We would switch from the naive belief that anthropocentric, omnipotent power exertion does not, sooner or later, harm ourselves, precisely for the reason that it is *omni*. That "war" is an outdated term and "omnicide" the only appropriate term for what we mean (Somerville, in Fox & Groarke 1985). Naturally we would follow the principle of "common security" in a deep sense (deeper, that is, than the realpolitik exposition of the Palme Commission) that mutuality is paramount in a global system endangered by our present technological power and intellectual-ethical powerlessness.

Responsibility, finally, would be located—once again—in the individual; it would be personal and close and reaching the entire system, "letting it be" because we understand what it *is*. No longer would it be distant, "dead," excusable in terms of organization size.

Part IV

Security and Society—Six Principles

16

Security Is about Survival and
Caring for Permanence

We know now why security cannot be built on a philosophy of "no care." This is a step in the direction of a reconceptualization, toward changing the ways we think.

The concept of security belongs to the category of "essentially contested concepts" (Buzan 1983). They contain a variety of normative, subjective, ideological, and even cosmological meanings that generate endless debates and that "render(s) empirical evidence irrelevant as a means of solving the dispute," as Buzan expresses it. It is part of their utility as concepts and bases of political decision making that they are so inherently ambiguous. And, not to be forgotten, like the concepts of democracy, justice, peace, and such, they signal something nice, something we all want, something that is legitimate (almost no matter how bad we might actually behave in the name of these value-based concepts).

It is not possible to arrive at a definition or operationalization of "security" to which everybody could subscribe. What security actually *is* is extremely difficult to determine, but that should serve as no argument in defense of the contemporary conceptualization. We have to analyze what *could be* implied by security and how it *could be* operationalized. Or, if you will, we have to look into the ways we think around the concept. In this and other chapters in Part IV, let us elaborate on some general observations.

Securing a high probability of survival and the lowest possible degree of violent conflict is, in the final end, what all security must be about. However, security is also about something less than the survival of humankind. If, for a moment, we compare with the equally contested and value-loaded concept of health, it is obviously true that health, in the final end, is about securing the survival of the individual. However, a person may be lacking in health without any probability of dying immediately. Thus both health and security is about meeting a variety of challenges or threats to the organism and the social organization, from minor disturbances up to life-threatening challenges.

Our hypothesis is that *if* we had really cared about survival, if security meant "caring about" instead of "no care," we would (1) hardly ever have developed instruments for "security" that threaten the very survival we were supposed to guard, and (2) we would, from the beginning, have tried to conceive of challenges in a broad framework and not have reduced them exclusively to that of military attack on our territory.

As we see later, there are so many other, more relevant and more probable threats than those our military and defense bureaucracies plan to meet. Survival and caring for permanence are aims that never ranked high in the defense planning of modern industrial society.

Security is increasingly about guarding against the risk of being involved in somebody else's war, that of the superpowers. But this does not exclude other concerns, as Kenneth Boulding explains:

> The historical evidence suggests that a subtle combination of defiance and submission in the face of threat is what makes for survival and for creativity, and that a victory is nearly always bad for the victor.
>
> Nevertheless, romantic illusions about war have persisted for a very long time and still continue. Partly perhaps this is the fault of the historians, who have so grossly neglected the history of peace. The playrights, the poets, and the novelists can be convicted too of glorifying the romantic and exciting aspects of war, and so producing in the human imagination a remarkably distorted view of reality (Boulding 1985).

Small countries, in principle like the bigger ones, have an urge to play a role. The gross mistake, however, is that they try to do it in the same game as the superpowers. They join alliances, buy the same modern technology, and some of them consider acquiring nuclear weapons. They take part in the game as if there were such a thing as a "small superpower," whereas, in reality, there are only prospects of survival if they play *another* game, measure strength in a different manner, run foreign policy on the basis of different power concepts, and so on. (More on that later.) What *is* important is to remember that when we talk about war in contemporary society, we talk about something in our imagination, something never seen before, but something that, unfortunately, many powerful people believe is thinkable, possible (even likely), and, stupidly enough, controllable.

If perceived probabilities of various challenges are combined with an analysis of a society's (local, nation-state, region) capacity to resist such challenges, and if necessary carry the burden of them being realized, then it should be possible to outline a "spectrum of security" or a number of *security fields* that could permit us to state with some precision: This is what we can manage and this is what we cannot manage and those are the things we should not even try to manage.

We can all think of such challenges that we cannot do much about because they are deemed (1) so unlikely that scarce resources must be allocated to something more probable or (2) so dangerous and overwhelming that there is very little or nothing we can do at all. On the other hand, there are such challenges that seem negligible or so slowly developing that we see no reason to guard against them (which may be wrong) and those that are thinkable but seem so harmless that we do nothing about them, and they, too, may turn out to surprise us.

There is hardly any doubt that our culture is endowed with what philosopher Harald Ofstad (1972) calls "contempt of weakness." We don't like to state openly that here is something we cannot manage; neither do we like to look weak in the eyes of others. Strangely enough, this is a situation we bring ourselves into the moment we try to "match" an objectively stronger opponent on *his* (or her) premises rather than on our own. The point is that it becomes a little less embarrassing to admit our weakness *on some scales and in some respects* if, at the same time, we can be strong in other respects, particularly if they are the ones where *we* happen to know that the other is objectively weak.

For example, there is an encouraging tendency for smaller countries to win, or at least not be defeated, in wars with larger ones. Vietnam succeeded against the United States, not because it was stronger if one would take a look at "the military balance," but because of strong morale, decentralization, world public opinion, third party political-moral support, another culture, and social structure—perhaps another basic view of life—that made it impossible to subdue. Most of all, the Vietnamese were defending their own soil. There was also a fundamentally different military strategy operating in this culture, all of which made it strong vis-a-vis the world's strongest power.

On the other hand, it should not be overlooked that most societies that have suffered from interventions were internally divided, often with one of the conflicting parties inviting the intervention. A country that is internally united is less likely to become a target of such aggression.

We are in no doubt that the Soviets were, in principle, caught in the same problematique in Afghanistan, although the two cases for historical, cultural, and many other reasons are not parallel. And wouldn't precisely the same "strength in being different" and in not trying to match a superior power on its terms apply also to Gandhi's struggle against the British, to Mao Zedong's Long March and the 1949 revolution? Wouldn't it also apply to *Solidarnosc* (Solidarity) in Poland in the sense that if that movement had taken to weapons and tried to look strong vis-a-vis the Polish government and the Soviet Union, things could have ended in a Soviet invasion and much bloodshed?

We raise this question because it is little studied and discussed, because it has really not been taken account of in the defense philosophy of smaller nations facing much stronger powers every day.

It *could* turn out that a careful analysis here would show that power and strength are much more complicated than we usually think. It would give a boost to self-confidence and the credibility of smaller countries starting out on another power game, (like New Zealand so succesfully did in 1985–1986 in banning nuclear weapons from its territory) and encourage others to follow.

Maybe, after all, the power of the powerful is vastly exaggerated? Maybe there is hope in the "powerlessness of power" these years? In superpowers actually becoming weaker and less credible? Maybe their immense technological power is so absurd that it is about to become counterproductive and undermine them as leaders in fields of politics, culture, economy, technological innovation, education, and particularly in terms of their legitimacy in the world society?

In summary: Security is about the probability of survival, about meeting a variety of threats within a broad spectrum and analyzing carefully what we should be and not be able to do while admitting weaknesses in some respects and developing strength in other respects.

17

Security Is about Society and
Its "Carrying Capacity"

We can do something in order to feel secure. And we can be human beings and societies in ways that are and express security. And we can be and act in ways that permit those we interact with to feel secure and insecure. It resembles naturally other essentially contested concepts like health and happiness; you can be healthy through the habits of a particular lifestyle (and some luck) or you may run around between doctors, psychiatrists, pill bottles, and exercise tracks "hunting" some kind of health that is not attainable within your day-to-day lifestyle.

In other words, there is a structural, "natural," integrative, or existential way and an action-oriented, instrumental, or fragmentized way.

Whatever we do in life, there are basic roads to reach positive value-realization. One may try to (1) become and act according to the good value, be the embodiment of it, (2) try to not do and become the negative value, but not particularly aim at the good value, and (3) feel forced to or objectively be in circumstances where one partly does a number of negative or counterproductive things, partly and simultaneously tries to "catch up" and compensate with some good, productive activity.

There are, of course, external and internal dimensions involved here. Security is about actors, about relations between actors, and it is about structures within and between actors from the micro to the macro time and space.

Suppose there is a human society situated on an island, no other human society being known. Provided a certain amount of natural resources are available to the inhabitants, one may imagine that this society's survival is dependent exclusively upon its own doings. In principle, we understand, it has no external challenge; it is 100 percent responsible for its own survival and overall security. It may be threatened only by what the inhabitants do

193

or fail to do, depleting the environment, killing each other in internal conflicts, failing to produce for basic needs, and the like. Whatever challenges, threats, or feelings of insecurity we find, they emanate internally, feed upon internal dynamics. If the society disintegrates, the last survivor can only think that it was of our own making and our own destruction! There is no one else to blame, so to speak.

You may think here that this is also an image of the world as such, of the entire system. And that is very correct.

In a certain way this is what "security community" is about. Political scientist Karl Deutsch does not mention external threats in his description of security:

> A security community is a group of people which has become "integrated." By integration we mean the attainment, within a territory, of a "sense of community" and of institutions and practices strong enough and widespread enough to assure . . . dependable expectations of "peaceful change" among its population. By sense of community we mean a belief . . . that common social problems must and can be solved by processes of peaceful change. By peaceful change we mean the resolution of social problems, normally be institutionalized procedures, without resort to large-scale physical force (Stephenson 1982, 32).

The point here is that security is of society; it comes from within social units. If it is not found there, in the very midst of human community, it cannot be obtained (neither by being or by acting) from outside, not from other actors, not from the relations with them. In this sense, *any society is its own security base.*

Security, in other words, is security being built into human communities qua their being communities. It has more to do with internal structure and functions than meets the eye in present-day debates about national and international security (for an excellent, broad discussion, see Stephenson 1982).

In this sense it is not unreasonable to expect the "good society." Society— by being a social organization—may display some qualities making it attractive to people (in terms of let's say welfare, freedom, identity), and if a number of indicators of "quality of life" in general are present our hypothesis would be that it would then also rank highly in terms of security. People would experience self-realization, permanent constructive development, peaceful conflict-resolution, and security. As such we would probably say that this is a strong society, rather self-reliant, in command of its own future to a large degree, and we would expect it to get along rather well with other communities—like the healthy human body and mind is pleasant to be with, representing no insecurity to ourselves. From a liberal perspective this has been analysed thought-provokingly by political scientist R. J. Rummel in his *Understanding Conflict and War* (1981).

A "security community" implies that there is a community worth securing and able to secure itself, and it implies a security for which the community is the sine qua non. The means we choose to secure our community have to be taken from that same community, in the sense of human, technical, natural resources, and in the sense of reflecting deeper cosmologies in that same community. Likewise, what we choose to secure and choose not to secure in the community are, naturally, indicative of what kind of community and cosmology we are confronted with.

Does it amount to truisms what has been said so far?

In substance few practitioners and experts in the field would disagree. However, there is a problem when this internal dimension is completely overshadowed by considerations having to do with external actors, their behavior, and our relations with them. When security problems are seen almost exclusively in the light of factors "external" to our community and when security is seen as instrumental, as built upon community from the top down, then the picture becomes blurred and, in the extreme, absurd.

Again the analogy with the human body and mind is in place. Health and well-being are not fundamentally "caused" by means of factors outside the human being; the body, of course, needs some inputs from outside, but it is in "processing" them that we may distinguish between the healthy and the less healthy person. Likewise, to combat illness there may be temporary needs for surgery or medicine, but it is through the balance between body/ mind itself and the environment that health is established, for instance through the natural capacity of the body to resist infections, regenerate after an "attack," as it is through exercise of the "community of organs" that fitness and excellence in performance are arrived at.

If we become ill (insecure) it is not always explicable by reference to external "threats" only. From time to time we may be predisposed, feel weak, and be more receptive, having developed a counterproductive lifestyle, feeling an inner emptiness, and so on. Much of the perceived insecurity we feel as individuals may come from "inside," be psychosomatic, although we are good at rationalizing it into environmental "causes" and explain them as either physical or psychic when, in fact, they are both.

By and large, we would hypothesize, the same applies to the social body. Whether individual or social, the body is the "processor," the one that transforms input from the environment into complicated thinking and action patterns. In this particular sense the body and the mind, the community and our ways of thinking (consciousness)—understood as one unit—is *the only security source,* the only security creating unit. It is from this community that every type of security flows.

The security to be gained from influencing others in various ways or entering into specific types of relationships with them is, in this perspective, secondary. Not unimportant, but secondary. It may add to the security community, but it has no power to be a "security multiplier" in the way the inner human community has. If the body or psyche itself is not well, good relations with your friends will be a help but not the permanent solution— no amount of love can cure a neurosis as psychiatrist Janov maintains.

Thus where conventional wisdom has it that the root causes of our perceived insecurity are located outside ourselves and our community, it deserves emphasis that insecurity is also a system characteristic, something that develops internally in the human communities. And where conventional wisdom has it that we ought primarily to control or at least influence our external environment, we emphasize that it is at least equally important to (re)gain control of the inner social body, its structure, and way of thinking.

With this in mind, we ought to engage ourselves more than hitherto in the issue. Which types of social, economic, cultural, and so on structures and system characteristics are more, respectively less capable of serving as security multipliers? Are some more prone to yield security by their being a system than others? Are some better than others in serving as a source upon which more instrumental security/defense measures can be added?

These are in a sense highly abstract issues. But, as we see, they became concrete in the context of practical security policies, and in several ways they have already surfaced in Parts I and II.

In summary: Security is about structure (the way we are a society or human community) and it is about instruments (action). The essential source of security, the reservoir of security energy is the community itself—through its interaction with the environment and other units. It starts from within. Thus security and community are inseparable. External relations are secondary in creating security; even if we can guard against external challenges this is not "enough" if we cause system breakdown by our own defense means and/or development policies.

If we think globally, there *are* no external challenges—only one whole system with subunits to secure, that is, to care for.

18

Security Is about Meeting Threats and Solving Conflicts.

We have argued that security is first and foremost a matter of how we organize ourselves. It amounts to saying also that when countries nowadays arm so conspicuously and "need" such strong enemy images, it is likely to have to do with an inner weakness. We believe that the two superpowers and their respective alliance systems increasingly lack legitimacy vis-a-vis world opinion, that they are no longer very strong as "ideal societies," that they are empires on their way down in the long-term perspective and that they *share* a number of features in this civilizational crisis, for example being growth-oriented and materialistic, male-dominated, elite-based (the capitalist and the revolutionary elite), built on subduing Nature and projecting their power and ideology on others through interventions, invasion, infiltration, and numerous civilian mechanisms. They share the armament-security dilemma. They also increasingly seem to lack support from their smaller allies, and they have lost or are losing wars in the Third World.

Now, this does *not* imply that we find it irrelevant to analyze threats from outside each of the communities; neither do we ignore the important task of trying to identify wise ways of meeting external challenges. (It would not be wise, either, to ignore bacteria and virus in the human environment.) Part deals with many examples and principles of conflicts and security. We shall elaborate further here with an eye on *threats*.

Kenneth Boulding distinguishes between the following responses to threats and other external challenges: (1) submission—we carry out the demands of the other, (2) defiance—"I won't do what you ask, and you can carry out your threat if you wish," (3) flight—we increase the distance to the threatener or drop out of the conflict formation, (4) counterthreat—"If you do something nasty to me, I'll do something nasty to you," and (5) diminishing the threat through, let's say, armor, city walls, and other defensive measures (Journal of Peace Research 2, 1984).

This is a fruitful way of approaching the problems. However, it needs refinement.

Threatening in the first place and counterthreatening in the second are offense. This is a controversial statement nowadays; there is the international norm of self-defense and it is usually considered acceptable to counterthreaten somebody who threatens us. If you do something nasty to me, I'll sue you; the basic principle behind our legal system. At present, international security rests on the fundamental idea that counterthreatening with mass destruction is the most stable, most rational conflict management strategy under given circumstances. This, of course, presupposes some kind of equality and symmetrical relations; the mouse cannot counterthreaten the cat.

If we put up a counterthreat to somebody else, it can mean essentially two things: either "I try to persuade you to back down from carrying out your threat against me" or "I am fed up with you now, I am (very tempted) to smash you once and for all." In the first case the counterthreat is conditional, if you behave and back down, I won't carry out my threat. In the second case "enough is enough," this was one step too far, our conflict is now beyond the point of no return.

It all depends on how far the conflict has developed. We usually don't react very strongly to the first minor threat, but if repeated several times, if escalated in seriousness and implications and so on, we are increasingly seeing it as a life or death issue, "them" or "us."

The two types of counterthreats, of course, are related. No threat or counterthreat is credible if the threatened—and perhaps even the threatener—knows that the threat won't be carried out in case of defiance. If I threaten to kill you I must seriously be willing to do so, if . . .

Second, the more tension in the relationship, the more likely it is that we take to "worst case" interpretations of the threatener, perhaps in order to mobilize our own solidarity or the support of third parties. What may be intended as a persuasion-oriented counterthreat by party A will have a tendency to be perceived by B as a response that does not invite sensible solution or compromise, but that in fact says; "Now, you B have gone too far, now I carry out my threat."

Thus any threat and counterthreat have the two elements of importance: persuasion, which puts the action back to the threatener in the first place, and punishment, which we are to carry out. It may be very difficult to distinguish between these two elements in concrete cases, but they are there.

They are both offensive in the sense that they aim at reaching the opponent in a potentially and/or actually detrimental manner.

What Boulding calls "diminishing the threat of the threatener" is, to be precise, a matter of diminishing the effects upon us when he chooses to carry it out. Here we meet a variety of options, actually a spectrum that is broader than that available in the offensive orientation.

A threatener usually threatens us because there is something of value we have that he (or she) wants to have. Or something we can do that he does not want us to do.

Possible responses are therefore to make ourselves less dependent on the threatener, more self-reliant (invulnerability), reduce the value of the object he or she seeks, or make clear that we are more useful to the threatener if left in peace (dissuasion), or finally we may think of various defensive means that cannot threaten the opponent before he directly interferes coercively with our society (self-defense), as discussed in Part I, Chapter 4, and in Part II.

Conflicts are about incompatibilities, about incompatible expectations among actors as to the (re)distribution of resources. Such resources may be material or non-material, but most often they focus on issues related to four very basic human need categories: Survival, welfare, freedom and identity (Galtung 1980).

Threats and counterthreats appear at certain "breaking points" in the conflict process. Up to a certain level the parties are likely to try other, more peaceful means. Threatening one another may escalate the conflict intensity and lead closer to a point of no return.

Since threats are integral parts of conflicts as such (you may have conflicts without threats, but hardly threats without conflicts), a number of "classical" conflict-management and conflict-resolution methods can be thought of. Galtung (1975) has the following typology concerning conflict management: conflict control, conflict institutionalization, turning latent conflicts into manifest ones, protracting conflicts, increasing conflict consciousness, that is, counteract elite definitions of the situation. And the following ones concerning conflict resolution: changing from zero sum to positive sum (making a "bigger cake"), bargaining to make the acceptable compatible, bringing in more actors (multilateralization), integrating the conflicting parties into one, one party absorbing the other, and protraction in the sense of making a manifest conflict latent with no violence or threats, probably what amounts to permanent "peaceful coexistence."

The typology in Table 5 summarizes what we have dealt with under this point. One effect is that it is important in any conflict to have a large spectrum of options available in order to reduce the likelihood that one or both resort to violence. Nothing should be left untried, and in many concrete cases it is simply not true, as often maintained by decision makers, that "we had no other choice."

Now much of this depends on circumstances, types of conflicts, cultural values, and many other things. Security against such challenges is a multifaceted phenomenon. Statesmanship is precisely about combining elements of such a typology into a coherent, time- and space-effective strategy.

Table 5 contains hardly more than a tentative list. We simply want to bring out the point that there are almost always *so* many ways to proceed when we feel stuck in a conflict. A broad spectrum is available, *and it seems to be the broader the earlier we think constructively about solutions*. The more intensive and polarized, the smaller the likelihood that something constructive for one or both parties comes out of the process.

We all live with conflicts, small or big, close or distant to us. Conflict is an integral part of any human relationship. It is strange that the "art of conflict handling" is so underdeveloped compared to the so-called art of war. To study when conflicts were actually handled constructively and when some kind of wisdom was brought in and things, therefore, did not run out of hand may be one of the most useful things we could do as researchers and as politicians. It is remarkable that so much energy has gone into the study of those few resolution methods that have to do with war, compared to the rich variety at hand in the above list!

Maybe, after all, we belong to a culture terribly illiterate in terms of understanding conflicts and what to do about them?

It would hardly surprise the reader were we to maintain that counterthreat B in Table 5 is generally the worst type of response to a conflict situation and that much more should be done in terms of furthering our understanding and performance as individuals and organizations dealing with A, C, D and E.

The "problem," of course, is that only B types of responses signal "strength," power, determination, and such, *and* outward orientation, offensiveness, and punishment behavior. It reflects so many aspects of what Western cosmology is all about. The other types of responses somehow signal wisdom but also conventional "weakness" in various degrees. So, unless we change the "ways we think," there is little chance that these more constructive measures will gain in importance and make us realize that type B, by and large, is obsolete in the modern world.

So, with a world in which everybody is so fascinated by the prospect of

Table 5

Typology of Responses to Threats and Conflicts

(A) Threat acceptance
1. Submission (giving in)
2. Defiance
3. Decoupling (distancing)
4. Flight (diffusion)
5. Rewarding (if he backs down)
6. Trade-offs
7. Strategic retreat (giving in for the time being . . .)
8. Accept (please carry out your threat . . .)
9. Business as usual (act as though we don't understand)
10. Prevention (withdraw before he makes a threat explicitly)
12. Persuasion and appealing

(B) Counterthreat
13. Pre-emption (first strike)
14. Retaliation (second strike)
15. Revenge (delayed second strike)
16. Punishment (anything up to nuclear war)
17. Threaten back (deter offensively)
18. Appeal to opponent's allies or own population or world opinion
19. Principled defence of oneself (defensive measures to prevent him from achieving his goals with us) leading to:

(C) Threat reduction
20. Self-sabotage
21. Reduction/minimization of offensive means and capabilities
22. Increase one's usefulness to others
23. Increase one's self-reliance (vulnerability reduction)
24. Defensive defense including nonviolence (Sharp 1973)

(D) Conflict/Threat management
25. Conflict control
26. Institutionalization
27. Change from latent to manifest conflict
28. Protraction
29. Change conflict consciousness (redefine situation)
30. Third party mediation
31. Do something unexpected but nonthreatening
32. Prepare to live with the conflict unresolved, make the best of it
33. Develop mutually benefiting relation unrelated to conflict issue
34. Invite negotiation before conflict intensifies
35. Study your conflict—your own attitudes, behavior, and definition of what the conflict is about

(E) Conflict/Threat resolution
36. Change from zero to positive sum game (increase values to be had)
37. Bargaining (making the acceptable compatible)
38. Multilateralization (bring in more actors)
39. Linkage (bring new conflicts into the picture)
40. Integration (the two parties become one)
41. Absorption (many possibilities, fusion of one into the other)
42. Seek a situation that makes later final resolution or peaceful coexistence more likely/acceptable
43. Principled negotiation á la Gandhi, and Fisher and Ury (1981)

controlling others (without understanding much of themselves and the overall situation or of conflicts as such), it takes quite a mental switch to realize
the importance of the essential things. To be able to control oneself and the
situation as well as understanding both. Which to a certain degree implies
being able to take the perspective of the other.

At this point it is reasonable to ask: What types of conflict can we identify
with some relevance to modern industrial society toward the end of the twentieth century?

The typology in Table 6 offers four basic concepts, and they will do to
argue a few points.

It is immediately evident that there are other conflicts and threats than the
external military one, that is, the "big invasion." It is likewise conspicuous
that there are threats that can*not* be met by any military means whatsoever.
The table makes the point that modern society is constantly "goal overloading" its official security policy. When asked what threatens us today
and tomorrow we are—as individuals as well as nation-states—prone to
point to external, identifiable "personalized" enemies. Asked about how we
secure our existence, we answer, by our national military defense. Whenever there is a threat, acquiring more weapons turns out to be the standard
solution. The single means becomes the answer to all challenges.

The relative proportion of its total security means that a society devotes
to military defense is indicative of its priorities. Similarly, most public debates focus on military threats, whereas threats of types II, III, and IV (Table
6) are not discussed from a society point of view.

With goal overloading goes the "radical monopoly of the military." Citizens have asked the state and the professionals within it to guard them. We
have, as citizens, let the military experts define what threatens us *and* let

Table 6
A Typology of Threats

TYPES	THREATS from outside		THREATS from inside	
direct violence	I	attack invasion occupation	II	terrorism criminal violence civil war
structural violence	III	embargos economic warfare ecological break-down global crisis	IV	alienation maldevelopment social disintegration

them select the means to produce security. Formally, the governments decide, but complex as the issues are, the real power is with the professionals.

The officer (in principle dressed in colored uniform) takes care of our collective survival by means of weapons and, when pensioned, enters the boards of military-industrial corporations, much in the same way as the doctor (in principle dressed in white uniform) takes care of our individual survival by means of medicine and, when pensioned, enters the boards of medical-industrial corporations. We all become clients, dependent. The right to define health and peace has been withdrawn from each of us, and—by and large—the capacity for prevention, safe and healthy lifestyles is reduced. We repair each other in military and medical operations. And as there are diseases produced by medical treatment, there is the disease called insecurity incurred from the very medicine (weapons and our general security and peace thinking) that was supposed to help us.

All this must be regained. The right to participate in our own lives must again become part of the essentially human responsibility. As there is a trend in preventive and holistic medicine, there must develop an insight that security means to care, be responsible, prevent, and think in terms of the whole (social) body.

But, you may object, societies do care about, let's say, the impending ecological crisis. It can be discussed whether this is a deep or a shallow endeavor in proportion to the challenge, but there is concern. This is true, but it is *not* part of an overall security philosophy. Things are fragmented and by overloading one agency—the military one—we have created a lot of new problems and brought ourselves further, not nearer, long-term solutions. The typical *"security monoculture"* of contemporary society is, indeed, very dangerous.

So, instead of reducing wild squandering of scarce energy resources by conserving and switching to alternatives within a broad spectrum of available options, major states *compensate their vulnerability* (i.e., reliance on other nations, e.g., oil imports) by setting up rapid deployment forces in order to be able to grab the oil themselves or prevent others from doing it, as if the oil were theirs and not part of the common heritage of humankind.

So, instead of decentralizing the vital functions of their countries and economies and thereby increasing invulnerability and the potential for self-defense and civilian strength, they centralize even more and go for "interdependence," which is, more often than not, deeply asymmetric, and furthers unequal development, maldevelopment, long-term ecological damage, and thereby increases the potential for conflict (for which again they need more weaponry).

So, instead of building systematically the "good" society that can stand on its own feet when the winds get high, in solidarity, in justice, and prosperity (without so much waste production and environmental degradation) they build societies split by internal (class) conflicts bound to be outward directed to "hide" their own weaknesses. And, instead of developing the social "carrying capacity" by means of robust technologies, they rely increasingly on sophisticated equipment vulnerable to sabotage, embargos of spare parts and expertise, programmers, and the like. Instead of keeping the old equipment in the hospitals so that instruments can be used again and again, we increasingly rely on one-time use and may ask: What would happen during a crisis or war?

We are near a hypothesis that can be stated in this manner: Civilian developments are such that they tend to undermine our own invulnerability and carrying capacity as a community. Much of what we term defense and security is nothing but compensation for the feeling of being increasingly helpless and indefensible should a major crisis develop. To arm is a very visible manifestation of this compensation, and from that point of view it does not really matter whether it is sensible or not to have more weapons. So, it could be argued, often the enemy is us and we arm against our own defenselessness, caused by civilian developments. The military–industrial complex constantly needs external enemies. Having enemies simply helps us look stronger in our own eyes. And that is important since we hate to look weak and defenseless!

In consequence it is only natural that threat analyses reflect much more "what society needs to boost its fragile, compensatory self-confidence-building measures" than objective circumstances in international politics. Threats and enemy images are instruments, often created more by us than by enemies, which help us define how much compensation we need internally.

The good society as well as the healthy body may have enemies and face dangers, but neither creates them systematically and thrives upon them to such an extent that it is a major occupation bordering on obsession without which they would hardly be able to understand themselves or the world.

19

Security Is about Time and Space,
Cycles and Fields

Static security concepts won't do in our world today. We have to think through what the time and space dimensions of security are. Let us explore some aspects and principles noted in Part II in a concrete manner. Here we approach an argument as to why the type of protective, dynamic defense presented in Part II not only meets some of the criteria for good conflict understanding and conflict handling, but also those that pertain to sensible security management.

If we start out with the time dimension, it is readily seen that the protective defense cares about an entire cycle.

- Security in peace time: the function of preventing "unnecessary" insecurity and dissuading threats and threateners externally, be they potential or actual. Under various circumstances this phase may be termed conflict regulation, solution, prevention, and dissuasion.
- Security during tension and crisis management: when the dissuasion function is perceived as shrinking, when everything becomes more intensive, stakes are increasing, "something has to be done."
- Security in high-level conflict, in defense, in offense, in struggle: when prevention turned out not to be enough and all other means have been tried, when we start or they start using destructive means.
- Security in settlement, final conflict resolution, or ongoing lower level conflict regulation–when a new phase in the process enters toward the phase where we seek:
- Security in normalization toward a new peace time–and so on.

Thus we are not talking about any static security aim, or security once and for all. It is an ever-changing, dynamic flexible thing. It's security in time cycles: peace-prevention-dissuasion-crisis-fighting-resolution-normalization-peace.

This type of cyclic or organic thinking stands in opposition to today's security philosophy in which society in general is highly likely to be completely destroyed somewhere in the middle of the cycle. We are prone to think that there is a substantial proportion of male thinking behind such a philosophy: Follow the rules of the game, stick to principles even if it means a breakdown of relations. Female thinking is, as we have maintained earlier, more likely to preserve relations, to attend to the situation rather than rigidly adhering to principles no matter the costs. Again, if the ethical basis is that of care and preservation, *protection* of what is to be secured in the first place is a must.

In very general terms, the aim is to survive through all the stages. What is done at one particular stage should be compatible with what is done at the next, so to speak. If we talk about security in peace time, it is logically true that it is better to seek prevention of insecurity instead of contributing to tension that may bring us toward war. The logic here is not disputed; the problem is what it implies in terms of practical decision making. Since human society wants some kind of security all through the stages, all through the cycle of security, we are forced to plan for proceeding through it, not because we like to fight war, but because security is interesting to us in future terms. Can we prolong this period of peace or must we also prepare for security during an eventual war?

Following is a comprehensive list of security *means* that are discussed in earlier chapters.

1. Military—conventional, paramilitary, guerilla, home guards, and the like, "techno-commandos," modules etc. All of them are known from the European debate in the early 1980s (e.g., Journal of Peace Research 2:1984 and see Part II).
2. Economic—the self/other reliance problem focusing on what are the basic minimum need satisfaction of the community, which the community should be able to provide for by its own capacity.
3. Political—the relations between citizens and the state operating security means, the problem of legitimacy, law and order.
4. Civil defense—shelters, evacuation plans, caring for victims, refugees, etc.
5. Civil preparedness—making society operate under the crisis condi-

tions, energy storage, hospitals, mass communication, production, distribution, etc.

6. Nonviolent defense—noncooperation, persuasion, strikes, moral pressure, political "jiu-jitsu."
7. Society's invulnerability level—decentralization, robust technology, infrastructure, population, dispersion degree of specialization, self-reliance in basic need categories.
8. Community, human beings—cultural identity, morale, belief in the future, crisis orientation or problem-solving orientation, participation, freedom, etc.

Within the traditional "national security" paradigm there is an emphasis on 1 and 3 and, in the best of cases, on 2. Nobody would deny that the remaining security means are relevant, but they are anyhow considered marginal in meeting the "preferred" external military threats, or they are considered close to impossible to do something about.

Modern industrial society is vulnerable, and its civilian "carrying capacity" in terms of resisting pressure from outside and in terms of carrying the activities of modern warfare is decreasing in proportion to the damage that modern security technology can inflict upon it. For a number of reasons, security measures such as 4–8 are, unfortunately, considered marginal compared to investing in purely military (often offensive-oriented) preparations. Civil preparedness is a kind of "cure" under the present circumstances without social or structural change. To reduce society's vulnerability in the future is a "preventive" measure aimed at building into present-day decision making about, for example, energy, technology, trade, and the like a security dimension. Does this or that alternative in our civil development add to or reduce our vulnerability in the future?

There is no doubt that some types of society, structure, and functions are more "defensible" than others. Our basic hypothesis is that one reason there is an armament "fix" in contemporary security politics is the more or less clear recognition that we are vulnerable societies difficult to defend. Therefore we build up ever higher "outward"-oriented security means to compensate for internal vulnerabilities. "Should war come, everything is anyhow lost, and there is little we can do," it's often said. And the fact is that this is probably more true than ever before: given the highly vulnerable societies we have developed.

Thus it can be argued that the prospect of war is taken very seriously by security managers in military terms, whereas it is not taken seriously in civilian-organizational and internal terms. We are supposed to fight wars that have no civilian, societal support. If, on the contrary, modern states were deeply concerned about survival, we would hardly have built society the way we have in the first place.

As said before, the deep source of security comes from inside. Weak human communities, whether mini- or maxi-states, whether militarily weak or strong, cannot build security on sand castlelike societal foundations. Security logically cannot be stronger than its source, and that is the very community to be secured!

The end/means discussion leaves us with Table 7.

But, then, there is the space dimension to be added. Its quality, the distinction into offensiveness and defensiveness, is elaborated on below. What we are after here is just a simple exposition of relevant "security layers," such as

- Inner human being
- Individual citizens
- Municipality/local society
- Nation-state or state-nation
- Region
- International
- Global or world order

Thus we are left with four by eight security fields to be covered throughout seven layers. No wonder, you may say, that purely military defense is not able to care for all this! It is, on the other hand, also no wonder that security can never be complete. If we ever tried, we would reach a "garrison society" desired by nobody.

Let's elaborate a little on the issue of layers.

Taking our point of departure in the international system, the "highest" guarantor of security is the state. "National security," so much in focus, is actually "state security," which has been given the task of securing the entity called a country, a society, a community. It so does by means of resources—human, technological, economic—given by society's members as a payment for being defended from outside threats. By means of social production, citizens have agreed to let "the state" care for their security, the single organization for the whole. However, as is often pointed out in politics, "the state" is both a servant (guarantor) and a master. It is both dependent on the citizens—resources and perceived legitimacy—and it commands such societal resources and is handed over such powers that it may, to a large

Table 7
A Typology of "Security Fields"

ENDS / MEANS	...Peace .....> ..... Struggle ......> .....Peace. .>				
	Normalization prevention dissuasion	Crisis, tension threats	Defense/ Offence Struggle	Conflict resolution/ regulation	Normalization ....> ...
Military					
Economic					
Political					
Civil Defense					
Civil preparedness					
Nonviolence					
Self-reliance					
Human beings community					

(Row group label at left: TRANSARMAMENT)

extent, make society and its citizens dependent upon it, rule them, threaten them, and so on.

Thus the state is a servant and master, both a security guarantor and threat. National security is always dualistic. There is no guarantee that the state's security is identical with the collective perception of security by its citizens. There is nothing new, however, there is surprisingly little research and debate about this fact. As long as the state is given the task of securing society at large, there is a risk that its security interests as state apparatus overrule security interests of the citizenry and that, since civil society and its citizens have declared themselves unable to achieve security by themselves and have turned to their state they have also declared themselves rather "helpless." Thus the inner security capacity of any human community as such has been underdeveloped due to the citizenry's reliance for their security upon the state, which has also its "own" interests detached from the people.

It should not surprise, therefore, that the state and its representatives habitually monopolize the security concepts and means and the correct images of the world in general and the threats in particular; neither is it strange that the state, almost as a matter of principle, abhors the idea that community itself can secure itself, as shown by its general rejection of ideas about nonviolent national defense.

With this in mind, it probably also becomes a little more evident why there is a habit of looking more at the strength of the military organization than at the (in) vulnerability of the community, the resource base as well as the object of security. Through a succesive development of a security monopoly by the state, civil community and the citizens have been rendered more and more helpless, and society rather less defensible.

Therefore, behind the contemporary protest against the arms race, we are also likely to find a signal of dissatisfaction with the lack of democracy, with insufficient participant relations and a doubt about the legitimacy of what the state, elevated above the citizenry, does more or less to the detriment of the human community, locally as well as globally.

It seems reasonable to see this as one more consequence of deeper lying cosmological patterns: the either/or and center/periphery component. Society has become a periphery to the central state, which in much of its activity treats other states as peripheral. As security by the state is not developed in cooperation with society as its source, security is not sought in cooperation with other states.

Above the state level, we find a significant degree of anarchy, mature or less mature, more or less oriented toward "everybody's war against everybody else." We find a global society having no collective security function paralleling that of the state vis-a-vis the citizens. We find that the states within the community of states behave in ways that the state would never "allow" its citizens to behave. The real problem is not whether it is so; it obviously is. The problem is whether it *has* to be like that.

Let's therefore try to look into the complex relationships between society, the state, and other societies and their states while holding the distinction offensive-defensive in mind.

Any unit, be it a society, a country, a region, can display strength or weakness internally. It may be more or less vulnerable. At the same time, it may employ specific means for defense—a supplement for whatever it "feels" it doesn't have in terms of inner strength. These means may be primarily defensive or offensive.

We rely here on the very simple but far from generally acknowledged formulation employed by Galtung (1984), which states that the security of A relative to B equals the invulnerability of A minus the offensive destructive capacity of B. Galtung argues that

> Security is simply here defined as one's own invulnerability minus the capacity of the other Party to destroy. I think that it is a fairly reasonable definition of security: it means the capacity to come out of a conflict unscathed, in other words the probability that human beings, society, nature and also one's own defense system will survive. One may later on decide to change them, but then out of one's own will. If the invulnerability level is insufficient, then one is insecure" (Galtung 1984).

This conceptualization departs radically from mainstream thinking: It starts out with "ourselves." And with a basically defensive orientation. Traditional balance of power reasoning, not to speak of deterrence philosophy basically asks: How can we destroy the opponent or threaten to destroy him to keep him at bay? As Galtung points out, it may have very much to do with the sad fact that destructive capacity is much easier to handle and measure. The "offensive," expansive, periphery-encroaching cosmology is reflected in this type of reasoning, basing itself on the acceptability of using violence and on the idea that conflicts are "their" fault—not "our mutual fault and problem"—for which reason it is "natural" to direct the means toward "the other." It reflects our cultural "contempt for weakness" (Ofstad 1972).

20

Security Is about Defensiveness and Protection

It will come as no surprise that this chapter title is our contention, based on the premises and principles put forward in this section. The "good defense" is one that not only reduces the probability of war, but also seeks to increase crisis stability and confidence-building measures. *Defensive security and protective defense holds the potential of contributing to the abolition of war as a social institution in the long run.*

What would we want the good defense to achieve?

First, of course, it should be compatible with the premises and principles elaborated on here. On the other hand, it should not be so "utopian" that it will never come about. Some may hold the value dear that defense should be all-nonviolent. So would we. But taking into account the fact that there is such an intimate relation between society and defense, we see no chance, in the short-term perspective, to bring about the complete abolition of violent means of conflict resolution. Obviously the majority of Europe's people would not vote for a completely nonviolent defense today. So, some kind of transition must be outlined, a type of defence in which, over the years, the military/violent component will become increasingly irrelevant and look obsolete. An exclusive reliance on nonviolent defense also requires reciprocal steps from potential adversaries. A transition to a purely defensive military posture can, on the other hand, be undertaken by any country independently without risk while pursuing efforts in cooperation with other countries to establish a better world order.

Second, it must be a defense in which there is real security. It must look credible as an alternative to the present as seen by our own fellow-citizens. It must be strong in some ways and admit its weakness vis-a-vis certain types of threats. It should aim at self-defense but defense in such a manner that it simply cannot threaten anybody, yet so that an aggressor would realize that he would not achieve his aims, only endanger himself if he launched an attack. It should be operative only on our own territory, in other words, never useful for attack or retaliation. That is, it should build on persuasion and self-defense rather than deterrence and offense.

Building up a new defense employing both civilian and military means and abolishing the old is what we call *transarmament*.

There are some who believe that the threat of retaliation is a stronger deterrent against aggression than merely defense. It is also often argued that offensive operations bring the fighting to the territory of the aggressor, whereas defense alone allows an aggressor to fight on our side of the border.

But these arguments ignore that a defensive military posture is far more effective in avoiding war, and in de-escalating war if it should ever start.

If another country feels threatened by us, it may want to destroy us and/ or our military forces, out of fear that otherwise we might take the first step against it. If we make an effort to "bring the fighting into the territory of the opponent" once a war has started, he will have every incentive to continue fighting as long as he is able to. If he stopped he would lose the initiative and would fear being destroyed by us.

If, instead, we can convince him through a purely defensive posture that there is no risk in withdrawing, because we will not pursue him across the border, he has every incentive to stop the fighting.

This is why a defensive posture is also in our own interest.

Third, it should be for, by and of the people, based on a broad conception of human security and amenable to many types of participation.

Fourth, it should—as a transition strategy—open the way for real disarmament and arms control. By offering a credible alternative, something to which nations and peoples can switch according to local circumstances, it gives humankind an opportunity to abolish all offensive weapons and doctrines. They will simply not be needed among civilized actors.

This is why we think it is a false either/or position to argue either for more of the present type of defense, for exclusive nonviolence, or no defense at all. We don't need more or less of a bad defense but another type of defense.

Defensive or protective defense is *not* a truism, neither a contradiction of terms. Self-defense ought to be the only proper defense in a civilized world that cares about the survival of everything and about "common security" in a deep sense.

Imagine the present world as a street in which everybody walks around with a submachine gun. Each is able, with precision, to kill persons far down the street, victims who cannot even guard against being targeted. And the first shot by one may lead to panic and everybody shooting at everybody. Who could be secure under such circumstances? Hardly even a super-armed police force patroling the street.

Imagine, then, a world in which all nations and regions had built their security and defense on the image of the very same street. Everybody strolls up and down "armed" with jiu-jitsu. Nobody can harm or even threaten anybody before one turns upon another concrete person and tries physically to grab his bag or knock him or her down. *Then* the self-defense starts. The criminal is surprised by the defense capability of the offended, victim, and soon he is down on his back. He is not killed but being taught a lesson and suffers the humiliation from having "lost" in the eye of the people gathering around him.

It may be unpleaseant and we would prefer if nobody needed be trained in effective jiu-jitsu. But, remember, nobody is killed, the method cannot be used for retaliation or attack, the street and all other people present are not blown into a desertlike wasteland. There may be more frequent attempts on people, but also a stronger social control, cooperation, and a vital norm against somebody offending such a rather pleasant norm.

What is protective defense *not*?

It is not weakness. It is not characteristic of a single weapon system but has characteristics built into society, thinking, and action. It excludes certain weapons and doctrines, but not all. It is not a way of creating vacuums—rather it increases our invulnerability and strength—while reducing our temptation and potential for harming others. It does not involve us in somebody else's conflict since it builds on the idea of caring for oneself and, thereby, caring for the totality. It is not an illusion (as the present type of offensive military posture) through believing that "my" security can be obtained to the detriment of "their" insecurity. It is a defense that does not need a particular enemy image or "addressee," but that is generally "unconquerable" from all sides.

Further, it is not a naive attempt to "just do good and be nice in a cruel and dangerous world." In several respects it is already practiced by Austria, Finland, Sweden, Switzerland, and Yugoslavia; there are many instances in which its main principles have been successfully employed against overwhelmingly "stronger" (more offensive, bigger, and technologically more sophisticated) actors: by Gandhi versus the British, by Mao during the war of liberation against Japan, by Vietnam against the Americans, by Solidarnosć vis-a-vis the Soviet Union, and by Afghanistan against the Soviets. These are not "ideal" examples fulfilling all criteria, but each of them has borrowed elements and been inspired by defensive thinking and doctrines, and all have been weaker in the traditional sense of the term than their opponent and nevertheless fared better than their mightier enemies.

A number of more concrete criteria of defensiveness can be outlined, although there are "gray zones" between offensiveness and defensiveness. Some of the essential characteristics of a protective defense posture have been presented in concrete terms in the models of Parts I and II. They are:

- Short range—basically ranges that do not transcend one's own borders.
- Limited destructive capability—since defense is used one one's own space, there are limits to destruction.
- High mobility and flexibility within limited range.
- Potentially long-time perspective—there is no "hurry" to drop bombs or suprise the opponent or kill millions within ten minutes; weapons are not activated before attack on them.
- Adaptation to local circumstances—since defense means self-defense, it is adapted to the peculiarities of that self, geography, topography, political culture, level of technology, etc. Each society around the world builds its own defense and a much more pluralistic, nonmilitaristic culture becomes possible.
- Participative—the whole population is given an opportunity to contribute to the defense of their country, military as well as civil; protective defense is social and democratic (but not social-democratic!) and since its function is to preserve, local populations primarily defend their own community.
- Self-sufficiency—any unit increases its ability to produce for its military as well as civilian defense needs on its own, not contributing to the militarization of other's military-industrial complexes and exports.
- Military and civilian defense methods interact, although probably separated in time and space; all components in this new type of protective defense are functionally and symbiotically linked to each other; it's a both/and, not either/or. Likewise, whatever society does for defense, it does not prevent a sound civilian development of society at large; rather the two support each other constructively. This is particularly relevant in Third World countries.

It deserves mention that a society, a country, or other unit can be strong for at least two reasons. As a civilian actor, it commands its own destiny in a highly self-reliant manner, as, for example, China, *or* because it has an extended pattern of interdependence around itself in which it is usually the stronger, that is, engages in asymmetrical relations, like let's say the United States. Likewise there are two basic ways of being weak, either through being torn apart from the inside as a very class-divided country or perhaps through lacking virtually all basic need satisfying resources within the country; *or* by being powerful enough to engage in very many interdependent, but underdoglike relations such as is the case with many peripheral nations.

Again, we are dealing with no clearcut categories. You may be strong through exploiting others in an "imperialist" fashion, but then again even empires are vulnerable. And you may be weak because of exploitation by others, but still having some power since you have one or two items of priority for others.

Therefore, we would like to introduce the distinction not only between defensive and offensive security but also between civilian, societal-developmental offensibility and defensibility.

Offensibility here signifies the ability to command and control the resources of others for one's own purposes and, thereby, reach a certain degree of invulnerability and strength in spite of reliance on others. Simply being big and having many relations may serve this goal.

Defensibility, on the contrary, implies that the actor is rather self-reliant without exploiting others in any important way through its civil relations.

These two concepts thus exclusively pertain to civil society and its internal-external relations.

We consider the distinctions between society and society's defense and between offensive and defensive postures absolutely fundamental. There are no technological "fixes" to the security problems we face today. Another "way of thinking" about society and defense must go hand in hand with restructuring forces, with transarmament (or the shift toward protective defense) and with policies aiming at increasing society's general invulnerability.

In short, strive to increase your overall self-reliance and limit yourself to effective self-defense. As we shall see this is *not* the same as selfishness, protectionism, and such; it is an idea appearing through global thinking and a caring philosophy (see chapter 21).

We also think that it illustrates another message directed primarily to the research community, namely, that it is meaningless to do abstract modeling of security and defense detached from society as such. We are forced to integrate security (offensive/defensive) and society (offensibility/defensibility) since society is the source of our security as well as the object to be secured. The best policy is to change the present course from "super-offensiveness" in which both we and the opponents become less secure, which is typical of most nuclear developments and particularly of the Reagan Administration's star wars idea, which increases the risk of accidental nuclear war.

Instead, countries and peoples should strive to reach postures of "super-defensiveness" in which both "we" and "they" become safe. By inviting each other to take mutually beneficial steps toward self-defense and non-offensiveness, we have a chance of not only preventing war in the short run but also of making war, increasingly obsolete and unthinkable in the long run and abolishing it altogether in the final end. Just policies, trust, non-threatening, and tension-reducing initiatives become *more* acceptable when we are safe ourselves in the sense of being as invulnerable and strong in the self-defense mode as possible.

And, over time, it reinforces good relations and trust in the wider community of countries and peoples. This is a plea for holistic security thinking, holistic also in the sense that we take into account systematically that the opponents also have a legitimate right to security, part of which only *we* can deliver. In enlightened self-interest.

This, we believe, is common security in the deep sense. Can it be much different if we always remember that we have in common the interest in preserving and caring for there being a world in the future?

21

Security Is about Accepting Limits and Furthering Mutuality

A basic theme going through both our three general premises and the five security principles is this: *We have to accept limits*! If we want to survive collectively, there are limits to how much we can destroy. If we want to secure our society we have to take into account its social carrying capacity and not overload it as a human organization. When we meet threats and challenges there are things we don't do while we expand our activities in fields that make it impossible for the opponent to achieve his aims at our expense. And protective defense basically builds on the idea that we should be strong *and* unable to threaten the opponent at home. Thus we talk about a new type of strength, about power over ourselves rather than over others, the world or nature.

True humanism accepts a priori that we are not omnipotent. There is something with which we should not tamper. The world should not simply be turned into a tool for us; rather, we accept to be one element in the universe. We may run into problems again and again if we don't accept that our task is to optimize in terms of quantity and maximize in terms of quality.

In this perspective, we may argue that what the world needs and what we have modestly tried to do in this book is to discuss a new security and defense philosophy, to engage ourselves in *humanistic security politics*. We believe that there is such a thing!

We would not attempt to outline a single philosophically based limitation principle here. We are not competent to do so, and perhaps it would not be very desirable to have one. Instead, we simply present a few that we think offer the gist of what we have in mind.

1. *Being humble and caring, "letting things be" in an active manner*. This is the principle outlined by Zimmerman with reference to Heidegger under premise 3.

2. *The "mutuality principle."* It is dealt with by philosopher Harald Of-stad (1972) and states, in short, that "one ought to act in relation to others according to such norms on the basis of which we would like others to act in relation to ourselves." As Ofstad points out, this is not so simple as it may sound. My wish as to how others ought to treat me cannot automatically be taken as a norm concerning my acts in relation to them unless we assume that my will about the way they treat me is rational and morally right. So, I would still need some "higher" set of norms on which to judge. In this sense it is very subjective as a principle.

But there is also an element of objectivity in it. The norm that is applicable for person A in situation X is also applicable for person A1 in situation X1 provided there are no relevant differences. This would be important in concrete defense and security policy terms. If we stuck to such a mutuality principle it would be nonsense to accuse an opponent of having offensive intentions against us because of a certain kind of doctrine or weaponry that *we* ourselves also had. If the mutuality principle carried some importance, *our* defense in rough terms would resemble that which we would find acceptable for the opponent to have.

But, of course, the mutuality principle goes against the power principle applied in international politics. Here it is almost a norm that it is legitimate to do to other (weaker, far away, "primitive," dangerous) countries what we would never accept them to do to us (if they had the capability).

In other words, if there is a generally accepted norm in the international community stating that invasions or interventions of other sovereign countries is prohibited, this ought to apply to everyone. For example, the United States bombed Tripolis in April 1986 and referred to the legitimate right of self-defense, but it would never allow Libya to bomb Washington on the basis of this or any other argument. And whereas the Soviet Union invaded Afghanistan, it would never allow Afghanistan to invade the Soviet Union.

From time to time it is useful to "turn things upside-down" to see the proportions of right and wrong as seen by ourselves and from the point of view of others or of general principles.

It deserves mention that "soft" Christianity embodies a principle very close to that of mutuality; however, within a completely different framework, namely the Golden Rule, "Do unto others as you wish them to do unto you."

Johan Galtung has drawn a distinction between "hard" and "soft" Christianity. "Soft" Christianity emphasizes those aspects of the Bible that appeal for mercy, forgiveness, love, for example, the story of the good samaritan. It is perhaps most typically represented by Saint Francis of Assisi. "Hard" Christianity emphasizes righteousness, the wrath of God, the punishment of nonbelievers and sinners, for example the prophecy of the battle of Armageddon. One of its typical exponents is the Spanish grandinquisitor Tomás de Torquemada.

At present, the religious right seeks a monopoly on references to biblical images, stressing "hard" Christianity. We must see to it that the "soft" version and its content are not constantly being suppressed and forgotten. Western cosmology, as we have described it, is more hard than soft, that is, the dominant version relies more on the imagery of punishment, judgement, mission, and the like than on love, care, forgiveness.

3. *Immanuel Kant's "categorical imperative."* It states that we should "act so that you *can* will that the maxim of your action be made the principle of a universal law." In other words, *given* a community of human agents, they ought to act according to such a general practice. But, as Jonas points out, *that* is not the same as saying that there *ought* to be a community at all. (In a sense it is a hypothetical imperative in saying something like: "If there is a community of human beings . . ."; see Mackie 1977 for an excellent discussion of the two types of imperatives).

Kant's imperative is an attempt at universalization of norms, and there are, of course, lots of problems involved. Mackie (1977) argues that universalization takes place in stages. First, there is the type of universalization that point 2 above exemplifies, something like the Golden Rule. Bernhard Shaw satirically commented: "Do not do unto others as you would have that they should do unto you. Their tastes may not be the same."

The second stage implies putting oneself in the other person's place. "To decide whether some maxim that you are inclined to assert is really universalizable, imagine yourself in the other man's place and ask whether you can then accept it as a directive guiding the behavior of others toward you."

Thus if you are a superpower asserting the maxim that nuclear deterrence is necessary for self-defense, imagine yourself in the other superpower's place and ask whether you can then accept it as a directive guiding the behavior of that other superpower toward you. Or, being rich and healthy I may find the maxim that everybody ought to pay for his or her medical care acceptable, but would I also were I poor and chronically ill?

According to Mackie, the third stage consists in taking into account different tastes and rival ideals. Here we put ourselves even more deeply into the place of others, and, like before, it is doubtful whether *any* principle would pass such a severe test. I may be a ruthless individualist thinking that there is no reason to help somebody who has driven off the road (for instance, because I am sure that I would never do such a foolish thing myself). But, at the same time, I can acknowledge the fact that everybody else in the world does not share this view, that there are some "soft types" who don't and that the one I am passing right now in the ditch belongs to this category and that he, therefore, expects me to give a helping hand. In other words, you are not a fanatic, but open to compromise with the value sets of others.

This example functions well with a positive orientation, helping another human being, being benevolent. But it could hardly find moral support if turned around. "I am a principled pacifist abhorring all kinds of violence. But since I understand that there are those who do not share my maxim, don't do violence, and since the person (or country) I am now facing surely belongs to this category, then I engage wholeheartedly in killing others."

We are, of course, constantly thrown back to basics. What is good and ethically acceptable and what is not? However, the reasoning just described is a very typical one and it has been almost universalized. We do the (admittedly in principle bad) thing we do to "answer" them, because they use such methods, because they belong to the categories that obviously don't share our principles of the good. Were it not because of them, we would always only do good! That is, we tend to act according to the so-called brass rule. "Do unto others as you would expect them to do unto you."

There is no doubt in our personal minds that this is the type of thinking that we must leave behind in the nuclear age and in the world political system. Do unto them as they do unto us in terms of "bad" behavior is a very dangerous maxim. This is why offensiveness can and ought never be an answer to offensiveness by "them."

Be this as it may, there is still another problem to return to. Reasoning in these terms still carries the illusion that there is a "we" and a "them" that may harm each other more or less should a war be fought, as if there is an "it," the universe, the biosphere, being and future generations that would survive. This touches upon the next, related but expanded principle formulated by Hans Jonas.

4. *The "stewardship" imperative or imperative of total care.* Jonas offers a number of formulations as an extension of Kant's imperative in order to demonstrate the essential-existential principle that there *be* a world and a future. "Act so that the effects of your action are compatible with the permanence of genuine human life" or "act so that the effects of your action are not destructive of the future possibility of a genuine human life," or "do not compromise the conditions for an indefinite continuation of humanity on earth," or "in your present choices, include the future wholeness of humanity among the objects of your will" (Jonas 1984).

It may be said that this norm cares for the final, outer limits while it permits lesser harm. But it hardly rules out the possibility that we may risk our own life (suicide or limited death in struggle) or that we may, under certain circumstances, kill others. It rules out destroying the possibility of existence in the future.

There is no doubt in our mind that our time and situation is such that a fundamental new global stewardship is necessary. But it is also true that we still need something of the old "neighbor ethics" and person-to-person responsibility that we discussed when mentioning the Nuremberg principles and the female ethical principles.

Thus there is a need for combining the various principles, seeing them as complementary, as part of a larger spectrum of fundamental existential responsibility and paying tribute to the overall ethics of care and limitation.

The moment we care and strive for genuine security and peace, the pursuit of limitless freedom and growth is not only unwise and short-sightedly dangerous. It is immoral.

5. *Gandhian principles.* If there is any philosophical system that can help us on the way, well known in the West and practiced with a considerable amount of success, it is that of Mahatma Gandhi. As a thought system it encompasses, more or less, all the above principles (for details, see Galtung and Naess 1955; Duncan 1951; Sharp 1979).

Satya means truth, and for Gandhi it is another term for God. Truth is God, the embodiment of love, cosmic order, the universal one. It is the object of self-realization, and to be religious in the Gandhian sense is to identify with humanity.

Brahmacharya implies sexual abstention but also broader self-control, self-limitation, and self-possession. By controlling our senses we become more able to meet God. Everything we do shall be based on deep consideration; self-realization implies purification, a struggle for inner freedom, independence and for integrity. Power over oneself.

Ahimsa is more outward oriented where Bramacharya goes inward. Ahimsa basically means nonviolence, "nonkilling," no offense, insulting, hurting, no merciless thought. Gandhi says those who follow this teaching have no place for an enemy. But ahimsa is more than that. It is empathy, sympathy, fellow feeling, or solidarity with everything living. Only through practicing ahimsa can one reach truth.

These are the three basic principles on which the Gandhian metaphysic and political philosophy are built. Satyagraha is the conduct that appears when a group is in intense conflict with another group and the group acts on the basis of ahimsa norms (Galtung and Naess 1951).

What is the metaphysical basis of all this? First, ahimsa and the other two principles exist because it is the only way in which we can realize identity and unity with creation, with being. The underlying teaching here is that what is right—or truth—for me is also truth for others, for the universe.

Second, Gandhi knew that he could be wrong and that he had only found one of several ways. We can only know part of truth, never the whole truth. If we make a mistake it is very important that its consequences do not harm others. Third, means and goals must always be one. If we choose the right means, the goals are achieved "automatically." So, there is no road *to* peace; peace is the road, as Gandhi stated it.

Fourth, only God can create life, we can't. Since this is so, we should not allow ourselves to terminate life.

We shall stop here. The basic building blocks of Gandhi's philosophy— relevant as it is both to defense, to society and development in general, and to the individual's search for meaning in life—have been put forward. It is not coincidence if the reader, at this point, feels that this resembles to a certain degree the thought of Heidegger, Jonas, and Schumacher. Eckartsberg and Valle (1981, 287–313) among others point out that there are clear similarities between Heidegger on the one hand and Eastern philosophy (Hinduism, Taoism) on the other.

So, also when it comes to ethics in the nuclear age, there is a considerable need for intercultural dialogue. We need an awareness of the limitations of Western paradigms and an openness toward other cultures.

Part V

Si Vis Pacem, Para Pacem

22

If You Want Peace, Prepare for Peace!

Conventional wisdom has it that if we want peace we should prepare for war. In peacetime it is called deterrence, in wartime it's war-fighting strategies. It does not say that we should prepare ourselves to avoid or prevent war; it says that we should be ready to fight—anywhere and at any time and with the doomsday weapons, if "necessary."

So, this is basically what realpolitik is about.

It is not too easy to find similar "wisdom" in other human and social relations. We don't seem to prepare for dictatorship because we want democracy. We don't seem to say, if you want ecological balance, prepare for environmental decay. Neither do we prepare ourselves every minute to die in order to live our daily lives.

It seems quite reasonable from experience to prepare against "worst cases," which, if they appear suddenly, will stand in the way of achieving what we wanted. But that is prevention. In prevention, we try to avoid situations from occurring that would make our cherished goal achievement impossible. Thus society established a set of laws and procedures to prevent somebody from becoming a dictator, but we don't let our governments plan how to make a coup—"just in case"—*because* we want democracy.

What about relations with others? If we want friendship we don't plan how to fight our friends in the meanest manner, even to the point of killing them. If we want a good marriage, we don't plan every day how to divorce and fight the one we love today. If I want an honest and fair trade relationship I don't plan permanently how to cheat my trading partner and exploit him or her to the point where the partner goes bankrupt.

But, again, what about games? In certain plays, games, and sports there is a point in doing the opposite of what looks goal-rational in order to confuse the other party and then, by surprise, reach the target or score a point. This is what may be called tactics, strategic retreat, "playing the game," simulate, trick the other. But, if so, the purpose of the whole thing is to gain victory, be the best, beat or humiliate the other. That may be fine in a game where rules and judges exist, but in the "real world" in politics where the behavior is *not* a game, the consequences may, literally, make a world of difference. And, mind you, the aim is not peace and cooperation in such games; it is victory, an outcome where the gain of one is the loss of the other.

Thus we seem to conclude that either the war/peace issue is absolutely unique and deserves a principle of its very own—and one that goes against all other human experience—or the "*si vis pacem, para bellum*" principle is sheer nonsense. The only commonsense maxim *seems* to be: "If you want peace, prepare for the prevention of war."

And that is a minimum-maxim. It states only that peace at least amounts to there being no war going on. Thus *war prevention* is very sensible but somehow not "enough." Trying to prevent something means reducing its probability (or perhaps its impact should it happen), but it does not amount to totally excluding the possibility. What we try to prevent is something that *can* happen.

Therefore, a maximum-maxim would say: "If you want peace, make war impossible." This is maximum in the negative sense, making something impossible." But we may ask: Is it a very "desirable" peace if there are still very many other types of violence going on in the world? If, as today, roughly 60,000 people (mainly women and children) die every day and unnecessarily from malnutrition, lack of shelter and medicine, and such, is that compatible with peace? Clearly, it is not. Still, it is a better situation than one that, in addition to these features, also is characterized by direct war fighting.

In summary, we are thrown back to the conclusion that the *si vis pacem para bellum* maxim not only goes against all the premises and security principles we have elaborated on, but *it is also the cherished principle of those for whom there are higher values or goals than peace or, as in the nuclear age, existence of what is and can be in the future*. It is, as such, completely incompatible with mutuality, limitation, or "letting things be" in the existential sense we have discussed.

At the same time we are forced to acknowledge the fact that there are regimes and individuals who operate on the basis of such a maxim. Without engaging in a delicate philosophical analysis here, it is reasonable to point out that this raises the problem of what should be the role of a *nondeterrence-based self-defense as long as the global abolition of war as a social institution has not been achieved*. We tend to see it simply as one element in a macro-change and as a model of an independent initiative inspiring others!

On the basis of what has been stated so far and on our considerations following from the analyses carried out through this book, we propose the following maxim for a peaceful future: If you want peace, prepare for peace by:

1. Short-term war prevention and confidence-building.
2. Self-defense on the premises and principles put forward, particularly taking account of the limitation principle.
3. Abolition of war as a social institution.
4. Constructive, positive peace measures based on the right to existence and development, peace thinking, and an ethics of care.

We need the constructive element, the short and the long perspectives. We need an *idea* of peace, not a clearcut definition or a principle on which somebody can produce a program, mobilize followers, and monopolize the "one and only way to peace." We need an open conceptualization, one that stimulates a cross-cultural, highly intensive dialogue and that is open to be practiced according to local circumstances.

We tend to believe that there is something about peace that deems it necessary to treat it like the old taoists treated Tao, "the Way": the moment someone says that he knows what it is we can be confident that it is *not* tao. Maybe, thinking deeply about it, we can only hope to take part in a process, a movement down the road? Perhaps the fascinating thing is that peace can never be an "end state." It is a permanent endeavor, the limitless devotion—much like striving toward wisdom.

We have deliberately chosen to discuss the concept of peace toward the end of the book. It indicates that we find it important to have an idea of what peace *is*, but a clearcut definition is not desirable. The important thing is the process, the multifarious nature of its character, and the limitless endeavor in coming closer to it.

We have emphasized time and again that security and society are one; there can be no security unless there is a "securable" society, one that can be secured. Society develops its security on the basis of the way it is organized and by means of the defense it creates through its surplus.

In other words, security and development—the something to secure—are inseparable. We take "society" to mean 'that which develops."

We have also stressed that peace cannot imply simply the absence of war and violent conflict resolution; it must be something positive, in and by itself. Even if all wars and all weapons disappeared tomorrow, thousands of people would still die from civilian maldevelopment throughout the world. Peace, likewise, encompasses the means of defense as well as the object of defense—society and its development.

One the basis of this, and in principle everything else we have presented here—we advance the following *approximate description of the idea of peace*:

> Peace is to develop scurity and secure development of the whole human being and all human beings in a permanent process taking its point of departure in a model of human and social needs and based on an ethics of global care, allowing for unity in diversity!

So, security and development should be seen as one. That human beings are in focus will hardly surprise anyone having followed us this far. We think that needs—individual and collective—are more important than markets or planning systems. Human needs include basically four types (Galtung 1980): (1) survival or existence (physical-ethical), (2) welfare (material-"economic"), (3) freedom (politics and rights), and (4) identity (psychological-cultural-mental). The human being is terribly rich, nonreducible to a "homo oeconomicus."

We talk about a permanent process, a point we have elaborated on before. We must avoid any conceptualization and operationalization of peace that some elite could monopolize, and we must deny anyone the right to claim that "now we have reached peace." Like wisdom, quality, doing good, and self-realization, peace *is* a permanent struggle with ourselves for some kind of perfection.

We talk not only of the whole human being but of all human beings. This is where the limitation principle and like principles appear. And it is where the philosophy of self-reliance enters the picture. How?

If we care for others it is absolutely unfair if some of us continue to "overdevelop" our lifestyles causing "underdevelopment" somewhere else. That is global maldevelopment. We must limit our aspirations in such ways that others are permitted to satisfy their human needs. (Don't do to others what you would not appreciate that they did to you!) The principle of self-reliance says that each unit should be able to care for its own human and social need satisfaction to the highest possible degree since, by doing so, it withdraws successively from the global exploitative maldevelopment system.

If from the smallest unit upward we tried to stand more on our own feet, we would allow others to do the same, practicing, in principle, Immanuel Kant's imperative.

Thus self-reliance is a radical proposal to solve at least parts of the so-called North-South or development problems of the world. (In reality they are structural problems between centers and peripheries in and between societies, nations, and economic-political ecological systems.)

Self-reliance is also a practical idea in terms of security. The local society, country, or region that adapts its lifestyle as much as possible to its own physical, social, and economic carrying capacity is less vulnerable than units that, because of their unwise maximization, become more and more reliant on others.

Therefore, we would maintain that self-reliance is a viable and desirable goal to aim at, for development as well as security reasons. If combined with self-defense along the principles outlined in this book, there are reasons that we come out with a fairly strong, proud, nonthreatening, and nonexploitative community. One that could well be an inspiration to others.

Self-reliance in development to combat global maldevelopment and self-defense in security to combat global militarization; would it be such a bad formula, after all? To some it may look very "selfish"—oriented, protectionist, autarchic. Nothing could be more wrong!

Precisely by having built into it a basic norm, the limitation principle, it embodies the practice of "thinking globally when we act locally." It takes into account the world and the norm that there be a future. It allows others to do the same according to their local circumstances.

Precisely like the human body that is healthy and strong, self-reliant, and doesn't need medicine from "outside" all the time, the social communities that would go in this direction would not harm others but invite others. They would be pleasant collaborators in the eyes of the others.

Our argument is that caring for oneself on the basis of an ethics of global responsibility, humility, and limitation is the truly internationalist, solidary, and humane alternative. It permits equality, justice, symmetry, and the like in ways we *know* that the present world system does not.

It allows, surprisingly enough, also for diversity in unity. Self-reliance is something that is practiced under local circumstances first. We ask what we can do ourselves (under the global ethics, of course). If there are things we can't do but would want to do and are sure won't harm others, we turn to others in horizontal relationships rather than vertical ones. That is collective self-reliance (the very negation of asymmetric maldevelopment-and-interdependence policies practiced by global capitalist economics).

The cultural strong point here is that development in the self-reliance mode permits cultural integrity, in opposition to global monoculture tendencies. We don't buy development from outside, as we don't buy weapons and doctrines from outside but secure and develop from inside first. What, then, is the unity about? It is about sharing the global limitation and mutuality imperative. We all become global citizens and "local global communities" through the way we conduct politics, regarding development as well as security. We are in unison worldwide in "agreeing" on being nonexploitative and nonthreatening, thus inviting others to do the same.

In this perspective, "helping the poor" is not done through development aid, capital, and technology transfer. It is done through structural changes in which we, the overdeveloped, learn to live according to global norms. It would even imply that we learn something from them, development aid from South to North in the form of cultural, social, and human inspiration (because trade and other economic ties will increasingly be solved locally and horizontally). Why not, for instance, send our children to schools in another culture for a year or two?

In this perspective "security" is not won through negotiations about arms limitations and control. We know it doesn't yield the desired results in time, although they should go on, there is so much we could otherwise do. Global security will be more likely the moment each builds a nonthreatening strong and protective defense that makes all the mass destructive and conventional offensive forces, doctrines, and operations irrelevant. And for what should we use intervention forces, the moment we are highly self-reliant?

We are simply talking here of principles and ideas that combine into *a transnational restructuring of the world system*, its development and security policies. But, finally, you may ask what this means for "world peace" (Galtung 1980)?

It means that world peace cannot be built only on a single concept leading to a global "policing authority" or world government. It means that each unit must become responsible for acting in such a way that others can safely do the same, namely, build the local preconditions that further collective safety and confidence. Thus world peace is something we see as a "fabric collage," knit together from many small, diverse, and lively "small peaces." In one there is Christian agape, in another dar-al-islam (peace), and in others again there is "shalom," "eirene," ahimsa, satyagraha, chung yung, ho p'ing and p'ing ho, wahei, ai; or there are pacts, federalism, international laws, social contracts, justice, nonviolence, and elements of a positive future peace in which war has been abolished forever. And there is a tremendous interaction and mixing of it all under respect for the ethics of global responsibility and limitation.

This is our way of conceiving peace, a vision or a dream. It is a plea for the strength of smallness and softness, for holism and a truly global ethics. But a vision that allows anyone to play a role in the long-term *transformation to a peace culture*.

It will not be realized in a lifetime. To work and live for peace is to be on the road that *is* peace and to see the potentials for the future in the present.

23

Barriers against Preparing for Peace

The constant preparation for war, the institutionalized "peacelessness," stands in the way of peace politics. We just need to think of the immense human, technological, economic, natural, and social resources—the time and the energy—allocated to war preparations in the name of "peace" or "security" to understand that the world is almost programmed for war, even omnicide. Doris Lessing in her seminal *Shikasta* tells us that disaster means dis-aster—fault in the stars (Lessing 1979, 29).

It is our contention that the single most important barrier against doing what ought to be done in the present situation is the predominant *world views, cosmologies, and ways of thinking of the Occident*. As long as we don't change, as Einstein also implicitly suggested, it is impossible to see how the dis-aster can be avoided. This has been argued in detail in this book.

Second, of course, there are *objectively very strong power structures*—power elites, dictatorships, repression machineries, military-industrial complexes, interdependent power elites in general. There is the technological imperative, "science as religion" and the "anarchic" structure of the international system in which each tries to maximize power at the expence of others and without the slightest respect for outer limits.

Third, there are the official *enemy images and threat perceptions* as well as the more sociopsychological need for "those who are different," strange, and dangerous to us. We all achieve parts of our identity as individuals and nationalities through defining ourselves as being different from "them."

Fourth, there is *lack of civil courage and psychological "surplus energy."* Stating clearly that this is a mad policy, immoral or counterproductive, and acting accordingly, that is dropping out and working for change, has its various prices. They vary from being fired, promotion becoming impossible, loss of status, being declared mentally sick, imprisonment, loss of income, and social marginalization to being expelled from one's country, or being tortured or murdered. The single individual is tied to "the system" in numerous sophisticated ways and it takes a lot of courage and mental energy to struggle with integrity and paying the price.

Fifth, there is the *lack of constructivism in our own thinking and lack of visions, eutopias, and images of desirable, viable futures*. We are all better at criticizing, pointing out that the present policies are bad and that ideas are not "realistic" or desirable than we are at helping each other and ourselves being creative, constructive, hope-inducing. In a crisis-ridden, deeply materialist culture ("program"), good ideas are in short supply.

There are simply too few future workshops and social invention seminars in the ministries of Defense and foreign affairs around the world! It may have something to do with the subject itself. In such a potentially very dangerous world, we have to be careful not to "rock the boat." Security politics is a "high impact" affair; experimenting here is much more potentially destabilizing than in the building or schooling sector. If a country should decide to change course, even marginally, it is signaling a kind of "insecurity" or perplexity that may start a chain reaction. Better go for the known, the conventional wisdom!

This comes close to saying *that the only thing that is more dangerous than the present course*, heading as we probably are for nuclear catastrophe in the shorter perspective and ecological breakdown in the longer perspective, *is to try to change it*!

Popularly speaking we are better trained through public schools and academic education at being skeptic and critical and seeing limitations in ideas and proposals than in being enthusiastic, constructive, seeing the potentials of new thoughts. The realist is considered the one who argues convincingly that "this proposal is not possible." The idealist is the one who argues that "this proposal is possible." And whereas realists are seldom being asked or forced to give evidence to their "status quo" thinking being possible in the future, the idealists must always prove that his or her proposal or idea is "realistic," possible, feasible. Thus the United Nations continues producing reports about the feasibility of disarmament and conversion while we approach the dis-aster because conventional wisdom has it that the present can be extrapolated more or less indefinitely and without risk.

Next, there are *situational factors and the knowledge problem*. There is always some good reason not to start changing things today or this year. First this, then that . . . and maybe, if we succeed with that, we may plan to undertake some limited steps. And there is always something happening that legitimized the policy of "no radical change under present circumstances." The rapidity and depth with which parts of contemporary society change should not surprise us, for example, the "third wave" technological revolution or the star wars idea. They are fast because they are isomorphic with the overall program. They don't require a reprogramming, no matter how revolutionary they actually are in their consequences.

The knowledge problem is more difficult to handle. Particularly as researchers we are apt to think that solid analysis and careful arguments should be helpful. But to whom? Few policy makers take the time to read reports carefully, particularly if they contradict their preconceived notions and ways of thinking.

Do large state bureaucracies and their managers really take interest in analytical, rational *arguments*, and—if they do—can we measure change in behavior in consequence of such an interest? By means of what types of input are rulers and ruled to be reached? Sometimes one may fear that one Three Mile Island accident changes world opinion more than thousands of expert reports and the protest of millions, or that one, even very small nuclear weapons accident may change the world more than a thousand SIPRI yearbooks . . .

It seems to be a common experience with people who have been close to death—their own or that of others—that they think more deeply, spend their time more consciously, and become more humble and grateful. They live more intensely, if they "get through" the crisis (Noll 1984; Weaver 1984; Alvnez 1971; Bowlb 1980; Voesteu Laum 1982; Qübler-Ross 1968, 1976; Hillman 1964; Pabst Battin 1982).

It is interesting to contemplate whether the present situation in which the risk of dying in a catastrophe is part and parcel of our lives could somehow produce the same effect *without* the catastrophe actually happening. If so, something constructive may come out of the crisis—but it takes very conscious, collective efforts to understand the implications of the situation, and we would probably lack the experience of deep grief that serves as the basis of the mentioned constructive, life-respecting energy in the experiences mentioned.

Do we *know that* we are approaching death? Is there anything in our global situation resembling that of the cancer patient? We may think so or we may doubt it. But none of us can say that he or she knows for sure what the answer is. It remains to be seen.

Surely there are many other factors preventing us from constructively engaging ourselves in change toward a peace culture now. Those in power seem, by and large, to prefer constant *crisis management and step-by-step reform* when confronting the risk of catastrophe. Thus we have an ongoing arms race, but *"repair"* on it by means of disarmament and arms control negotiations. We are in the midst of a world ecological crisis and we know that much of what we all do every day contributes to it; however, instead of rapidly stopping these practices, we engage in "repair" on nature (pollution reduction technology, regeneration of areas, and such).

Perhaps the historians, psychologists, and cultural workers of the future will have very good reasons to wonder about us: How could it take them so long to recognize that they were on their way to catastrophe and then they built one barrier after another preventing them from acting differently, while, at the same time, loudly and constantly deploring that their world did not change more rapidly?

24

Strategic Considerations

A strategy is basically a scheme outlining who is to do what, when, where, how, why, and at whose expense. In crisis situations there is a natural tendency to "jump to solutions" immediately. Perhaps we don't have that much time . . .

We believe that the most convincing and frutiful standpoint is the one that says we carry out analyses of alternatives meticulously since the future deserves the best possible knowledge and, perhaps, wisdom. Panicking will not yield such quality. Furthermore, doing solid work as if the world is not approaching a catastrophe is psychologically rewarding. And should it happen that the catastrophe fails to come off, so much the better. Maxim: Work in defiance of the "dystopias" around you.

These years there is a vivid research and public debate about "defensive defense" or "nonoffensive defense" (Journal of Peace Research 1984, 2 for an overview). It is not defense as such that is in focus; rather the restructuring of that limited component that is military. We find it absolutely improbable that some kind of real alternative defense and security will be realized unless broader "ways of thinking" are challenged. It seems that the studies, which are excellent on their own premises, are reflections of the fact that some kind of acceptability in the eyes of real politicians is necessary to avert catastrophe.

This is to be questioned. Good research should not limit itself to what is acceptable with a particular group. If so, it is not open, not free.

What is research process all about? Is it very different from any other problem and solution analysis? Since nothing is so practical as a good theory, we shall advance the one Galtung has developed as a model.

Perfect action and good research relies on the interplay of at least three things: (1) facts and various kinds of knowledge, (2) theories and conceptualizations, and (3) values, emotions, preferences, and visions. The interplay between facts and theory is *empirical analysis*. The interplay between facts and values is *criticism*, and the interplay between theories and values is *constructivism*. In other words, it is all about asking and answering three questions: What is the world like? What is wrong with it? And what should it look like? When we put it all together in a never-ending searching and seeking process, we have a fair chance to *act rationally* (Galtung 1977).

Galtung points out that under empiricism, data is normally more important than theory (we change our theory if it does not "fit" reality). Under criticism values are stronger than data (since we are critically aware of things being inhuman, warlike, unfair, etc), and in constructivism values and theories are about equally strong.

However, if we emphasize that constructivism is at least as important as any other part of the process, we have an idea of a potential, preferred (not just extrapolated or foreseen) world. That is what does the trick, so to speak. Instead of changing our theories (and partly, therefore, also our visions) when they don't "fit" the data from reality, *we may strive to change reality to fit our visions, a potential future desired by us all through dialogue*. A good theory is not the one that accounts correctly for empirical reality but the one that *also* enables us to see and work for the realization of a desirable future (see Fig. 15).

But this is just a model of how we may perceive of an action theory. What is the process of social change like? Based on elements from planning

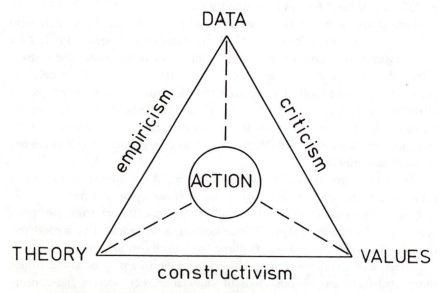

Figure 15. Relationship between theory, data, values, and action.

theory, strategic thinking, mobilization and revolution theory, future research and world order model thinking, we may present the following "classical" stages.

1. *Problem awareness.* There is an increasing awareness that something is going wrong. Analyses are carried out, causes of the problems identified, public discussion takes place, and we arrive collectively at the conclusion that "something must be done."
2. *Evaluation of the foreseen future.* Present tendencies are extrapolated, likely consequences are analyzed under various time perspectives. What is possible? What is likely to happen? Time and space, scenarios under various assumptions are described. There are gaming, historical analogies, and simulations placed before us. "Dystopia"—the non-desirable future is described. We must avoid the catastrophe!
3. *Development of images of desired, preferred, potential "futures."* What do the preferred worlds look like—goals, values, alternatives. Ideas, proposals, fantasies, values, norms, brainstorms, emotions, hopes are given a free play. After a period of "wild thinking" we try to arrive at a synthesis, focusing on a number of futures that we try, then, to describe in details. We identify negative and positive aspects of each and look for compatibilities. In other words, what does the "realistic utopia" (eutopia) look like and how do we communicate it?
4. *Evaluation of alternatives.* What new conflicts can we envisage? What is realizable in the short, medium, and long-term perspective? How sure are we that the preferred futures are "better" than the present? What could go wrong? What kinds of opposition will the struggle for alternatives meet? Finally, we choose one alternative, one type of solution to the problem facing us. However, we remain flexible enough to revise the proper solution if new information or better ideas justify it.
5. *Strategy.* Who (actors) are going to do (activity) what (goals), why (analysis) when (time), where (space), how (resources)? How far can we go when (tactics)? At whose expense (new conflict potential) and under what circumstances (how to defend the change process itself)? In short, this is the phase in which the operational plan is developed.
6. *Mobilization.* The change is set in motion according to the plan. Objective parties become subjective actors, old structures are revealed as obsolete, polarization appears, tension, confrontation are imminent. The first stages of a real conflict develop.
7. *Struggle.* All kinds of nonviolent actions start—talks, negotiations,

appeals, demonstrations. Parallel structures, the seeds of the "new" to come are sown. In other words, a "peak point" in the conflict with the "old" world is reached. This is the turning point, the critical phase in which change is likely to break through—or stop.

8. *Appearance of the new reality or solution.* The old world gives way, conflicts are played out on all levels. The potential future unfolds like a flower. A new awareness emerges together, of course, with a lot of new problems. Adjustments are being made—and a new enthusiasm carries the developments further. Those in charge of the old system are given new jobs, reschooled or what not—but brought into and offered a role in the new situation.

9. *Evaluation.* What does the new reality look like compared with what we planned, with the model. Does it really solve the problem, do we really avoid the catastrophe? Is it really any better? Control mechanisms are developed to guard the falling-back-to-the-past tendency in many change processes. What new problems are we facing now? What must still be improved on? To which degree did we manage to achieve our top goals and priorities?

10. *Starting all over again* . . . but at a higher level and with a new awareness. Life is recognized as a permanent change process, nothing ever becomes perfect (dull). Humankind is always on the move, and so are we. Peace—if this is our "problem"—is a process, never a perfect attainable situation.

Although we have numbered the stages in this process, there is no such "perfect" and ordered sequence to it all. Actual political change processes are full of "jumps" back and forth. All we can try to do is to be analytical and systematic in our attempts to outline concrete strategies and then be constantly aware that schemes like this are there to indicate how far we always are from them!

However, this is not the same as maintaining that we don't need strategies or theories. Among the reasons why the world does not change in the peaceful direction as rapidly as we would like to see is the very ignorance of theories, models, and carefully worked out concepts of change strategies. Expectations are wildly unrealistic; we become disillusioned and give up, sometimes simply because we never thought through *how* to contribute to change in the direction of our preferred worlds. This applies to "outward" social change as well as to the "inward" psychological change, discussed under premise 2.

It is very difficult to point out where and when change can most effectively start. It depends! So many people are used to expecting that their governments know. We don't think they do; some are not even interested in bringing about change. It is our deepest conviction that governments and other power-holders will not change unless there is a strong, well-informed, and critical-constructive widespread opinion.

As peace researcher Robert Johansen has pointed out, to expect current military and civilian leaders to take the initiative in changing the present system would be as illusory as if people in the nineteenth century had expected the slave traders and owners to take the initiative in abolishing slavery!

To work for peace often means doing both/and. It is important to influence your politicians and make nation-states move in the right direction. But it is at least equally important to work "above" the governments, for example, directly with people in other countries, and "below" in all types of networks and communications. This is the *transnational* perspective. In our actions we try to work through ordinary channels, but we try, also, to develop all the softer ties through grass-root organizations, international organizations, movements, professional groups, individuals, friendship ties, and so on. The peoples' diplomacy, supplementing the governments' diplomacy.

Whenever we criticize, we try also to be constructive. It is important to discuss priorities, but it is very important also to understand that there is no single right way of doing things.

Many people tend to believe that there must be a "program," a plan of action. We are doubtful about that. Centralizing everything into one program runs the risk of marginalizing creative people and watering down ideas to compromises. Often programs are developed and power struggles start about positions or the right interpretation of the program. The real issues and the immense task in front of us slide into the background and minor tensions take the energy and attention of too many. It already happens here and there in the peace movements.

But isn't it important to gather, unite on single issues, be many and strong? Isn't it important to get many signatures or be thousands in demonstrations? Of course! But is it more important to gather 100,000 people in the capital than 10,000 in each of the ten largest cities? We doubt it; perhaps there is a very vital danger in "imitating" the force or power thinking of the "old" militarized world. Maybe the work for peace much more clearly should embody "a new way of thinking," for instance, the idea of many small drops of water scooping out the stone. The point in this image is that there is no *need* for force centralization.

Where to start? So many programs say first things first, and everybody quarrels about what is most important! Top-heavy organizations develop, the creativity and enthusiasm of the masses are lost. Because of the wish or urge to centralize, be powerful, break through, we believe that this mirrors a very actor-oriented, short-term, and single-issue perception of the work for peace.

We see the work for peace as a social movement, a cultural, long-term renewal, something sedimenting a new set of human values in all corners of our own society and in other Cultures. We see the ideal peace worker as *any* human being, not only as a grassroot organizer, a diplomat, or a soldier. We don't think that peace is for the few. Everybody has a role to play in carrying the seeds, the water drops into even the smallest crevices in society.

We tend to come to conclusion, based on some years of theoretical and practical experience, that there are no experts in this field. There is no single expertise by means of which we can gain the necessary and sufficient insights to help humanity out of the calamity. It will only be done *through a universal, pluralistic, reorientation of the ways in which all of us think and act, a new "fundamentalism" concerning peace. No matter our social rank, race, nationality, ideology, we move toward a transformation and turn survival and a humane existence forever into a great cross-cultural civilizing mission. A global ethic of care, caring about a peaceful existence.*

Is it comparable to anything we witnessed before? We may think of it as a transformation as great as that from the feudal age to modern capitalist formations in Europe at the end of the Middle Ages. We may think of it as equally significant as the change from agricultural to industrial society. We may compare it to the abolition of slavery, absolute monarchy, or formal colonialism.

We talk, in other words, about a change from a militaristic culture to a peace culture, in our minds, collective thinking and action and in our images of a humane world future.

We believe that a well-considered movement for peace gives everybody who wants a chance to contribute. Because everyone of us is a force for peace. With this in our mind it is fair to say, in conclusion, that we may lose much if we fail, namely, the world as we know it up to here and now. But if we succeed, if we win peace we are winning something infinitely greater and more beautiful; this here and now plus everything it could become in the future.

25

What Can We Do?

Most books on security and peace end up with lists of what to do. They suggest nuclear-free zones, freezes, reduction in arsenals and military expenditures, nonintervention regimes, arms control initiatives, and the like. By such proposals they orient our thinking toward governments and formal politics, toward a level at which we ourselves are not responsible, at least not in a direct manner.

Basically this is fine, but it confers responsibilities unto others: our representatives or experts, other countries or international organizations. We think it is also important to try to list some concrete suggestions as to what each one of us, and the small groups and communities we are close to, can do, since we have argued that peace is not just a matter of security politics, not just a question of what others do or don't do, but, also, is about development of the whole society reaching from each one of us to a global cultural change. Toward a peace culture.

Individual action in everyday life will not automatically bring about a lasting world peace. But only human beings can do what we have suggested with reference to Albert Einstein, namely, change our ways of thinking, become the programmers ourselves.

Modern political and economic systems are so huge and often so impersonal that we must constantly try to regain the importance of individual responsibility and participation. Too often we get the question: But what can I do? Is there any chance of reaching the decision makers? Do they care if we do reach them? Is it important what ordinary human beings do in this world?

These questions reflect a high degree of alienation in a culture that is, after all, not so very democratic as we like to believe it is. Of course, it is part of the struggle for peace to appeal to governments and others "up there."

But there is also an important dimension in thinking and acting in a new way in the smaller settings of which we are all parts.

Peace politics, after all, is also a matter of seeing private and collective ethics and action as part of one continuum. Following are some modest proposals.

1. We can make peace and war prevention the primary topic of conversations with family members, friends, colleagues, as well as strangers we meet. We should not criticize or confront them, but ask them for their own views. We can help people to think more deeply by raising challenging questions. We can inform them about our own conclusions if they are interested, but should not try to force our views on them, since that tends to backfire.

2. We should get as much information as we can about the problems of war and peace from as many different sources as possible. We should try to understand how people think who reach the opposite conclusions from ours.

3. We can join peace organizations and other popular movements for change. Information about local organizations may often be obtained from schools, churches, labor unions, newsletters, journals, local TV, and such (A list of 7,000 U.S. peace groups can be found in Conetta 1988).

4. We can write letters to newspapers. Small local papers are often more likely to reprint letters to the editor than big national papers.

5. We can establish contacts with reporters and people in the media. If we are able to capture their interest, we can reach many people.

6. With some preparation, we can speak to groups and at public events. It is important to open dialogues publicly with people of different opinions.

7. We should not feel intimidated because we do not have access to classified information. The most important issues about war and peace do not deal with technical details about weapons, but with human nature. We should be eager to receive additional information and to be corrected. We must not be afraid of criticism, but see it as a starting point for an exchange of views. We may try to identify both where we agree and where we disagree with someone. If we remain silent, of course, others will decide for us, and not necessarily always the way we would have wished.

8. We can write to elected representatives, call them by phone, or visit their offices. Personal meetings are very important in an increasingly

anonymous society with long distances between rulers and ruled. A supportive comment when they have taken a step in the right direction is often more effective than an angry letter, which has a tendency only to create negative energy or end up in the wastebasket. Constructive proposals are often better than protests and criticism. We can also campaign for representatives whose positions are close to our own. By speaking to candidates for public offices, we may be able to persuade them to adopt some of our ideas and proposals. Confidence-building at the personal level is important.

9. We can establish friendly personal contact with people in other countries, particularly in countries with which our country has tense relations or a conflict. We can also seek friendships with people in our own country who belong to different groups, such as a different political party, different social class, different profession, ethnic group, or race.

10. We can provide assistance to people who suffer from war, and inform others about their suffering.

11. We can take steps toward limiting the causes of war, by contributing voluntarily to the removal of injustices. If we do so visibly, we may inspire others to do the same.

12. It is simply important that we keep working persistently, taking one step after another, and never give up. Our humanity and survival depend on it. We should do something for peace *every day*.

13. We can seek not only to analyze problems here and now but also anticipate long-term consequences of certain trends, that is, argue on behalf of the potential future, so to speak. It is important to train our capacity to see solutions that others have difficulty in finding, perhaps drawing extensively on our own experience from participating in conflicts and problem solving.

14. We may try to mobilize funds from many parts of society and create confidence with others that there is nothing strange or dangerous in working for or supporting peace activities. Each of us should contribute according to our abilities, e.g. for example, to a peace tax or foundations, so that our message can reach a wider audience in an attractive form. Remember, sometimes people do think that the medium is the message. It is important always to try to reach those who are not yet aware of the problems or who don't think they have anything to bring or who are of the opposite view.

15. We can try, from time to time, to evaluate—perhaps with the help of friends and colleagues—whether our own personal conduct, work,

and lifestyle is perceived as compatible with the greater cause we are working for. We must take care not to exploit others, for instance, in our work for peace and justice. And we should try to improve on our own ability to foresee, solve, or live with conflicts.

16. We can try all the time to raise new issues and solutions. It will help to keep peace politics alive, it will attract new people and attitudes, and enrich our own perspectives. And it may challenge the "monopoly" of the experts or power circles since it brings into focus issues where they will also be learners.

17. We can try always to state our motives and aims in a clear and open manner so that our nonviolent activities can never be misunderstood by others. It means studying carefully those who have written about and practiced wisely methods of conflict-resolution, negotiation-strategy, and nonviolent action as a political strategy. It is important not to back down from one's own goals or plans, but carry them through as a supplement to those of the establishment. Much is to be learned here from Gandhi—as usual!

18. Since it is important not to end up being disillusioned, bitter, or defeatist, we can try to define goals and methods in such a way that we do not become excessively vulnerable. If we aim broadly, we may often be able to gain support from someone, and if we "loose the battle" on one issue, there may be several others to switch to and "win" on. The psychological dimension is most important. And so is patience! We should avoid all actions that lead to "all-or-nothing" or "now-or-never" or "either-or" positions.

19. We can try to travel to faraway parts of the world and get acquainted with lifestyles, cultures, and ways of thinking that are non-Western, or different in various respects from our own. The purpose should not be to "go native" but to be open and inspired in our own work back home. Things can be seen and done in *so* many ways, and looking at our own culture "from outside," at least for a while, is a humanly and politically rewarding experience. A way of understanding better what it means to think globally.

20. We can try to think less than usual in terms of how to organize things and raise funds, and start out *doing* things. It takes very little to set up a study circle, read and discuss important literature, and invite people who know more than you do to begin with. Reserve, let's say, one hour per week for some kind of knowledge accumulation and/or being together with like-minded, concerned people like yourself.

You will soon experience that there is not that much reason to be impressed with the knowledge or wisdom of the average decision maker. Try to see yourself as an expert on your own security, local society, and visions of the future, and share it with others.

21. Although peace thinking and peace activism are about serious issues, we can try to introduce humor, play, and life-optimistic activites into them. We should take care not to be too serious or even pompous. Try to remember that peace means life, fun, development, happiness, trust, love, friendship, visions, self-realization, hope. Peace is about preserving our wonderful planet with all its potentials and rich humanity. What we do for peace here and now should, ideally, be an expression of such a perspective, sowing the seeds for it.

22. Write down your personal visions, your images of both the bad and the desirable future. Share it with others and elaborate on the constructive elements. We should not daydream away the "realities" of the present, but if we make use of our hopes and share them in a concrete manner, we may stimulate and support others. The worst form of repression is the one that succeeds in making us believe that there are no alternatives to what we do now. We can choose to go to lots of conferences and meetings about nuclear issues and foreign policy, but we can also drop just one of them and join a "future workshop" or "imaging the future" symposium. We might learn something that power-holders don't know that they need!

23. We can prepare ourselves for tough conflicts in some respects. Since the work for peace and nonviolence can, in some countries, imply that you are thrown our of your job or don't get a promotion, it may be wise to plan your life on income from more than one source, so you are not vulnerable to the "rules" of the employer (i.e., stopping your activity) or to being kicked out. Local support groups of friends and family are important, but so is a down-to-earth thing as an income, perhaps combined with a lifestyle that is not too demanding and therefore compatible with global norms. In other words, we can prepare a kind of self-defense and self-reliance and be useful to others in our own micro-world, rather much as we have argued in the book concerning larger units. Working for a peace culture in a militaristic-nuclearist culture is to adapt to conflict as a lifestyle. Why not try to turn it into an important learning process?

When you have a glass of fresh water, half-full, in front of you, you may take one of two general views of the situation: (1) Oh, I have already drunk half of it and there is only this little left—how sad! or (2) Wonderful, this first half was refreshing, I look forward to enjoying what is left!

We believe that the second approach is the most humanly rewarding and the one that will release most constructive energy. Working for peace is to see possibilities, openings, new ideas where a militaristic culture and mindset closes off.

Please, therefore, write to us.

What do you do at the personal level for peace, how did you come to work and think this way. What or who inspired you and have you inspired others?

Write and tell what you would suggest to others to do, whether they are individuals, organizations, or governments. What are your own peace proposals and how do you define peace yourself?

Authors write the books, and perhaps they are asked to talk about them and they get reviews. Those are, of course, important responses. But we would also be happy *to help establish a broad-based discussion and idea-sharing network by means of which we could all develop our constructive ways of thinking about peace.*

Since this book was published in the Federal Republic of Germany in 1987, in Denmark and in the United States in 1988, and is to be published in Japan in 1989, there is a possibility of starting a truly global dialogue. Depending on the response, we might be able to publish your responses and have them shared by all in the network and outside in the media for instance.

Please send your thoughts, ideas, proposals, points of view, or whatever you feel like to: TFF, Vegagatan 25, 223 57 Lund, Sweden.

References

Abt, Clark C. *A Strategy for Terminating Nuclear War*. Colorado 1985.

Afheldt, Eckart. Veiteidigung ohne Selbstmord—Vorschlag für den Einsatz *einer* leichten Infanterie, in Carl-Friedrich von Weizäcker: *Praxis der defensiven Verteidigung*, Hameln 1984.

Afheldt, Horst. *Verteidigung und Frieden*. München 1976.

———. *Defensive Verteidigung*. Reinbek bei Hamburg 1983.

———. *Atomkrieg—Das Verhängnis einer Politik mit militärischen Mitteln*, München/ Wien 1984.

Alford, Jonathan. *NATO's manpower problem*. Contribution to the Annual conference on Non-Nuclear War in Europe. Groningen 1984 (manuskript).

Altenburg, Wolfgang, and Karl Feldmeyer. Die Risikogemeinschaft darf nicht zerstört werden—Ich habe grosse Sorge wegen SDI, *Frankfurter Allgemeine Zeitung*, November 29, 1985.

Alternative Defence Commission (ed). *Defence Without the Bomb. The Report of the Alternative Defence Commission*. London/New York 1983.

Alvarez, A. *The Savage God—A Study of Suicide*. London 1971.

Ås, Berit. On female culture—An attempt to formulate a theory of women's solidarity and action, *Acta Sociologica*. Copenhagen. 2–3, 1975.

———. A five-dimensional model for change: Contradictions and feminist consciousness, *Women's Studies International Quarterly*. nr. 1, 1981.

———. A materialistic view of men's and women's attitudes to war. *Women's International Studies Quarterly*, nr. 3–4. 1982.

Axelrod, Robert. *The Evolution of Cooperation*. New York 1984.

Baker, Miller, Jean. *Towards a New Psychology of Women*. Boston 1976.

Barnet, Richard. *Real Security*. New York 1981.

Barth, Volker: *Bundeswehr und Öffentlichkeit—Zum Legitimitätsrückhalt des Bundeswehr in Zeitvergleich* (unpublished manuskript). Hamburg 1985.

Bastian, Gert. *Frieden Schaffen! Gedanken zur Sicherheitspolitik*. München 1983.

Baumol, William J. *Welfare Economics and the Theory of the State*. London 1952.

———. *Superfairness: Applications and Theory*. Cambridge, MA 1986.

Beaufre, A. *Introduction à la Stratégie*, Paris 1963, in German, *Totale Kriegskunst im Frieden. Einführung in die Strategie*. Berlin 1963.

————. *Dissuasion et Stratègie*, Paris 1964, in German, *Abschreckung und Strategie*. Berlin 1964.

Berger, Peter, and Thomas Luckman. *The Social Construction of Reality*. London 1966.

Bettelheim, Bruno. *Surviving and Other Essays*. New York 1979.

Beyond War: *A New Way of Thinking*. Palo Alto. CA 1985.

Bigler, Rolf R. *Der einsame Soldat—Eine soziologische Deutung der militärischen Organisation*. Frauenfeld 1983.

Blake, Nigel, and Kay Pole, (eds). *Dangers of Deterrence—Philosophers on Nuclear Strategy*. London 1983.

————. *Objections to Nuclear Defence—Philosophers on Nuclear Strategy*. London 1984.

Bohm, David. *Wholeness and the Implicate Order*. London/California 1985.

Born, Wolf-Ruthart. *Die Offene Stadt, Schutzzonen und Guerillakämpfer, Regelungen zum Schulz der Zivilbevölkerung in Kriegszeiten—Unter besonderer Berücksichtigung des am 10.6.1977 von der Diplomatischen Konferenz in Genf verabschiedeten I. Zusatsprotokolls zu den Genfer Konventionen*. Berlin 1978.

Boulding, Kenneth. *Human Betterment*. London/California 1985.

Bowlby, John. *Loss—Sadness and Depression*. Middlesex/New York 1980.

Bracken, Paul. *The Command and Control of Nuclear Forces*. New Haven 1983.

Brock-Utne, Birgit. *Educating for Peace—A Feminist Perspective*. Oxford/New York 1985.

Brodie, Bernard. *The Absolute Weapon*. New York, 1946.

Brossolet, Guy. *Das Ende der Schlacht* in *Verteidigung ohne Schlacht*. München 1976.

Browne, Malcolm. The star wars spinoff, *New York Times Magazine*, August 24, 1986.

Buchbender, Bühl, Quaden. *Sicherheit und Frieden. Handbuch der weltweiten sicherheitspolitischen Verflechtungen*. Herford 1983, 1985.

Bundesminister der Verteidigung (ed). *Weißbuch 1983 Zur Sicherheit der Bundesrepublik Deutschland*.

Bundy, McGeorge, George F. Kennan, Robert S. McNamara, and Gerard Smith. Nuclear weapons and the Atlantic alliance, *Foreign Affairs*, 60, No. 4, 1982, 753–68.

Burke, Peter (ed). *The New Cambridge Modern History—XIII Companion Volume*. London/New York 1979.

Buzan, Barry: *People, States and Fear—The National Security Problem in International Relations*. Sussex 1983.

Capra, Fritjof. *The Turning Point—Science, Society and the Rising Culture*. London 1982.

Catudal, Honoré Mark. *Nuclear Deterrence—Does It Deter?* Berlin 1985.

Chilton, Paul (ed). *Language and the Nuclear Arms Debate—Nukespeak Today*. London 1985.

Clark, Jan. *Limited Nuclear War—Political Theory and War Conventions*. Oxford 1982.

Clausewitz, Carl von. *Vom Kriege*, Bonn 1980/*On War* (London, 1908). Middlesex 1971.

Cohen, Avner, and Steven Lee (eds). *Nuclear Weapons and the Future of Humanity*. Totowa, NJ 1986.

Conetta, Carl (ed.) *Peace Resource Book. A comprehensive Guide to the Issues, Organizations and Literature 1988–1989*. Cambridge, MA 1988.

Dach, Hans von. *Der totale Widerstand, Kleinkriegsanleitung für jedermann*. Biel 1958.

Darnton, Geoffrey. The concept of peace, *Proceedings of the International Peace Research Association Fourth Conference (IPRA)*. Oslo 1973.

Deudney, Daniel. *Whole Earth Security—Toward a Geopolitics of Peace*. Washington, DC 1984.

Deutsch, Morton. The prevention of World War III: A psychological perspective, *Political Psychology*, 1, 1983. 3–31.

Die Grünen (ed). *Entrüstet Euch—Wir wollen leben. Analysen zur atomaren Bedrohung—Wege zum Frieden*. Bonn 1983.

DOD, Department of Defense. *Report to the Congress on the Strategic Defense Initiative*. Washington, DC 1985.

Duncan, Ronald. *The Writings of Gandhi*. Oxford 1951, 1971.

Easlea, Brian. *Science and Sexual Oppression—Patriarchy's Confrontation with Woman and Nature*. London 1981.

———. *Fathering the Unthinkable—Masculinity, Scientists and the Nuclear Arms Race*. London 1983.

Ebert, Theodor. *Soziale Verteidigung—Historische Erfahrungen und Grundzüge der Strategie*. Waldkirch 1981.

———. Ziviler Widerstand im besetzten Gebiet, in Carl-Friedrich von Weizsaecker (ed). *Die Praxis der defensiven Verteidigung*. Hameln 1984.

Enloe, Cynthia. *Does Khaki Become you? The Militarisation of Women's Lives*. London 1983.

Erikson, Erik H. *Gandhi's Truth*. New York 1969.

Falk, Richard, Gabriel Kolko, and Robert Jay Lifton (eds). *Crimes of War—A legal, political-documentary and psychological inquiry into responsibility of leaders, citizens and soliders for criminal acts in war*. New York 1971.

Feldman, Josef. Eléments de la stratégie suisse—V. La Protection civile, *Revue Militaire Suisse*, 129, No. 9, 366–374.

Ferencz, Benjamin B., in cooperation with Ken Keyes, Jr. *Planethood. The Key to Your Survival and Prosperity*. Coos Bay, OR 1988.

Fesefeldt, Joachim. Die nukleare Schwelle—Mythos oder Wirklichkeit?, in Werner Kaltefleiter (ed), *Libertas optima rerum*, Schriften des Instituts für Sicherheitspolitik an der Christian-Albrechts-Universität zu Kiel. Herford 1984.

Fischer, Dietrich. Invulnerability without threat—The Swiss concept of general defence, *Journal of Peace Research*, 3, 1982.

———. *Preventing War in the Nuclear Age*. Totowa, NJ 1984.

———. Weapons technology and the intensity of arms races, *Conflict Management and Peace Science*, 1, 1984.

———. *No First Use of Nuclear Weapons*. Santa Barbara, CA 1986. Reprinted in David Krieger and Frank Kelly (eds). *Waging Peace in the Nuclear Age. Ideas for Action*. Santa Barbara, CA, 1988, pp. 125–42.

———. Dissuasion: toward an active peace policy, in Avner Cohen and Steven Lee (eds), *Nuclear Weapons and the Future of Humanity*. Totowa NJ 1986.

Fischer, Louis. *The Life of Mahatma Gandhi*. New York 1950.

Fisher, Roger and William Ury. *Getting to Yes—Negotiating Agreement Without Giving In*. Boston 1981.

Forschungsgruppe SALSS. *Spezialisierung auf die Defensive: Einführung und Quellensammlung—Ein Übersichtsgutachten* (manuscript). Bonn 1985.

Fox, Michael Allen and Leo Groarke (eds). *Nuclar War—Philosophical Perspectives*. New York-Bern-Frankfurt 1985.

Frei, Daniel, In cooperation with Catrina Christian. *Risks of Unintentional Nuclear War*. United Nations Institute for Disarmament Research (UNIDIR), Geneva 1982.

Frei, Daniel. *Friedenssicherung durch Gewaltverzicht? Eine kritische Überprüfung alternativer Verteidigungskonzepte*. Bern 1983.

———. Neue Überlegungen im Licht von Tschernobyl, *Neue Zürcher Zeitung*, 6. Juni 1986.

French, Marilyn. *Beyond Power—On Women, Men and Morals*. London 1985.

Friberg, Mats and Johan Galtung, (eds). *Alternativen*. Göteborg 1986.

Gallois, Pierre M. Muß die Bevölkerung geschützt werden? *Truppenpraxis*, 2, 1985.

Galtung, Johan. On the strategy of nonmilitary defence: some proposals and problems, in Bartels (ed). *Peace and Justice—Unity or a Dilemma*? Nijmegen 1968, also in Galtung, *Essays in Peace Research*. Vol. 2, Copenhagen 1975.

———. *Peace: Research, Education, Action—Essays in Peace Research*, Vol. I, Copenhagen 1975.

———. *Methodology and Ideology—Theory and Methods of Social Research*, Vol. I, Copenhagen 1977.

———. *The True Worlds—A Transnational Perspective*. New York 1980.

———. *There Are Alternatives. Four Roads to Peace and Security*. Nottingham 1984.

——— and Arne Naess, *Gandhis Politiske Etikk*. Oslo 1955.

Gati, Charles. Soviet empire: Alive but not well, *Problems of Communism*, 2, 1985.

Gay, William C. *Philosophy, Nuclear War and Disarmament—A Starter Kit*. The University of North Carolina at Charlotte, Dept. of Philosophy, Charlotte, NC 1985.

Generale für Frieden und Abrüstung (ed). *Sicherheit für Westeuropa—Alternative Sicherheits- und Militärpolitik*. Hamburg 1985.

Gerber, Johannes. Die Bundeswehr im Nordatlantischen Bündnis. *in Die Bundes-wehr—eine Gesamtdarstellung*, Bnd 2. Regensburg 1985.

Gilligan, Carol. *In a Different Voice—Psychological Theory and Women's Development*. Massachusetts/London 1982.

Glover, Johathan. *Causing Death and Saving Lives*. Middlesex/New York 1977.

Glucksmann, André. *Le discours de la guerre. Théorie et stratégie*. Paris 1967.

———. *La force du vertige*. Paris 1983.

Gorbachev, Mikhail. *Perestroika. New Thinking for Our Country and the World*. New York, 1987.

———. Press conference in Geneva, *Soviet News*, Novemeber 27, 1985.

———. Session of the USSR Supreme Soviet, *Soviet News*, November 27, 1985. Both sources quoted in Stephen Shenfield, The militarization of space through Soviet eyes, in Stephen Kirby and Gordon Robson (eds), *The Militarization of Space*, Boulder, CO 1987.

Gordon, Michael R. Nuclear star wars, *National Journal*. 25. 1985.

Grimshaw, Jean. *Feminist Philosophers—Women's Perspectives on Philosophical Traditions*. Sussex 1986.

Günther, Ingo and Günter Vollmer. *Verteidigung statt Vernichtung! Wege aus der atomaren Konfrontation*. Starnberg 1983.

Hahlweg, Werner. *Guerilla—Krieg ohne Fronten*. Stuttgart 1968.

Halkes, Catharina J. *To a New Image of Man Based on Feminist Theology* (manuskript). Groningen 1977.

Hannig, Norbert. *Abschreckung durch Konventionelle Waffen—Das David-Goliath-Prinzip*. Berlin 1984.

Hardin, Russel, John Mearsheimer, Gerald Dworkin, and Roberg Goodin (eds). *Nuclear Deterrence—Ethics and Strategy*. Chicago, London 1963/1985.

Henderson, Hazel. The warp and the weft—The coming synthesis of eco-philosophy and eco-feminism, *Development—Seeds of Change*, 4, 1984.

Hillman, James. *Suicide and the Soul*. Dallas 1964.

Hook, Glen D. *Language and Politics—The Security Discourse in Japan and the United States*. Kursio/Syuppan, Japan 1986.

Huber, Reiner K. and Hans W. Hofmann. *On Reactive Defence Options—A Comparative Systems Analysis of Alternatives for the Initial Defence against the First Strategic Echelon of the Warsaw Pact in Central Europe*. München 1984.

Hueber, A. Friedrich. *Soziale Verteidigung—Chance oder Illusion? Eine kritische Untersuchung* (manuskript) Graz 1985.

Humphrey, Nicolas and Robert Jay Lifton (eds). *In a Dark Time*. London/Boston 1984.

Huth, Paul and Bruce Russett, What makes deterrence work? Cases from 1900 to 1980. *World Politics*, Vol. 36. 4, 1984.

IISS (International Institute for Strategic Studies). *Strategic Survey 1984–85*. London 1985.

Irving. David. Von *Guernica bis Vietnam—Die Leiden der Zivilbevölkerung im modernen Krieg*. Müchen 1982.

Jaspers. Karl. *The Atom Bomb and the Future of Man*. Chicago/London 1963.

Jervis, Robert. *Perception and Misperception in International Politics*. Princeton, NJ 1976.

Jochheim, Gernot. *Die Gewaltfreie Aktion—Idee und Methoden, Vorbilder und Wirkungen*. Hamburg 1984.

Johansen, Robert C. Building a new international security order: Policy guidelines and recommendations, in Carolyn M. Stephenson, *Alternative Methods for International Security*. Washington, DC 1982.

Jonas, Hans. *The Imperative of Responsibility—In Search of an Ethics for the Technological Age*. Chicago/London 1984.

Jones, Lynne (ed). *Keeping the Peace—Women's Peace Handbook*. London 1983.

Journal of Peace Research 2:1984. Special Issue on Alternative Defense, Oslo.

Kalckreuth, Jürg von. *Zivile Verteidigung im Rahmen der Gesamtverteidigung—Aufgaben und Nachholbedarf der Bundesrepublik Deutschland*. Baden-Baden 1985.

Katz, Nathan (ed). *Buddhist and Western Psychology*. Boulder 1983.

Keller, Evelyn Fox. *Reflections on Gender and Science*. New Haven/London 1985.

King-Hall, Stephen. *Defence in the Nuclear Age*. London 1958.

Kissinger, Henry. The future of NATO, *Washington Quarterly*, Vol II, 4, 1979.

Klumper, Anton A. Social Defense in the Netherlands 1940–45, in Schmid, Alex P. Social Defense and Soviet Military Power. Leiden 1985.

Koestenbaum, Peter. *Is There and Answer to Death?* New York 1982.

Kübler-Ross, Elisabeth. *On Death and Dying*. New York 1969.

———. *To Live Until We Say Good-Bye*. New York 1976.

La Rocque, Gene and Hylke Tromp (eds). *Nuclear War in Europe*. Groningen 1982.

Lackey, Douglas P. *Moral Principles and Nuclear Weapons*. New Jersey 1984.

Lessing, Doris. *Shikasta—Re Colonised Planet 5—Canopus in Argos: Archives*. London 1979.

Liddle-Hart, Basil H. Lessons from reistance movements—Guerilla and non-violent, in Adam Roberts, (ed), *The Strategy of Civilian Defence—Non-Violent Resistance to Aggression*. London 1967.

Lifton, Robert Jay. *The Broken Connection—On Death and the Continuity of Life*. New York 1979.

——— and Richard Falk. *Indefensible Weapons—The Political and Psychological Case Against Nuclearism*. New York 1982.

Luckham, Robin. Arms and culture, *Current Research on Peace and Violence*, 1, 1984, Tampere Peace Research Institute.

Lutz, Dieter S. (ed). *Kollektive Sicherheit und Europa—eine Alternative—Beiträge zur Utopie einer neuen Friedens- und Sicherheitsprogrammatik—Pro und Contra*. Baden-Baden 1985.

————. *Strukturelle Nichtangriffsfähigkeit*. Hamburg 1988.

Löser, Jochen. *Weder rot noch tot—Überleben ohne Atomkrieg—eine sicherheitspolitische Alternative*. Müchen 1981.

McAllister, Pam (ed). *Reweaving the Web of Life—Feminism and Non-Violence*. Philadelphia 1982.

Mackie, John. *Ethics—Inventing Right and Wrong*. Middlesex 1977.

Mao Tse-tung. *Selected Military Writings*. Peking 1963.

Marsella, Anthony, George De Vos, Francis L.K. Hsu, (eds). *Culture and Self—Asian and Western Perspectives*. London/New York 1985.

Maslow, Abraham. *The Psychology of Science: A Reconnaissance*. New York 1966.

Mechtersheimer, Alfred. *Zeitbombe NATO—Auswirkungen der neuen Strategie*. Köln 1984.

Mellon, Christian, Jean-Marie Muller, and Jacques Semelin. *La Dissuassion Civile*. Paris 1985.

Merchant, Carolyn. *The Death of Nature—Women, Ecology and the Scientific Revolution*. San Fransciso/London 1980.

Mez, Lutz. *Ziviler Widerstand in Norwegen—Untersuchung zu Organisation und Form der sozialen Bewegung in Norwegen unter besonderer Berückschtigung von Konzepten Sozialer Verteidigung*. Frankfurt 1976.

Miller, Alice. *Prisoners of Childhood*. New York 1981.

————. *For Your Own Good: Hidden Cruelty in Child-Rearing and the Roots of Violence*. New York 1985.

————. *Thou Shalt Not Be Aware! Society's Betrayal of the Child*. New York 1986.

Morgan, Patrick M. *Deterrence—A Conceptual Analysis*. Beverley Hills/London 1977.

Müller, Albrecht C. von. *Grundzüge einer europäischen Sicherheitspolitik für die 80er und 90er Jahre*. Max Planck Institut, Müchen 1983.

Murty, Satchidananda, and A.C. Bouquet. *Studies in the Problems of Peace*. Bombay/London/New York 1960.

Nakamura, Hajime (ed. Wiener, Philip P): *Ways of Thinking of Eastern Peoples: India, China, Tibet, Japan*. Honolulu 1964.

Naroll, R., V. H. Bullough, and F. Naroll. *Military Deterrence in History*. New York 1974.

Nisbet, Robert. *Social Change and History—Aspects of the Western Theory of Development*. London and New York 1969.

Noddings, Nel. *Caring: A Feminine Approach to Ethics and Moral Education*. Berkeley 1984.

Noll, Pete. *On Dying and Death* (in German). Zürich 1984.

Nolte, Heinrich. *Graf Schlieffens. "Cannae" und Deutschlands "Verlorene Siege"* (manuskript). Detmold 1984.

Nolte, Wilhelm. Autonome Abwehr, in Hans-Heinrich Nolte, and Wilhelm Nolte: *Ziviler Widerstand und Autonome Abwehr*. Baden-Baden 1984.

Nolting, Hans-Peter. *Lernschritte zur Gewaltlosigkeit—Ergebnisse psychologischer Friedensforschung: Krieg, Folter, Unterdrückung und wie man ihnen entgegenwirkt*. Reinbek bei Hamburg 1984.

Øberg, Jan. *To Develop Security and Secure Development* (in Danish). Copenhagen 1983.

————. Deterrence—Punishment, anthropocentrism, patriarchy and absurd theatre. TFF, Lund 1986.

Oesterreichisches Bundeskanzleramt (ed). Landesverteidigungsplan. Wien 1985.

Ofstad, Harald. *Our Weaknesses: Norms and Values in Nazism—and in Ourselves* (in Swedish). Stockholm 1972.

Olson, Mancur. *The Logic of Collective Action*. Cambridge, Mass. 1965.

OTA, see U.S. Congress: Office of Technology Assessment.

Pabst Battin, Margaret. *Ethical Issues in Suicide*. New Jersey, Tokyo, London, 1982.

Palme Commission. *Common Security*. London, 1982.

Pietilä, Hilkka. *Tomorrow Begins Today*. ICDA/ISIS Workshop at Nairobi Forum, Helsinki 1985 (manuscript).

Prigogine, Ilya and Isabelle Stengers, *Order Out of Chaos—Man's Dialogue with Nature*. New York/London 1984.

Rapoport, Anatol. *Fights, Games, and Debates*. Ann Arbor, Michigan 1960.

Rawls, John. *A Theory of Justice*. Cambridge, MA 1971.

Reagan, Ronald. Reagan would internationalize SDI system, *Wireless Bulletin*, nr. 47, 13. March 1985.

Reardon, Betty A: *Sexism and the War System*. New York 1985.

Roberts, Adam. *The Strategy of Civilian Defence—Non-violent Resistance to Aggression*. London 1967.

————. *Nations in Arms: The Theory and Practice of Territorial Defence*. London 1976 (revised 1986).

Rummel, R. J. *Understanding Conflict and War: The Just Peace*. Beverley Hills and London 1981.

SAS: see *Studiengruppe Alternative Sicherheitspolitik*.

Schell, Jonathan. *The Fate of the Earth*. New York 1982.

————. *The Abolition*. New York 1984.

Schilling, Hans-Jürgen. Zum Flüchtlingsproblem in kriegerischen Konflikten, in *Das Parlament—Beilage: Aus Politik und Zeitgeschichte*, 8:1981, Bonn.

Schmid, Alex P. *Social Defence and Soviet Military Power: An Inquiry into the Relevance of an Alternative Defence Concept*. Report from the Center for the Study of Conflict. University of Leiden. Leiden 1985.

Schumacher, E. F. *A Guide for the Perplexed*. London 1977.

Schwarz, Urs. *The Eye of the Hurricane: Switzerland in World War II*. Boulder, CO 1982.

Sharp, Gene. *The Politics of Nonviolent Action*, (3 vols). Boston 1973.

————. *Gandhi as a Political Strategist*. Boston 1979.

————. *Social Power and Political Freedom*. Boston 1980.

————. *National Security through Civilian-Based Defense*. Omaha 1970/1985.

————. *Making Europe Unconquerable. The Potential of Civilian-Based Deterrence and Defence*. London 1985.

Sherif, Muzafer and Carolyn Sherif. *Social Psychology*. New York 1969.

————, G. Harvey, B. White, W. Hood, and C. Sherif. *Intergroup Conflict and Cooperation—The Robbers Cave Experiment*. University of Oklahoma 1961.

Small, Melvin, and J. David Singer. *Resort to Arms: International and Civil Wars, 1816–1980*. Beverly Hills, CA 1982.

Spannocchi, Emil. Verteidigung ohne Selbstzerstörung, *Verteidigung ohne Schlacht*. München 1976.

Sperry, Roger. *Science and Moral Priority*. Oxford 1983.

Stephenson, Carolyn (ed). *Alternative Methods for International Security*. Washington, D.C. 1982.

Studiengruppe Alternative Sicherheitspolitik (SAS) (ed). *Strukturwandel der Verteidigung—Entwürfe für eine konsequente Defensive*. Opladen 1984.

Szasz, Ferenc Morton. *The Day the Sun Rose Twice*. Albuquerque 1984.

Thompson, Robert. *War in Peace. An Analysis of Warfare Since 1945*. London 1981.

Tinbergen, Jan and Dietrich Fischer. *Warfare and Welfare—Integrating Security Policy into Socio-Economic Policy*. Brighton, England 1987.

Toynbee, Arnold and Daisaku Ikeda: *The Toynbee-Ikeda Dialogue: Man Himself Must Choose*. Tokyo/New York 1976.

Uhle-Wettler, Franz. *Gefechtsfeld Mitteleuropa—Gefahr der Übertechnisierung von Streitkräften*. Gütersloh, 1981.

Unterseher, Lutz. Landstreitkräfte zur Verteidigung der Bunderepublik Deutschland—Ein Modell für die 90er Jahre, in Studiengruppe Alternative Sicherheitspolitik 1984.

U.S. Congress, Office of Technology Assessment. *Anti-Satellite Weapons, Countermeasures and Arms Control* (OTA-ISC-281), and *Ballistic Missile Technologies* (OTA-ISC-254). Washington 1985.

Valle, Ronald S. and Rolf von Eckartsberg (eds). *The Metaphors of Consciousness*. New York/London 1981.

Vetschera, Wolfgang R. Das Theorem der Inkompatibilität—Zur Unvereinbarkeit von atomarer Militärgewalt und fortgeschrittener Gesellschaft in Wolfgang R. Vetschera (ed). *Sicherheitspolitik und Streikräfte in der Legitimitätskrise—Analysen zum Prozeß der Delegitimierung des militärischen im Kernwaffenzeitalter*. Baden-Baden 1983.

Vogt, Wolfgang R. Das Theorem der Inkompatibilität—Zur Unvereinbarkeit von atomarer Militärgewalt und fortgeschrittener Gesellschaft, in: ders. (Hrsg): Sicherheitspolitik und Streitkräfte in der Legitimitätskrise—Analysen zum Prozeß der Delegitimierung des Militärischen im Kernwaffenzeitalter. Baden-Banden 1983.

Waldrop, M. Mitchell. Resolving the star wars software dilemna, *Science*, Vol. 232, May 9, 1986.

Walzer, Michael. *Just and Unjust War—A Moral Argument with Historical Illustrations*. Middlesex 1980.

Watson, Thomas J., Jr. *Can the American Political System Adapt to the Nuclear Era?* Providence 1986.

Weaver, Hank. *Confronting the Big C*. Ontario 1984.

Weizäcker, Carl-Friedrich von. *Wege in der Gefahr—eine Studie über Wirtschaft, Gesellschaft und Kriegsverhütung*. München/Wien 1976.

———— (ed). *Die Praxis der defensiven Verteidigung*. Hameln 1984.

Welwood, John (ed). *Awakening the Heart—East-West Approaches to Psychotherapy and the Healing Relationship*. Boulder 1983.

Wernicke, Joachim and Ingrid Schöll. *Verteidigen statt vernichten—Wege aus der atomaren Falle*. München 1985.

Wilber, Ken. *The Spectrum of Consciousness*. Wheaton/London 1977.

Worchel, Stephen and Joel Cooper. *Understanding Social Psychology*. Homewood, Ill 1983.

Zielonka, Jan. *Civilian Defence Strategies* (manuscript). Straßburg 1985.

Zimmermann, Friedrich (Interior Minister of the FRG). Speech of May 30, 1983, in *Zivilverteidigung* No. 3, 1983, p.5ff.

Index

About the Authors

Dietrich Fischer was born 1941 in Münsingen, Switzerland. After Studies in Mathematics, Physics, Astronomy and Computer Science in Bern and New York he obtained his Ph.D. in Computer Science from New York University in 1976, with a thesis on optimal price strategies for developing countries exporting raw materials. From 1976–86 he taught in the Department of Economics at New York University. He has also been a consultant to various United Nations Agencies on questions of disarmament and development. From 1986–88 he held a Social Science Research Council/MacArthur Foundation Fellowship in International Peace and Security Studies at Princeton University. Now he is an Associate Professor of Computer Science at Pace University in White Plains, New York. He is a founding member of the Exploratory Project on the Conditions of Peace and director of its working group on questions of common security.

His previous books are *Preventing War in the Nuclear Age* (1984) and *Warfare and Welfare: Integrating Security Policy into Socio-Economic Policy* (1987), with Jan Tinbergen. Through speaking and writing, he seeks to promote the concept of an "Active Peace Policy."

Wilhelm Nolte was born 1940 in Zerbst (today in the German Democratic Republic). He is a professional soldier in the German Bundeswehr. After commanding a tank unit, he edited for several years an information service on defense and security matters as a staff-officer. Today he is Director of Documentation at the Military Academy in Hamburg.

Besides a series of articles, lectures and radio interviews on security policy, he has developed the concept of "Autonomous Protection" and presented it in the volume *Civilian Resistance and Autonomous Protection* (in German, 1984) with a historical account of civilian resistance by his brother Hans-Heinrich Nolte, a historian.

Jan Øberg was born 1951 in Arhus, Denmark. He is a sociologist and peace researcher. He got his Ph.D. from the University of Copenhagen with a thesis on "Myths of our Defense." His research work focuses on peace theory, peace policies, socio-economic development in the global context, disarmament and development, and Third World development. For many years he has been the director of the Lund University Peace Research Institute (LUPRI) in Sweden and Secretary of the Danish Peace Foundation in Copenhagen. Together with his wife Christina Spännar, he has founded the Transnational Foundation for Peace and Future Research (TFF) in Lund. He is also a member of several consulting groups for the governments of Denmark and Sweden and of research groups, including the Club of Rome.

His many publications include *To Develop Security and Secure Development—an Essay on Militarism and Peace* (in Danish and Swedish, 1983).

TFF

The Transnational Foundation for Peace and Future Research (TFF) is a private non-profit organization.

TFF wants to make possible quality research on global peace goals such as security, development, transition to nonviolence and related questions.

The founding of TFF can be understood as a constructive protest against the neglect of peace and conflict research at the national and international levels.

With books, seminars, courses, lectures and consulting and with future workshops, TFF intends to increase the interest and understanding for burning world problems and to make its findings accessible to decision-makers, popular movements and the public at large.

The TFF fellowship program brings together researchers from East and West, North and South, enables them to pursue their research in a stimulating environment, and makes room for new questions and new groups from time to time.

The foundation focuses its activities on two major program areas:

(A) WORLD IMAGES, SECURITY, PEACE (WISP)

(A1) Images of a world with security and peace

(A2) Alternative defense philosophies

(A3) Nordic Common Security

(A4) New European Peace Order

(A5) Militarism in industrial society

(B) CIVILIZATION—DEVELOPMENT—DIALOGUE (CIDIAL)

(B1) China and world politics

(B2) Micro-electronics and world peace

(B3) Somalia—social change to self-reliance in crisis

(B4) Lund in the world—the world in Lund

Peace and future research are significant, although not sufficient conditions for the development of a world that is more peaceful for all.

Worldwide, there is over 100 times more military research than peace research. Military research can exhaust enormous resources, including economic resources.

TFF, the first research foundation of its kind in Scandinavia, depends on economic and other support from individuals, groups, administrative bodies, professional societies, movements, private and public foundations.

Please write or call us if you

—wish to obtain further information about the foundation

—wish to apply for a fellowship

—wish to receive the TFF newsletter regularly
—wish to become a supporting member of TFF

If you sympathize with the ideas and goals of TFF, please let us know via the Swedish postal account number 494 9484-2.

TFF, Vegagatan 25, S-22357 Lund, Sweden, Tel. 011-46-46-145909